WRITING YOUR WAY

WRITING YOUR WAY

CREATING A WRITING PROCESS THAT WORKS FOR YOU

DON FRY

WRITER'S DIGEST BOOKS
WritersDigest.com
Cincinnati, Ohio

 Published by Writer's Digest Books, an imprint of F+W Media, Inc., 10151 Carver Road, Blue Ash, Ohio 45242. (800) 289-0963. First edition.

16 15 14 13 12 5 4 3 2 1

Distributed in Canada by Fraser Direct
100 Armstrong Avenue
Georgetown, Ontario, Canada L7G 5S4
Tel: (905) 877-4411

Distributed in the U.K. and Europe by F&W Media International
Brunel House, Newton Abbot, Devon, TQ12 4PU, England
Tel: (+44) 1626-323200, Fax: (+44) 1626-323319
E-mail: postmaster@davidandcharles.co.uk

Distributed in Australia by Capricorn Link
P.O. Box 704, Windsor, NSW 2756 Australia
Tel: (02) 4577-3555

Edited by: Scott Francis
Cover designed by: Joshua Roflow
Interior designed by: Rachael Smith
Production coordinated by: Debbie Thomas

DEDICATION

For Joan, the love of my life.

ABOUT THE AUTHOR

Don Fry has taught over ten-thousand writers worldwide to write better and faster with less agony. Don first taught medieval English literature, mostly *Beowulf* and Chaucer, at the University of Virginia and at Stony Brook University. Later, he headed the writing and ethics faculties at the Poynter Institute in St. Petersburg, Florida, and edited the Institute's series Best Newspaper Writing. In 1994, Don became an independent writing coach, working with newspapers and magazines, radio and television stations, and nonprofit organizations. He spread the idea of coaching writers throughout the world, especially in Singapore, Scandinavia, and South Africa. Don has published hundreds of articles and seventeen books before this one, which he wrote as a blog.

He lives in Charlottesville, Virginia, with his wife Joan, a writer and occasional radio columnist, who cooks divinely. He creates absurd wooden sculptures to amuse himself.

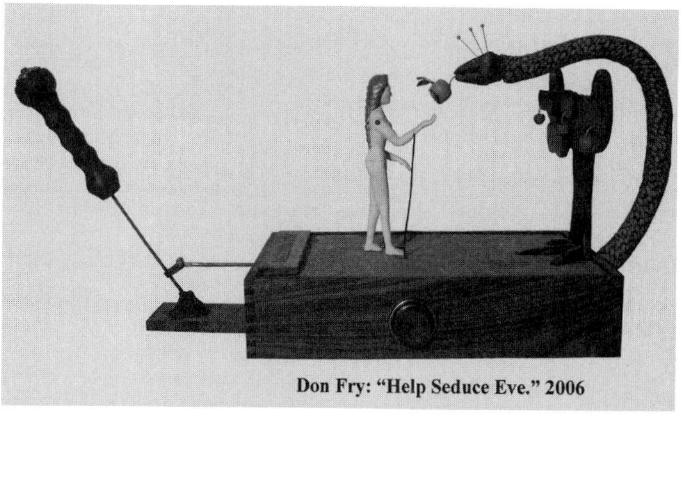

Don Fry: "Help Seduce Eve." 2006

TABLE OF CONTENTS

one

HOW THIS BOOK CAME ABOUT

I learned to write before I learned to read.

My father attended Navy radar school in Cambridge, Massachusetts. He enrolled me in the second grade in a local Catholic school, although we were Methodists. Navy children couldn't attend public schools in Massachusetts because their parents didn't pay taxes. Only the private Catholic school would accept me.

In my hometown of Raleigh, North Carolina, pupils learned to read and print in the second grade. But in the Cambridge school, children were taught to read and print a year earlier. So I entered my second year of school as the only illiterate in the class.

That year, the pupils learned to write script with a fountain pen. The nun, despite the fact that I fell in love with her, mocked me in front of the class as an example of what it meant to be Protestant, Southern, and illiterate.

One day, she wrote words in script on the blackboard, and we had to draw pictures of what the words represented. She put up the first word, which could have been in Sanskrit as far as I was concerned. So I cheated. I peeked at the picture drawn by the kid sitting next to me, evidently a crude B-17 bomber. I was a whiz at drawing warplanes, so I produced a magnificent Flying Fortress. Unfortunately the word on the board was *potato.*

I survived that semester and learned to read and print, although I've never gotten the hang of longhand. The saving grace was that learning to read by phonics made me a perfect speller.

I wrote my first piece a year later back in Raleigh, when I was eight:

I wonder where the robin goes,
All the winter long.

Maybe where the tulip grows.
They'd listen to his song.

My flame-haired third-grade teacher, Miss Kirkpatrick, read this piece of gibberish aloud to the class and launched my career as an author. Many people, perhaps including you, become writers because they never get over their first public praise.

In the eleventh grade, Phyllis Abbott Peacock took me under her wing. She was legendary for discovering talent, such as the novelist Reynolds Price, and tried to turn us all into another Thomas Wolfe, our local writer-hero. She required absolutely correct spelling, usage, and grammar to produce a perfect surface. She saw flawless prose as evidence of flawless character.

She demanded brevity. This tiny, birdlike woman would jump up and down in class, flapping her hands and chanting, "Cut, cut. Cut, cut."

At Duke, I studied with another legend, William Blackburn, who disassembled poems and sentences before his amazed students, and showed how the words interacted. And I learned how to push the words apart to find the *persona* underneath.

I served as the communications officer on an Atlantic Fleet destroyer, where Mrs. Peacock's "cut, cut" mantra served me well. I had to encrypt every message I wrote, which put a premium on clear and short prose. I had to get to the point, because the point was the whole message, something like Twitter.

I never taught writing as a graduate student or as a professor of English. But one day, my wife, Joan, asked me to teach her how to write. I was shocked. Her parents, the novelist Dorothy Baker and the poet Howard Baker, wrote all the time, and Joan grew up resenting the fact that they ignored her while immersing themselves in books. At the age of eight, she kicked her father in the shin and yelled, "Don't read!"

She hated writing and writers, and she married me on the twin conditions that I'd never ask her to type my stuff, or read anything I wrote.

A local weekly had recruited her to write food columns, and she accepted without realizing that she was in over her head. Writing ain't cooking. She drafted her first column, which had three beginnings and three endings. Before I agreed to help her, she had to swear to take my advice as suggestions only, and that we would stay married.

We walked through her draft as I explained how to make sentences work, how to use paragraphs to develop thought, and how to structure the whole piece so readers would understand it. You don't have to tell Joan anything twice, and she quickly developed her own style. She wrote her column for two years and parlayed that experience into public-radio commentaries. And we've managed to stay married for forty-seven years.

One day, my favorite graduate student, Roy Peter Clark, came to my office with a paper he'd written for another course. He called it the best thing he'd ever written and demanded that I read it on the spot. I barely managed to get through the first page before I said, "Roy, I can't understand a word of this. It's too dense and knotty, it doesn't make any sense."

Roy replied jubilantly, "Yes! I've done it. Form follows function, and I've caught the density and opaqueness of my argument in the density and opaqueness of my prose!"

I threw his paper out my office window, and we started a conversation that changed our lives and continues to this day. We talked about how readers read, how to achieve clarity for readers, and how to make the readers' understanding the first goal of writing. We were both medievalists, and the reader became our Holy Grail.

I directed Roy's dissertation (on farting in Chaucer, the definitive work on the subject). By a series of accidents, he (Roy, not Chaucer) ended up directing the writing program at the Poynter Institute in St. Petersburg, Florida. He invited me to sit in on his first writing seminar for newspaper reporters. He wanted me to do what I had taught him: question assumptions.

My research up until then focused on *Beowulf*. In Roy's seminar, I made a stunning discovery. Instead of speculating on what an ancient, thoroughly dead poet thought as he composed, I could interview living professional writers about what was in their heads as they wrote. And I could help them write better.

I changed professions and became a writing coach.

I interviewed writers to understand their writing processes, and learned quickly how different their methods could be, and often how self-defeating. Each writer had his or her own combination of techniques that got a piece written, but most of them knew only one way to write, the way they were taught or the way they always did it. They used somebody else's writing process instead of one suited to them.

I discovered writers who had no way to know what they needed to know; they just collected information until they ran out of time. Many writers destroyed their confidence by critiquing every sentence as they typed it. Half the writers did nothing to figure out what they wanted to say; they just typed whatever fell out of their fingers and let their editors try to make sense of it.

So I began to help writers solve their problems by finding out what worked and what needed work, and designing ways to change their methods.

- A food writer paralyzed herself by worrying about whether her second cookbook would sell as well as her first; I shifted her attention to what she wanted to say, and away from what she feared.
- One writer, who wrote lengthy pieces, always took a month of weeping to write a perfect and fabulous first sentence, by which time she hated the whole project; I taught her to draft her opening and perfect it later.
- One star writer turned his stories in late to prevent editing; he believed that editors had to write as well as he did to deserve to edit him. I showed him that editor and writer skills are not the same, and brilliant work requires both.

Everywhere I discovered writers damaging themselves and their writing and their careers by faulty methods, assumptions, and attitudes. A Danish writer decided to commit suicide because he was totally blocked. He hadn't written a single word in two years. I showed him how not to think about failure. Later, he told a friend I'd saved his life.

One day I realized that most of my publications showed how to help writers, not how writers could help themselves. So I decided to write this book, about how to write in your own way and create your own voice.

My hyperdigital son, Jason, suggested that I publish it serially as a blog, a preposterous idea. "I'm not the blogging type," I said, "inflicting daily drivel on people with nothing to do." Actually, I had never read a blog.

Then I read Jason's two blogs: faithandfearinflushing.com, which is about the New York Mets, not religious plumbing, and reinventingthe newsroom.wordpress.com, which tracks digital cultures. And suddenly I got it. Blogging would let me write whatever was hot in my mind that day, not the next item in an outline. Readers commented on what I wrote, giving suggestions and offering their own examples and experience. Old friends and former students chimed in. I haven't had so much fun writing since my poem about robins.

two

YOU ARE WHAT YOU WRITE

Here's a radical idea: You can escape your teachers. You can write in ways suited to you, rather than ways you were taught.

Your teachers taught writing methods suited to themselves, not to you. Like Mrs. Peacock, they taught you how to write more correctly, but not better. But you can write better and faster if you base your writing process on your strengths, and change your weaknesses, or compensate for them.

Joan Didion said, "Style is character."[1] You are what you write and how you write it. Everything you publish creates your public *persona*, how you present yourself to the world. What you write and how also creates your inner *persona*, the storyteller that speaks in your head, the voice that keeps telling you who you are. This book's original title was "I write, therefore I am."

In this book, you'll discover how to create your own writing process, your individual collection of techniques, habits, and attitudes. You'll learn how to create your own voice to match your new writing process.

This book is for writers like you who want to improve, to make your writing easier and faster and more compelling. Beginners can learn from it, but it's not a primer. I assume that you already write, and the fact that you're reading this sentence suggests you want to change the way you do things, that you want to improve.

I make no assumptions about your writing conditions. You may be a student writing term papers and e-mails. Perhaps you work in a publication's office as a staff writer, with a full production crew of editors, photographers, graphic artists, and copy editors. Or you may write by yourself for yourself, with nothing ever made public. You may write books or one-paragraph condolence notes. You may be thinking about a short memoir featuring your cat. The principles and techniques are roughly the same, and I leave it to you to adjust them to best suit you.

I may suggest that you ask an editor for help with a sentence; if you don't have one, ask a friend. I know one writer who consults her dog. She solves her problems by hearing herself define them, as Cesar wags his tail in approval.

This book has two parts: techniques for writing and devices that create voice, or how you sound to your readers. You can sample things that interest you, perhaps skipping around the book and trying things out, but reading the book from start to finish first will help you understand how readers read, how writing works, and how different devices produce different effects.

Fiction writers and journalists can learn and profit from this book, but I have not aimed it at them alone. This book translates many techniques from fiction and journalism, such as characterization and interviewing, to make them useful in nonfiction prose.

Most books on writing teach correctness, with strict standards of grammar, usage, and language. They divide things into right versus wrong, insisting on such matters as the distinction between *that* and *which.* I prefer to discuss the effects that words and constructions have on readers. *That* versus *which* is more a matter of formality than correctness.

This book makes some assumptions, which I have turned into principles:

- We write for our readers.
- Writers are responsible for their readers' understanding.
- You can't explain what you don't understand.
- Writers write better if they use methods suited to them.
- Writers improve by magnifying their strengths.
- Fast writers have fewer problems.
- Honest communications and teamwork enhance writing.

Think about those principles for a minute. Isn't that the kind of writer you want to become? Use this book to transform yourself into the writer you want to be.

three

WRITING YOUR OWN WAY

Like you, I climbed the ladder of school and adjusted myself to each teacher's demands. Lots of angry red marks appeared in the margins of my papers.

"Write it like this."

"No sweat, ma'am."

I had over fifty instructors by the time I finished high school, with eight years of college and graduate study yet to come. It's a wonder I could write at all.

You don't write in your own way. You write the way your teachers, or books on writing, taught you to write. Unfortunately the methods you learned may not suit you at all. If you haven't learned other ways to write, you can only write the way you know. You have no freedom.

Think back to your school years. Most writers, including you and me, were taught to outline a piece before we wrote it. Remember this?

OUTLINE FORM

I. Big Stuff
A. Medium Stuff
1. Small stuff
a. smaller stuff
b. more smaller stuff
c. even more smaller stuff
2. Small stuff
a. smaller stuff
b. smaller stuff
B. More Medium Stuff
II. More Big Stuff
III. Even More Big Stuff
etc.

Outlines help some writers organize their thoughts. But outlines imprison others and keep them from thinking clearly.

I was taught to write in high school by the brilliant Phyllis Abbott Peacock, who demanded a full outline before I put down a single word. She created me as a writer, and I'm eternally grateful. But I've spent my whole life escaping her techniques.

Some of the methods you think you have to use may actually hurt you. They make you slow, damage your confidence, and cause errors. I once coached a television writer who would type a sentence, and then search on the Internet to see if it was correct. He plodded along, checking each sentence before he wrote the next one. Needless to say, it took him forever to finish anything. He didn't know any other way to write accurately, so he had to use that technique. I taught him how to write the whole piece and then check it. This new knowledge freed him to write quickly and well.

This book shows you how to create "Your Own Writing Process" using a five-step template:

WRITING PROCESS

- **IDEA**
- **GATHER**
- **ORGANIZE**
- **DRAFT**
- **REVISE**

In the IDEA stage, you decide what you want to write about and how. You might come up with your own idea and develop it, or the idea might come from the outside, when you get an assignment. You figure out what the piece will be like. Is it a book on ocelots, a magazine article on rhubarb, a radio script on Martin guitars, a memoir of your wretched childhood, a proposal letter for a new spillway, or an e-mail to your uncle about the tree that fell on his car? Then you decide what you need to find out, and how.

In the GATHER stage, you collect material from various sources, such as observation, documents, interviews, the Internet, *etc.* I named this step "Gather," because you bring the information together.

In the ORGANIZE stage, you decide what you want to say and how to say it. This is the hardest part of the whole process, the place where many writers fail, mostly because they don't organize their work at all.

The next two stages, DRAFT and REVISE, involve typing. You DRAFT a rough version, then REVISE that draft to finish the piece.

Each of these five stages involves many actions. Your writing process is your own batch of techniques, tricks, and habits that get a piece written. You don't need a writing process that worked for your teachers. You need your own writing process that works for you.

This book will show you many ways to work through all five stages. You choose and design your own collection of techniques according to what suits you, and then you continuously tune your process to match your writing needs. That's what I mean by "writing your own way."

But wait, there's more, as they say on television. You can also write in your own voice. *Voice* is the way writing sounds to readers. Voice is what makes writing individual and compelling. Your voice is how you present yourself to the world.

Your writing process is a collection of individual techniques, and your writing voice results from using individual devices consistently to create a personality. The second half of this book will show you how to create your own writing voice, and how to tune and change it.

HERE'S MY WRITING PROCESS

(WARNING: My writing process will seem weird to you. Anything you break down into steps will sound strange. For example, how do you walk? You move your left foot forward and shift your weight to it. Then you hold the left foot in place, pivoting at the ankle, as you move your right foot ahead of your left. See what I mean?)

You design your own writing process based on two personal factors: amplifying your strengths and changing or avoiding your weaknesses. So you begin by listing your strengths and weaknesses. I'll use myself as an example.

My writing process is based on two strengths: memory and organization. If I want to remember something, I can read it once and hold it in my head for about four hours. I annotate my notes as I take them, and then

I annotate them again at the end of GATHER stage. At the beginning of the ORGANIZE stage, I read only the notes I've marked as important and memorize them. Then I close my notebook and ORGANIZE, DRAFT, and REVISE from memory. Then I check things against the notes, and they're mostly right. This technique allows me to work faster, because I don't waste time looking things up in my notebook.

You're thinking, "Wow, I could really speed up if I used that trick." But it takes a terrific memory to do it that way.

YOU CAN ONLY USE TECHNIQUES YOU'RE QUALIFIED FOR.

My wife, Joan, is jealous of my second strength, the ability to organize things quickly. Recently, I tackled our hall closet, which contained about five hundred objects: jackets for two seasons, raincoats, seventeen hats, shoes and boots, gloves, twenty-two cartons of Tab, binoculars, wrapping paper, five flags and their staffs, four Whole Foods grocery bags, three cameras, two flashlights, and a partridge in a pear tree. I sorted it all, donated half of it to the SPCA, and repacked it in one afternoon.

I deal with information in much the same way: sort it into groups and throw most of it out.

My weakness is typing. I type four words a minute. Four, yes, you heard me, four. FOUR. That doesn't mean that letters drop out of my fingers at four words per minute. I mean that by the time I type them and then go back and correct all the errors, it adds up to four words a minute. (That last sentence came out like this: "I mean t hat by the ime I TYPE THEM AND go back and fix repar alll the errose,,....")

So I use my memory and organizing strengths to speed up my whole process, balancing my weakness: poor, slow typing. I strengthen what's strong to compensate for what's weak.

You're thinking, "Why don't you learn to type better, Don?" Well, I've tried, but I don't get any better, so I compensate. And that's what you can do.

CORRECT WEAKNESSES IF YOU CAN, OR COMPENSATE FOR THEM.

Here's my general writing process, which is actually quite fast. My IDEAS mostly come from noticing something, such as an odd sentence, or discovering a new technique or helping a writer solve a problem. Things happen to me and turn into ideas. Then I start saving related materials in a messy way, just tossing them into a folder or copying them into a file. I think about the evolving idea as I do other things, such as take a shower or build a bathroom stool. Eventually the idea jells in my head, and I start asking key questions: What's this likely to be about? Who would read it and why? Where would I publish it and in what form?

I'm a freelancer. I don't work for publications, so I don't pitch ideas ahead of time to editors. I prefer to write whole pieces (even books) before I talk to editors or publishers or agents. Sometimes, just for fun, I write about something that interests me, such as the PBY-5 Catalina in the Pacific War, with no publication in mind.

As I begin the GATHER stage, I make up a list of questions I need to answer to become a temporary expert on the subject. I try to talk with somebody knowledgeable ("a pathfinder") to lay out the ground and suggest people to talk with. Then I search the Internet, prowl a few libraries, interview sources, and buy related books. (For large projects, I build a bookcase.) As I learn things, I add questions to my list.

Halfway through GATHER, I stop and ask myself, "If I had to write this today, what would it be about, and what would be the sections?" Then I focus my GATHERING around those two questions. I know I've got enough material when I have the right questions and full answers to them. I usually have several endings in mind by then, maybe even a beginning or two. I annotate my notes again, memorize the important ones, and close my notebook.

During the ORGANIZE stage, I wander around mumbling. One day at the Poynter Institute, a student asked, "Why does Don walk up and down talking to himself?" The director replied, "Oh, he's writing." Actually, I was planning what to write and how.

I usually answer three questions:

1. What's this about?
2. What are the parts?
3. How long does this need to be?

As a visual thinker, I answer that second question with a diagram in my head, with the sections pictured as boxes. Then I'm ready to type, and it all just pours out onto the screen, at four words a minute. My mentor Fredson Bowers, who bred Irish wolfhounds, quipped, "When you gotta whelp, you gotta whelp."

To compensate for my typing, I DRAFT at top speed, the characters dropping out of my fingers at about twenty-five words per minute. (Slow, yes, but better than four.) I don't worry about typing or spelling or sentences or sense. I just blast it down as fast as I can.

I want a perfect beginning, but I find it hard to come up with one for a text I have to imagine. So I write the beginning last, even if I started typing with one in mind. I usually type the second paragraph first and go from there. There's usually a good beginning in my head by the time I reach the ending. If I give in to temptation and type the beginning earlier, I might waste time revising it over and over.

Then I fix the typos and take a long break, sometimes ten minutes, sometimes months.

I start the REVISE step by reading the whole piece aloud. I print a copy and read it out loud with a pencil in my hand, putting a check in the margin beside anything that doesn't sound right. Then I crawl through and fix all the rough spots. Because I ORGANIZE well, I seldom move anything around, maybe a phrase here and there. I open my notebook and check a few things, mostly quotations and numbers. Then I take a long break, usually overnight, and polish it up. Done.

That process works best for most of what I write, articles and columns. I modify it for books and novels, where the long time scheme renders my memory less reliable, and I need to revise more.

As I predicted, my writing process probably sounds weird to you, but yours will sound just as strange when you spell it out. Mine isn't weird; it's tailor-made for me. My process turns a sloppy typist into a fast writer.

NOT NECESSARILY IN ORDER

You don't have to do the five steps of your writing process in order. Most writers, even the most rigid outliners, skip around. Events can disrupt the sequence, requiring reorganizing and more gathering. If the cake collapses in the test kitchen, you have to back up and rethink your recipe.

Most writers would like to have all the information before they type anything, a perfection rarely achieved and potentially self-destructive. The novelist John Gardner, who was also a medieval scholar, lamented that he never wrote a book on Dante because he couldn't imagine reading all the scholarship in one lifetime. His assumption cost him (and us) a good book. We always write from partial knowledge.

It'll help you to have a test for knowing when to end each step and move on to the next stage:

> **IDEA:** I can move on because I know what I'm after.
> **GATHER:** I have the material I need.
> **ORGANIZE:** I know what I want to say and how.
> **DRAFT:** I've written the framework of the whole piece.
> **REVISE:** I've finished it enough to share it.

In the IDEA stage, it helps to know whether you're explaining something or telling a story (or both), what it's likely to be about, what medium it might appear in, approximately how long it should be, initial sources, who might be involved, and likely problems you may encounter. You usually start out with much less than all that, but you can GATHER quicker if you know what you're after.

You end the GATHER stage by asking yourself whether you have enough material, using tests discussed in detail later. Gathering information, especially talking with people involved, usually changes the idea. The topic turns out to be larger or smaller or deeper than you first imagined. Sometimes the notion you start with doesn't pan out at all. So you break the sequence of steps and return to the IDEA stage and redefine it.

Some people write a little during the GATHER stage, just to test what they have and if they understand it. The trick is drafting, rather than revising and finishing this test writing. It's really a form of note taking. I sometimes draft a paragraph or two to see if I have the tone right.

ARE YOU A PLANNER OR A PLUNGER?

Here's a distinction that could change your life. There are two kinds of people: PLANNERS and PLUNGERS. In their lives, PLANNERS decide what to do, and then they do it; PLUNGERS do things and figure them out later. In their writing, PLANNERS create a plan and follow it; PLUNGERS discover what they want to say by typing.

In the ORGANIZE step, planners usually figure out what they want to say and how by jotting down some sort of outline or plan. Plungers skip this step and start typing to decide what to say. Plungers organize by drafting.

The point of the DRAFT stage is to *get it down*, so you can *get it right* in the REVISE stage. An analogy using sculpture explains this concept: If I give you a hunk of clay and ask you to create a portrait head, would you model the eyes first? Of course not. You'd shape the contours of the head, followed by the shapes of the face, and then the details of lips, nose, ears, and eyes. Trying to finish details without the underlying structure makes writing hard and slow.

GET IT DOWN, THEN GET IT RIGHT.

You'll often discover during DRAFTING that you've missed something, so you jump back into the GATHER stage. Or sometimes what you're trying to say won't land because it's just flat-out wrong or there are holes in the information. You may have to go all the way back to the IDEA stage and refocus the piece.

Events can bounce you out of the DRAFT. You're typing along, and an e-mail arrives with new information. *New* meaning something you didn't already know or *new* in that it just happened, a fairly common experience thanks to social networks pouring events into the hopper. Sources call back during drafting, and everything shifts. So you gather some more and reorganize.

For some people, REVISION never ends because they can never achieve perfection. But the test is not perfection for you, but readability and understanding for your readers. You probably can't judge when to give it up; that's what friends and editors and colleagues and spouses are for.

The REVISION stage also involves typing, and it subjects you to many of the same traps that the DRAFT stage does: new or missing information, unfocused ideas, *etc.* When revision breaks down, it's usually because you're trying to say something you don't believe or understand. So you back up to ORGANIZE.

Some writers march through these steps in order. But most follow their needs wherever they lead them.

The next chapter addresses the first step in the writing process, the IDEA stage.

Four

STAGE ONE: MASSAGING THE IDEA

Ever noticed how some people keep finding things? You walk down a street with them, and they spot the $50 bill that you didn't see. How do they do that? Well, it's not just luck. "You can see a lot," Yogi Berra allegedly said, "just by observing."

Some writers keep finding good ideas that others don't, and you're about to learn how to become one of those apparently lucky authors.

In the IDEA stage, you come up with your own idea or accept an assignment. You develop it either alone or with someone else, preferably an editor who will be part of the production team. You imagine the process to come: gathering information, organizing it, and typing it into a finished piece, followed by editing and layout. Books may involve further steps, such as finding an agent and securing a publisher.

The sequence is about the same when you're working alone, such as writing a blog, in which case you're the entire production team. The quality and speed of the whole project depends on how well you begin and how smoothly your writing and production processes work.

The best ideas are yours, rather than assignments from others. Ego drives us as writers, and we wrap our egos around our own stuff. People who come up with their own ideas have more control over their careers.

One day, I watched my colleague Roy Clark stand on a sidewalk in St. Petersburg, surrounded by a gaggle of beginning writing students. Roy wanted to show them that they live among ideas ripe for picking. He turned slowly in a circle for thirty minutes, pointing and asking questions:

- What are all those antennas on top of Woolworth's?
- Why are people standing in line in front of H&R Block, the tax preparer, in July?
- How do these trees planted in a sidewalk get water?
- Why are the concrete blocks in this sidewalk hexagonal, and what's inscribed on them?
- Where does that cat live? What do strays living downtown eat?
- Who shops in The Wig Villa, and what do they buy?

Roy taught the students to question the world around them. If you see the world in terms of people interacting for reasons, you'll find all the ideas you'll ever need.

Curiosity, attention, a little bravado, and a willingness to break routines lead to great ideas. You lurk, listen, ask questions, and find experts. You can prowl the Internet, but the best ideas come from face to face interaction with people.

The best ideas are subjects that other writers haven't written about, or haven't noticed. The following techniques work because they dynamite you out of your routine ways of thinking and dealing with the world. They make the world "strange," so you can see it fresh.

1. MAKE THE CONTEXT LARGER OR SMALLER:

Think larger and smaller at the same time. Enlarge the context to find the bigger subject in a wider perspective or a longer time frame. Narrow the context by finding individuals who exemplify something large. For a business magazine, you might explain a bank merger in terms of its earlier mergers and acquisitions, or explore the effects on one employee. Open an account in the new bank and write about what happens to you. Find out if any bank merger ever improved customer service. Your memoir about your pets might expand to the whole farm or shrink to only the horses, or to one cat.

2. EXPLAIN COMMON THINGS:

Ask experts to explain how ordinary things work, preferably things invisible to the public. For example, how does your town's water-purification system work? What happens to recycled plastic? How do wine aerators work? What do lifeguards look for? What makes chocolate taste good?

3. MAKE THE INVISIBLE VISIBLE:

Find people who operate prominent objects and processes where you live. For example, interview the operator on top of a T-crane. Find out how college students game the registration system. Search out the person who controls traffic lights before and after large events. Talk with football trainers about how they deal with on-the-spot injuries.

4. MINE YOUR EMOTIONS:

Explore your own reactions. If something bothers or puzzles you, find out why by interviewing people with similar reactions. You'll discover you're not alone in stupidly opening junk mail, never changing your passwords, buying lottery tickets, or your fear of high bridges. I've always wondered if my parents were really my parents, which turns out to be a fairly common doubt.

5. STUDY THE PAST IN THE PRESENT:

Think about things, such as a monument or a photograph, to find the past continuing to influence the present. My father died, and I poked through all his Navy gear, discovering that everything I knew about what he did in World War II was wrong. Look at a picture of your mother at your current age; then look in a mirror. It'll lead to thoughts about what you inherit, and what you don't.

6. CHOOSE THINGS RANDOMLY:

Read a different magazine every week at random. I learned this trick from Don Murray, the first writing coach. Picture Don as a tall, fat man with a Santa Claus beard, dressed in shorts and shower shoes. He'd back up to a newsstand rack and buy the first magazine he touched. Then he'd pay particular attention to the fringes: little ads, personals, letters to the editor. The randomness leads you to worlds you haven't imagined, such as the symbolism behind professional wrestling, families who shelter strangers' dying babies, the physics and chemistry of sand traps, how grocery stores position candy in the checkout line to attract toddlers, or how to hire a hit man. You can use this trick in a public library, but don't dress like Don Murray.

7. STORE THINGS RANDOMLY:

Develop a storage system for ideas you can use later, such as a drawer full of 3 x 5 cards, notebooks, a "Miscellaneous" hanging file (I use this one), or computer caches. Encourage yourself to browse by not organizing it at all. Roy Clark calls this "composting," turning over the trash until it matures. I often gather great quotations that have nothing to do with what I'm working on, so I write them on a card and toss it into my "Future" file, along with the name and phone number of the speaker. My stash also includes clippings, recordings, jottings, pictures, maps, and even pieces of gadgets.

8. FOLLOW ALTERNATIVE PATHS:

Take alternate routes to your normal destinations, and try out different types of transportation, especially slower ones that let you see more. Leave your car at home and walk to work, or ride a bike. Climb stairs instead of taking elevators, take the service elevator, or enter through back doors. The best idea collector I ever met was Mike Foley, who jogged five miles every morning before work, taking a different route every time and jotting down things he saw on a pad.

9. CULTIVATE WEIRDOS:

Your mother taught you never to talk with strangers. Good advice for children, bad advice for writers. Strike up conversations with people you don't know, even cultivating weirdos. Introduce yourself to airplane seatmates, to people carrying a sign or wearing a nametag. "Wait a minute," you object, "I'm too shy for that." I am too, so I say to myself, "I'm a writer, so I have a license to talk to strangers," and just forge ahead.

10. LOWER YOUR STANDARDS:

Accept any piece of paper handed to you on the street. Read junk mail. Watch awful TV shows and ask why they appeal to anyone. Get beyond easy condescension. Ask why teenagers who don't cook watch the Food Channel. Attend get-rich-quick workshops and pay attention to the audiences. Buy TV gadget offers, test them, and try to get your money back.

11. EAVESDROP ON STRANGERS:

Lurk in busy places and eavesdrop to find out what people are doing and thinking. High school grandstands, food courts in malls, and baggage-claim areas all have diverse mixtures of people. In a lecture or business presentation, watch for the reactions of members of the audience and interview them later. Many Silicon Valley companies have a favorite hotel where they lodge candidates for jobs; you can grab scoops in the breakfast room just by listening. I once rode on a bus behind two teenagers. One girl turned and surveyed the passengers, including me, looked back at her companion and lamented, "No movie stars here." Bingo: several ideas about fame, absurd expectations, and vanity.

12. MAKE YOURSELF INTO SOMEBODY ELSE:

Role-play the lives of people with viewpoints different from yours or your readers'. I once spent half a day in a wheelchair and learned about hazards I never imagined. Did you know you can burn your knees on hot water pipes under a sink? Bob Graham, the former governor of Florida, did manual labor one day a month to understand his public.

13. SEEK RANDOM FRIENDS:

Extend your personal life outside your writer friends and your own economic group. You might join a Civil War reenactors group, take a course in blacksmithing, or sing Handel's *Messiah* in a chorus. My sister, Sandra, sampled most of the churches where she lives, by attending services over a year.

14. SCARE YOURSELF SAFELY:

Make a list of things you fear and find a way to experience them safely. You might spend a Saturday night in a hospital emergency room, just observing. You could design a dinner party that includes a dish that might flop, such as a soufflé, and write about the disaster or about cooks' anxiety or about culinary triumph. I'm terrified of damage to my eyes, but I once wrote an article on blinding giants in Homer's *Odyssey* and Norse sagas.

15. KEEP MOVING AROUND:

Move around at any event to get as many viewpoints as possible. Stay far away from any other writers present. Don't be satisfied with what you learn in the press box or a corporate skybox; get out with fans and the action. Find the staging areas for a parade and where it breaks up.

16. COLLECT AND SCATTER BUSINESS CARDS:

Dele Olojede taught me a great technique. He asked for a business card from everybody he talked with and stored them in a random file. Later, he would pull cards out at random, and call people to ask what they were up to. It's flattering to get such a call, and Dele scored about half the time.

All of these techniques jar you out of your normal vision, because that's where the ideas are, invisible in plain sight.

But we also need to keep our eye on ordinary life because it's just as rich and interesting as some of the oddities above. How do you find ideas about ordinary people and everyday events? How can they be normal and yet interesting?

My friend Jim Nicholson used to write obituaries about ordinary Philadelphia citizens who had two things in common: They were dead, and not famous. He chose them by closing his eyes and poking his finger onto that day's list of the deceased. I objected, "Now wait a minute, you write a piece on an ordinary person chosen at random? How often do you fail?"

"I don't," he replied. "Everybody's interesting."

NOTICING IDEAS OTHER PEOPLE MISS

Some writers consistently come up with good ideas about subjects that other people haven't noticed. It looks like luck, but it isn't. Here's how they do it.

First, some people naturally notice things, both details and patterns. My childhood pal Edward Spencer and I kept finding stuff that other kids didn't: cash, puppies, a kayak, even a colossal steel boiler. (Well, it seemed colossal to a five-year-old.) Edward caught details that others missed. In the woods one day, he heard faint squealing and found five abandoned collie puppies, which we later sold. My skill was patterns; I could spot four-leaf clovers just by glancing at a patch of grass. I noticed breaks in patterns, where others failed to see the patterns at all. So I discovered things that were hidden, like an abandoned laboratory, and Edward found things that were small, such as a dime. We found things because we looked for things.

The best writers profit from deep curiosity, which drives them to notice details and patterns. And the writing game has a tinge of outlaw culture, which makes writers look where others don't. It's called "contrarian thinking." Here's a simple technique: When you recognize that you're looking in the same direction as everyone else, at the same things they're looking at, stand up and turn 180 degrees, and see what you see and they don't.

Point of view determines what you see and hear, and you can find original ideas by placing yourself where others aren't. If you stand in a group watching a boat, you'll see the boat; so get aboard the boat. Photographers say, "Be there, get close, f8."

One of the richest sources of new ideas is sources of old ideas. People can extend your vision by telling you what they notice. Late in a good interview, ask your subject who else you should talk to, and then ask what that source is likely to tell you. You also want to follow up on what subjects say when they think the interview has ended. They tend to bring up things you didn't ask or even know about, but they want to talk about.

Dick Bothwell, a Florida weather writer and humor columnist, would call ordinary homeowners to ask about rainfall in their backyards, and then ask, "By the way, what are people talking about, up where you live?" No wonder he always knew what was going on at ground level.

In your daily life, you'll notice details or patterns, but you might not ask about them because they don't seem relevant to what you do or write about. You're not after whole ideas from these inquiries, just interesting sparks. The questions you ask yourself as you begin to notice connections can make the most unlikely material into ideas nobody has but you.

MAP YOUR OWN MIND

Sometimes in the IDEA stage and often in the GATHERING stage, you have so much material available that you don't know where to start. You need a map of the territory, a way to see connections and find patterns, or to find the most promising areas to develop. This technique is called "mind mapping." Essentially, you lay out areas of interest or events, and draw arrows to show what causes what.

What would happen if all American women decided they're fed up with preparing Thanksgiving dinner and would rather watch football on television? This map explores possible consequences:

THANKSGIVING DISASTER

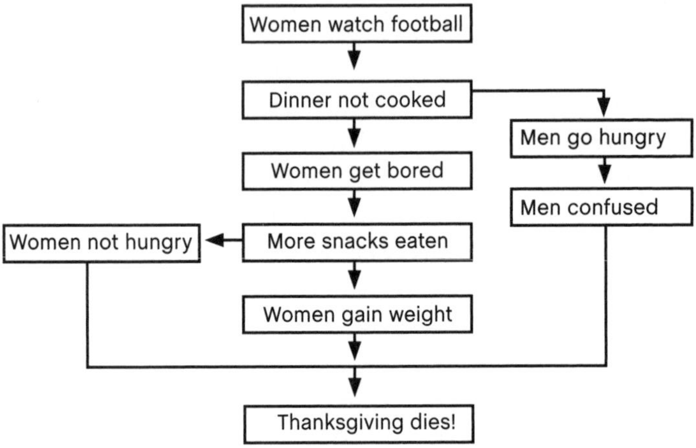

You can also use mind mapping to determine which part of a range of material to focus on and write about. Let's use adopting feral cats as our subject:

ADOPTING FERAL CATS

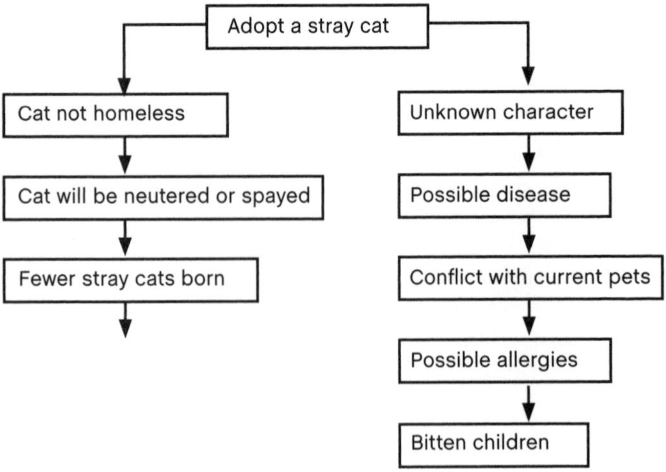

You could ask which of these consequences of adoption most interests you, or which might intrigue your readers, or which fits a publication you're aiming at, or which promises rich material. Then you select part of the map and write about it. You might also use it, as I did, to talk your spouse out of adopting more strays. (It didn't work; we have three.)

The bigger the project, especially for books, the more mapping will help you.

PITCHING IDEAS SO EDITORS CATCH THEM

Sometimes magazine editors assign pieces to staffers or freelancers, and sometimes writers "pitch" ideas to them for acceptance. Pitching a book to agents and publishers involves written proposals, which include outlines, a sample chapter, bios, and more. The secret of successful pitching is the same as for selling anything: Spark their interest.

Editors' jobs are repetitive and tend to dull their imaginations, so everything starts sounding alike to them. But editors do like to read and publish good pieces. So the pitch has to ignite their enthusiasm while fitting templates of what they normally publish. Nowadays most pitches happen through e-mail, which is harder than in person because you can't see and hear each other.

First of all, you establish your authority by the idea, the information, and the way you present it. Before you try it out, do enough at the GATHER stage to know what you're talking about: at least a few calls, maybe a little searching and reading, and some planning. The more complex the idea, the more preparation you need.

What are the parts of a pitch, keeping in mind that you haven't done much gathering yet?

- What the piece might be about
- The genre and likely size
- Who might read it and why
- A tentative gathering plan
- Graphic, video, and sound possibilities

So you might begin a pitch like this: "I want to write a short, funny column about clothing myself using stuff that university students lose on sidewalks and lawns, like scarves and gloves, Redskins caps, strappy red sandals, underwear...."

"Strappy red sandals, underwear," you just landed it.

Editors think in pigeonholes of genre and size and subject and treatment, so you aim your pitch at the appropriate slots by talking their lingo. When their eyes start to light up, you talk about what this piece might REALLY be about: obscenely rich students, America's throwaway culture, drunken coeds carelessly shedding garments.

Many writers fail by crafting pitches that are small and dull, so their ideas sound like everything that's boring their editors to death. So get your editor to imagine a photo of someone (not you) wearing everything picked up early one Sunday morning in a football weekend.

(My wife, Joan, did land this pitch to a local NPR station, minus the picture.)

You can tailor your pitches by knowing your editors' tastes and quirks. Study what they usually publish, how they play it, what they praise, and their hobbies and obsessions. One editor I knew had model airplanes hanging all over his office ceiling; any pitch about aviation would land (take off?) with him. You also need to know your editors' dislikes; some food-magazine editors will never allow directions for killing a lobster near their pages.

Most word people don't know enough about handling pictures and sound to include them in their pitch, although every ambitious writer should make it a point to learn how in this infancy of electronic publishing. But you can *talk* about how cracking a (dead) lobster might need illustration or how a map of Baja, California, would help readers or why you need a video of repairing the Hubble Space Telescope.

Phrasing your pitch in an assured way should convince the editor that you've done some preliminary gathering, that you know what you're talking about, and that you can deliver the piece, superbly written, on time.

Some ideas are harder to land and require special techniques to convince editors. Pitch complicated or controversial pieces with a short memo followed by a chat. Your editor may have to consult senior managers, or even lawyers, and your memo will get your idea up to higher levels intact, in your own words.

Sometimes your pitch fails, which doesn't mean you should abandon the idea. Chalk it up to bad timing and try the pitch again, later, in a different form. You can try a different editor at the same publication, unless policy forbids such "editor shopping." Some editors resent it, so be politic.

If you expect your pitch to fail, and you really want to write the piece no matter what, do just that. Write it without pitching, and submit it. Editors will publish almost anything a staffer submits, if you write it well.

Pitching books to agents and publishers requires more information and persuasion.

The bottom line: Editors want good pieces, and writing well makes landing the next one easier.

SURVIVING DUMB ASSIGNMENTS

Sometimes you get an assignment you really don't want, because your heart isn't in it. Do you really want to devote ten seconds of your life to the new packaging of Tide? It means nothing to you and sounds boring. So you probably do what most writers do in that situation: You procrastinate, making it worse. Here are some bad strategies for dealing with dumb ideas:

1. Keep delaying until your editor forgets.
2. Write something sort of related to the assignment, hoping your editor won't notice.
3. Do some gathering, then confer with your editor, presenting the assigned material dully, but related material brilliantly.

The three tactics above involve guerilla warfare and will probably lead to worse assignments, or no assignments. Here are some better tactics:

4. Do some gathering and then discuss the assignment with your editor, moving sideways toward what really interests you.
5. Get angry about the subject rather than the assignment.
6. Ask yourself how this assignment touches your life or the lives of people you know.
7. Start gathering information immediately before you drown in self-pity.
8. Narrow the context by finding the specific and the particular.
9. Expand the context and explore the context rather than the original subject.
10. Brainstorm with a friend about potential approaches.
11. Ask how the subject has been handled in the past, then transcend it.
12. Imagine potential readers, why they would read this piece, and what they might want to know.
13. Find somebody whose life will be affected by this subject.

14. Do the assignment as quickly and simply as possible to get it out of the way.
15. Talk with real people. Remember Jim Nicholson, who said, "Everybody's interesting."

Give the idea a chance. Talk with people and let it bloom.

I once asked Murray Kempton, the famous curmudgeon columnist, how he dealt with dopey ideas from editors. He said he immediately leaves the building and starts talking to people on the street "to gather material to throw in the editor's face to show him how dumb his idea was!" I asked him if his technique worked. He replied, "You know, once I start talking to people, the idea gets pretty good."

BRAINSTORMING YOUR IDEA

The IDEA stage works best if you get help from another person, although you can do it alone. In a magazine, it usually involves an editor giving an assignment or accepting a proposal. Ideally the editor brainstorms with you to achieve mutual agreement on the project, and to narrow or broaden your gathering of information. You want to leave such a session knowing what the piece is likely about, its scale, and your deadline. Are you writing a wedding announcement, 250 words with two photos on coleslaw, a blog post, an eighteen-inch feature, a three-part series, or an atlas of *Star Wars*? Smart writers also discuss potential visuals at this stage, just to get the production thinking started.

The other person need not be an editor, but it helps. This session, called a "briefing," launches the production process. The editor will follow up by commissioning photos and graphics, allocating space, and scheduling when the piece will appear. The secret of flawless teamwork is early and constant communication between editor and writer, updating each other and adjusting the whole production sequence.

NEVER SURPRISE AN EDITOR, EXCEPT WITH QUALITY.

The briefing session sets expectations. You always want your editors to know what to expect from you and to get what they expect (plus a little more). And you always want to know exactly what editors expect from you, especially if you're a freelancer.

DON'T LET A BRIEFING END UNTIL YOU UNDERSTAND WHAT YOU'RE EXPECTED TO DO.

There are two models for these conversations. In the first, an assignment editor tells you what she wants, when, how long, and any other pertinent details. You ask questions to make sure you're both on the same wavelength.

In the other model, you pitch an idea to the editor to get it approved. A helpful editor will ask about likely sources, treatment, length, possible visuals, *etc.* Then you reach agreements on deadline, length, reimbursement, and any other important factors. Freelancers should ask for a memo, or even a contract, of what you've agreed, to prevent heartaches, screaming, and heavy rewriting later.

Here's a sample briefing, from a (fictional) magazine called *Bait*:

EDITOR: Okay, what've you got?

WRITER: An amazing invention, a new kind of fishing lure. Get this: It projects a hologram of bait fish underwater to attract larger fish and hook them....

EDITOR: You're kidding me....

WRITER: No, I'm not. I've got an interview with the inventor this afternoon to see the actual gadget.

EDITOR: What's this likely to be about?

WRITER: Well, all our readers fish, and it might be a tip-off of a great new product coming. Or it might be a business piece. The guy actually invented it for the tuna industry.

EDITOR: Big piece? Little piece?

WRITER: Can't tell until I see how real this is, and how close to getting funded. I'll call you this afternoon after my interview, and we can discuss it.

EDITOR: Who else have you talked to?

WRITER: A friend at Rapala tipped me off. And he gave me some names in the tuna industry.

> **EDITOR:** Got a picture?
>
> **WRITER:** Not yet, but I'll see if I can get a snapshot with my phone camera. Later, we'll need a photographer who can shoot underwater.
>
> **EDITOR:** I like it. Keep me informed.

Notice that the writer has done some gathering and planning and arranging ahead of the briefing. She knows what she's talking about, and that's the secret of pitching.

KNOW WHAT YOU'RE TALKING ABOUT.

The editor asks prompting questions. Done well, briefings are short and launch writers knowing what they're after, with the supervisor's approval. Briefing also launches the editor, who now knows what's likely to happen, and can start thinking about schedules and photos and graphics.

Lots of freelancers, including me, don't have editors. How do you brief without one? You can brief with a friend, or you can ask yourself questions to organize your thinking and help you design the next phase, which is GATHER. Here are some good questions that recognize you don't have much information yet:

- What's this piece likely to be about?
- What's the genre?
- Who's likely to read it, and what do they already know?
- What visuals would help readers understand it?
- What sources, both documents and people, do I need to start with?
- How much space will I need?

If a friend asks you these questions, you're more likely to answer them honestly and specifically. If you're friendless, write down your answers. Everything seems clear inside your head; you have to get it outside yourself to see what's fuzzy. If you start the next phase with vague ideas of what you're after, you'll make lots of false starts and take forever. Books take much longer to produce, and writing down your intentions at the start will keep you focused.

And that's the IDEA stage. Next, get ready to GATHER.

Five

STAGE TWO: GATHERING STUFF

You're probably drowning in information, not just in piles of data, but also in data that's not useful. Everybody is, especially writers. The Internet deluges us, e-mail pours in, and social networks swamp our attention. I have chosen the word *GATHER* for this next stage because it implies purposeful collecting and selecting, rather than trying to manage a flood. It's also an agricultural metaphor: Writers gather fruit to cook into nutritious things to read.

In the GATHER stage, you collect information and focus it. The idea sharpens as you learn things, and what you learn as you go along leads to increased clarity and more directed gathering. Suddenly, you realize you have what you need, and you can move to the next step, *i.e.*, you can ORGANIZE it to say what you want.

The way you begin to GATHER can determine the speed and success of a whole writing project. How do you move from acceptance of an idea to gathering material to write it?

STARTING TO GATHER THINGS

Since you haven't done much gathering yet, your work will be tentative for a while. The magic question "What's this about?" becomes "What's this likely to be about?"

Some writers create a GATHER plan to develop the idea. Here are some of the things you might think about:

1. What written sources do I need; which ones do I need first?
2. Who can lay out the ground for me and suggest sources, *i.e.*, who's my "pathfinder?"
3. Who's involved in what I'm writing about, *i.e.*, the actors?
4. Who else has a stake in these issues?
5. What sources do I need to talk to, and in what order?

6. What commentators can supply context and interpretation later?
7. Who might read this piece, and what can I assume they know?
8. What visuals (photos, graphics, charts) might help my readers?
9. What's my target length, and when is my deadline?
10. And the magic question again: What's this likely to be about?

You vary your list to fit your project.

All this planning may sound like overkill if you're writing, for example, a short piece on fortune cookies, with two recipes and a photo. You don't need pathfinders or commentators, but you might want someone who can test the recipes to make sure they work. And you'll need several photos, even if you only print one. Fortune cookies have tricky shapes, so you might need a diagram on how to fold them. The more of this you imagine early, the faster the GATHER stage goes.

Or suppose you're writing a book over a period of years. You need more detailed answers to those questions. But remember where you are in the writing process, at the beginning of GATHER. As you gain information and understanding, the list of what you need will change and grow. That's part of the fun of writing books.

Now take the opposite case. It's 10:12 A.M. Assignment: Write a three-hundred-word dispatch informing the university community of the hurricane emergency shutdown beginning at noon. Deadline: five minutes ago. Obviously, you don't have time for planning. Well, slow down a little, you do have time. As you rush toward your office, ask yourself these key organizing questions:

- Which essential personnel should remain? (I know that.)
- When will classes cease? (Noon, except for the law school.)
- Will the hospital close? The emergency room? (Need it.)
- Format? (One short paragraph and a bulleted list)
- How will this dispatch be transmitted? To whom? (E-mail everybody, plus local police and media.)

Arriving in your office, you call the law school and the hospital, and gather the information you lack. Then you type. You planned on the run.

All this is "planner thinking," of course. Some writers prefer to plunge right in, making phone calls and letting things develop. If you have lots of time, just flopping around can work. You can regroup from false starts. But undirected gathering is slower and more likely to miss important things.

Questions that develop the idea don't take long; in fact, you should keep asking them all the way through the GATHER stage. The questions themselves give you confidence that you know what you're after, and you'll know when you've got it.

> PEOPLE WHO THINK ABOUT WHAT THEY'RE DOING AS THEY DO IT, WORK FASTER AND BETTER.

FINDING PATHFINDERS TO GUIDE YOU

You have three kinds of live sources: actors, commentators, and pathfinders. Stories consist of actors performing actions in time for reasons. So for greatest punch with the reader, writers try to use the actors themselves as primary sources of information. They were there, and they're the characters. The commentators frame the situations and issues surrounding the action; they tell you what it all means. So what's a pathfinder?

Pathfinders are experts who know things without being involved in the immediate action. If you get to them early, the gathering goes a lot faster and easier. You ask them to map out the ground for you, identify the actors and commentators, and help you gain access to sources. You flatter pathfinders by asking their advice and reward them by not mentioning their names or quoting them. Thus pathfinders can influence events without risking involvement or disclosure.

Suppose you're writing a piece for a health magazine about a new kind of stent used in heart surgery. Your pathfinder might be a cardiologist who knows all about stents but doesn't implant them. She could tell you how stents work and how *this* stent is different, the players involved, the likelihood of success and problems, and the names of experts who might explain things. If you're lucky, she closes the conversation by telling you to drop her name so sources will talk to you. You don't quote her or mention her, but you send her a copy later with your thanks.

Today's source, properly treated, may become the pathfinder for your next piece, and vice versa. Smart writers develop a crew of pathfinders for different subjects, and call them first. They save time and prevent false starts and mistakes. Pathfinders enjoy pathfinding.

COLLECTING HELPERS

Writers generally talk to somebody official, usually an editor, at the beginning and end of producing a piece. They brainstorm at the front, and answer editing questions later. Such debriefing involves talking with an editor just before you type and after you turn the piece in; more on that later.

Different specialists help you in different ways in the middle of the writing process. At the very beginning of gathering information, librarians and researchers can enrich your materials and save you lots of time. They listen to what you're up to and tell you what information they can get for you, usually online. They can suggest sources you would never know about. They can find things in back files and previous issues of periodicals faster than you can. A good reference librarian is a godsend, and you should cultivate at least one. I collect librarians, lots of them.

Photographers make great companions while you're gathering materials. Many writers discover that their best quotations come from sources speaking to their photographer, and photographers know that they see more and better with another set of eyes to spot things. A photographer will make you more likely to see visual information, and just one photo may save you and your readers three hard paragraphs. While driving to the scene, brainstorm with your photographer about what you're after and ways to treat it. Driving back, map out the piece with photographers to guide photo selection and test your ideas. If possible, help select the photos and write the captions. Television crews do this kind of planning on the fly all the time.

You probably won't have a photographer with you (most of us don't), but you can carry a camera, or use the one in your phone. It'll remind you to see things and think visually, even if you don't take a single shot. Writing coach Rene Cappon once equipped his entire staff with cheap film cameras. He ordered them to carry their cameras with them all week. For five days, they all wrote stories full of visual details. But he didn't give them any film. Not magic, but awareness.

Graphic artists are great brainstormers simply because they don't think like writers. They think in patterns you'd never come up with. They can package complex information into graphs, charts, diagrams, videos, and pictures that explain things better than words. For example, look at your left wrist; now think about its internal structure; now imagine all those bones moving, and then broken, and then repaired surgically. Impossible to describe with words alone.

Most writers think of copy editors as people who come in at the end of production, but they're also helpful in the middle, especially with questions of format and usage. You flatter them when you ask them for advice early, and they'll treat your pieces better later. Copy editors know everything, not just the rules of their publication, but also the corporate memory of treating the subject. A copy editor in Seattle may know more about Boeing than Boeing employees. Their skill with headlines and captions can pop your disorganized thinking into focus, just by talking with them, and you want that clarity early, while you're still typing. Copy editors can perform magic on key sentences that won't work.

Here's a copy editor trick you can do by yourself. When you have a problem with a sentence or paragraph, cover your screen and ask out loud, "What am I trying to say here?" Answer the question orally, and the solution will pop into your head. This technique works even better and faster with two people, especially if the other one is a copy editor.

Why don't you, as a writer, ask for help in the middle of your writing process? You don't want to seem stupid. You think that only weak writers need help. You don't have any helpers. You don't have time to save time. Forget these excuses. Ask for help. And give help in return.

WRITING IS TOO COMPLICATED TO DO BY YOURSELF.

You may not have access to any of these helpful specialists, especially if you're a freelancer like me. But sometimes you will, and you should let them help you while you've got them. Seek them out and cultivate them; they'll help you write better. Remember to thank them, invite them to parties, and buy them drinks.

INTERVIEW FOR RICH MATERIAL

There are two kinds of writers: those who interview, and those who don't. Interviews open paths to information you can't get otherwise. Writers often ask me what makes some pieces deep, compared to the general run of writing, which is shallow. Deep pieces result primarily from skilled interviewing.

Interviews enrich writing by giving you access not just to information, but also to character. They add human touches with quotations and anecdotes. We spend our entire lives learning to judge other people's characters from *how* they say things, not just *what* they say.

What do you want from an interview? Information, understanding, and some quotations, in that order. Effective interviewing techniques ensure that you leave the session with the information you need and understand, with some quotations to enliven your piece.

Interviewing, like writing, has its own process.

INTERVIEWING
PREPARATION
CHAT BASE CLOSE IN CLOSE OUT [SURPRISE]
ANNOTATION

PREPARATION includes everything you do before the interview begins, and ANNOTATION happens after it ends, when you assess, fill out, and correct your notes. The interview begins with CHAT, or small talk, followed by a long session of BASE, where you gather facts and establish a relationship that creates trust. CLOSE IN doesn't necessarily happen. It involves asking difficult, uncomfortable questions. CLOSE OUT cleans up unresolved issues, confirms statements, and gets material back on the record. And subjects often SURPRISE you at the very end.

PREPARATION COMES FIRST

Have you ever noticed that some of your friends catch social cues better than others? How do they do that? They listen and watch better. And you're about to learn the skill of deep listening and watching too.

Listening is the key to interviewing. The more you know going into an interview, the better you can listen. Good listening allows you to ask good follow-up questions, which will get you to the place where the best stuff lies. Preparation includes reading documents, especially by or about the person you're going to interview. You schedule difficult interviews later, so you can learn more about your subject in the easier ones.

Listening also involves looking. Survey and inventory the waiting room before the interview. Reception rooms express the personality of the person who controls them. For example, you notice a signed photograph of your subject playing pickup basketball with Barack Obama. So you start the interview like this: "I noticed a picture out there of you shooting hoops with President Obama." And your subject smiles and talks volubly about all the former presidents he knows, and you're deep into CHAT.

CHAT UP YOUR SUBJECT

Beginning an interview with small talk relaxes some of the tension inherent in interviews. The subject doesn't know you or trust you, so you ease your way in. Preparation helps you find common ground. Keep chat short and friendly.

LAY DOWN THE INFO BASE

Asking about basic information takes up most of any interview and also creates a relationship between you and the subject. Everybody you interview is afraid of you, because they don't know what you'll do with what they tell you. Your manner can disarm their anxiety, or make it worse. Subjects who trust you will tell you more.

You use body language and little prompts to encourage subjects, convincing them how professional you are, and how fascinating they are:

- Lean toward the subject.
- Maintain eye contact.
- Nod your head and say, "Uh-huh."
- Smile and laugh (sincerely) at funny bits.
- Take it slow.
- Let the subject see you taking notes.
- Keep saying, "Tell me more about that."

Sounds like dating, doesn't it? Interviewing and courtship use many of the same skills.

"Now wait a minute," you object, "television interviewers don't act like that. They ask hard questions right away, and stay in the subject's face." Right you are, but most television interviewers are in the entertainment business. They're after faces and conflict, not information and character.

Here's the tricky part: You have to react sincerely, or the subject will spot you as a phony and a manipulator. End of interview. Francesca Gino, a specialist in negotiation at the Harvard Business School, says, "When one feels like a fake, he or she is likely to behave like a fake."[2] If you think of yourself as a manipulator, you'll look like one. So think of yourself as a professional forming a bridge between this subject and your reader. Treat both fairly.

ASKING RUDE QUESTIONS

Here's the hard part. CLOSE IN follows BASE, when you realize that you and your subject are ready for tough questions. Many writers fail to write deep pieces because they can't (or won't) ask hard questions. They don't know how or they're afraid of conflict or their mother's rules of politeness get in the way. But proper techniques and attitudes will let you ask tough questions and follow them up with harder ones.

You avoid hard questions until you think your subject's ready to answer them. But how do you know the magic moment has arrived? Watch the subject's body language:

- Enjoying the conversation
- Hands and arms away from the body
- Shoulders down and relaxed
- Leaning in and smiling
- Volunteering things you didn't ask about

Your date's starting to like you.

Your subject's ready, but are you? Your mother taught you not to ask rude questions, and here you are sitting with an important person, about to ask why he added melamine to baby formula. Your mother yells in your ear, "NO, NO, NO, DON'T ASK HIM THAT!" You say to yourself, "Quiet, Mother. I'm a professional writer. I have a license to ask hard questions."

Then you soften the tension a little and ask the zinger: "You know, this next question may seem a little harsh, but I do have to bring it up. Why did you add melamine to the baby formula?" Then you just sit there, maintaining eye contact, and wait.

And wait.

And wait.

And keep your mouth shut and wait.

And the subject will either throw you out or answer the question.

Human beings find silence excruciating, so it's hard for you to shut up. Here's how. Count under your breath. Or say silently, "Shut up, shut up, shut up." Or think about a polar bear, anything to keep you from speaking. My colleague Roy Clark is half Italian and can't talk without moving his arms, so he shuts up by tucking his hands under his thighs.

If you're still in the room, the next follow-up questions will probably yield the treasure. Listen, ask the follow-ups, shut up and wait, listen, follow up....

> THE KEY TO DEEP INTERVIEWING IS DEEP FOLLOW-UP QUESTIONS.

CLOSE OUT AND MOP UP

CLOSE OUT is the cleaning-up phase. Now's the time for you to review anything you're unsure about. Ask the little questions that didn't fit before. You'll read about "off the record" later. Here's where you get confidential matters back on the record.

Ask the source if you can call back later in case you need to check something. You might say you work at home at night, so would she mind if you called her at home. Swap business cards if you haven't already. How you end the interview determines whether you get back in again. It's all a matter of trust.

See how you create trust? By coming on slow and easy and unthreatening. Interviewers who come on hard-ass collect a lot of "No comment."

SURPRISE AT THE END!

At the very end of CLOSE OUT, a magic moment often happens. You close your notebook and stand up to leave, thanking the subject. Suddenly she starts talking about something you didn't ask, because you didn't know about it. You open your notebook and ask good follow-up questions until this phase runs out.

Why does this wonderful revelation happen? The subject has something she wants to talk about, but dopey you didn't bring it up. I always prompt for it at the end, like this: "Thank you for being so open with me. By the way, is there anything else you'd like to talk about?"

ANNOTATE YOUR NOTES TO MAKE SENSE

As soon as the interview ends, if possible, sit down onsite and annotate your notes. Expand contractions and abbreviations. Inventory what you got and what you missed. If you're still at the scene, you can probably get what you need in a document or by asking an assistant or a secretary.

> I learned the best of what I know about interviewing from John Sawatsky. If you ever get the chance to attend one of his workshops, he'll change your life, as he did mine. Thanks, John.

ASKING QUESTIONS IN INTIMATE SPACE

Where would you interview someone for the best results? The more meaningful the site to your subject, the richer the interview. This principle is called "intimate space." The closer you get to your subject's heart, your subject's real self, the more information and insight you'll gain, especially important in profiles.

Important people have all sorts of screens and defenses to keep you out of their intimate space. So you work your way in, often over a long period of time, sometimes with a series of interviews.

What's the least intimate space? Written answers to written questions. You can't see the subjects or their surroundings, and the answers are probably written or vetted by staff. The source controls everything, and you can't ask follow-up questions. Some writers refuse to submit written questions, but sometimes it's the only way to get access, especially to hostile or military sources.

Next is telephone interviewing. Again, you can't see the subject, and the subject can't see you. Visual clues play a huge role in establishing trust, especially for deep interviews. Videophone connection, such as Skype, provides crude visual clues.

Some interviewers are terrific with just sound clues, but most aren't. You want to interview, if possible, on site. Let's say that the subject is the male CEO of a company. You want to interview inside his building, which has different levels of intimacy in different places. A corporate meeting room reflects the culture of the company, not the subject. Decorators designed it to reflect corporate values. Meeting rooms tend to be rather bare, lacking in clues to your subject.

Corporate boardrooms have the same problem but are more intimate in that they have more signals on the walls, such as portraits, awards, certificates, and prizes. The décor makes statements about the company, but probably says little about your subject, beyond his approval. You can probably get most of what you see there in documents or from the Internet ahead of time.

His office is more intimate; it's where he works. Again, it will be professionally decorated, with corporate iconography, but it will also include personal touches, such as diplomas, pictures (especially signed ones), and trophies. It's full of things he's proud of.

The subject's desk is a gold mine of clues, and you need to see it. What's on it, and what isn't? My desk has statuettes of Thomas Jefferson and Johann Gutenberg, clues to what I'm really about. If you interview me in my study, you might ask what those two figures mean to me. If you look up, you'll notice a model galleon with a golden hull and silver sails hanging from the light fixture. What's that about?

Subjects often decorate their offices with their hobbies. I remember the adjacent offices of two executives. One had airplane propellers on the ceiling, and the other had animal heads glaring from the walls. You can develop such clues to character during the initial chat.

Some subjects have two offices, one public and the other a private retreat. Thomas Jefferson kept a mansion all to himself at Poplar Forest in Lynchburg, Virginia, where he could escape the public. These private lairs are more intimate still.

Some executives manage by walking around, a kind of moving intimate space. You'll learn a lot by following them, watching not only what they do and say, but also how others react to them. You'll see the actors in action.

Now, for a leap in intimacy, enter your subject's private life. Interviewing at home may be more intimate, and the house or apartment has levels of closeness: living room, parlor, office. Julia Child's kitchen combined the intimacy of a home and a workplace. A friend of mine interviewed in a bedroom and learned about scent on a pillow.

In his book *Off Ramp*, Hank Stuever passes along a tip from Susan Ager:

> Always ask, at some point, to use the bathroom when you're interviewing somebody. Ask this in their home, especially,

> but also in their office or workplace, whether you need to use the bathroom or not. If you're in the subject's home, it's just another way further in—down the hall, on your right, past all these fascinating pictures of the children when they were in high school, including the one your subject didn't yet mention, the child who drowned in 1973. The little pearly soaps in the dish by the sink; the potpourri Glade; the old issue of *Cosmopolitan* opened to the horoscope.[3]

What could be more intimate than a bathroom? Interviewing inside the subjects' passions, such as beside their model-train layout, in their walled peony garden, or on their sailboat, the "Millie B.," out of Wiscasset, Maine. If you want to get close to me, we'll talk inside my messy sculpture studio.

YOUR EXTERNAL PERSONA AND YOUR INTERNAL PERSONA

Your *persona* is the speaking voice your readers perceive as they read you, but it's not the same as you, the author. It's a fictionalized version of yourself directed at outsiders. You also use your *persona* when speaking with other people. Your external *persona* (or mask) chats with their *persona*.

You also have an *internal persona*, how you represent yourself to yourself. It's an artifact that you create and modify. It can push you through barriers to get what you need, especially during sticky interviews.

My son Jason, sixteen at the time, attended a summer course for student writers in St. Petersburg, Florida. He liked to hang around Al Lang Stadium, right up the street, where his favorite New York Mets used to practice during spring training. One day, he lurked outside the empty stadium's gate, staring at the pitcher's mound. He wanted to stand on that hillock and see what home plate looked like to pitchers, but the sign over his head commanded "No Admittance!" He looked at the mound, then at the sign, then the mound, then the sign. Then he asked permission and got it. He swaggered onto the field and stood on the mound.

How did he do that? He thought of himself as a writer, not just a kid, not just another baseball fan. His writer *persona* made him act like a writer, someone who gets access because he asks for it. Put on the face of a tiger, and you are one.

Many writers never produce deep pieces because they hesitate to approach people or ask hard questions. Your mother warned you never to talk to strangers and not to bother people you don't know. And she might have a heart attack if she heard you asking tough, intrusive questions. My very Southern mother would have disowned me if she knew I talked to strangers about that most taboo of subjects: money. Even worse, I write about it.

You deal with your mother's restrictions by defining your own *persona*, not as a child, but as a writer, and living it. You say to yourself, "That's what writers do, Mom. I am one. I have a license to ask hard questions, and stand on the mound."

EFFECTIVE QUESTIONS GET GOOD ANSWERS

John Sawatsky taught me that the way you ask questions in interviews determines how good an answer you get. Not only that, but some ways of asking actually suppress good answers.

In general, you want your subjects to give you accurate, full, and honest responses. You want to find out what they know and think. And you don't want canned stuff written by staffs for them to memorize and spout back at you.

Effective questions tend to be open-ended, active, neutral, simple, and short.

Open-Ended Questions don't limit subjects to one path, but allow them to choose where to go. Such questions often lead you to things you didn't know about, and give you clues to your subjects' personality and experience. Here's an open-ended question: "What formed you as an artist working in glass?"

Active Questions make the subjects think. They require exploration and invite follow-ups, where the treasure usually lies. Here's an active question: "How do financial considerations influence what you choose to paint?"

Neutral Questions avoid value judgments that can lead to digressions. Suppose you ask, "Had you seen Van Gogh's *Starry Night* (my favorite painting) before you painted *Brightly Night*?" The artist may respond to your parenthetical remark about your taste and say, "Actually, it's not *my* favorite." Then you have to ask the question again in different form. A neutral version would be "What artworks, if any, influenced your *Brightly Night*?" And you get to Van Gogh eventually.

Simple Questions focus a little more by limiting the avenues the subjects can pursue. "Why did you switch from painting on canvas to painting on glass?"

And **Short Questions** tend to get the best answers of all, because they startle your subjects a little but don't distract them. The most effective short question, in my experience, is "Why?" Then I sit back, shut up, and wait. I also use "How?" and "Oh?" a lot. My favorite question is more a prompt than a question: "Hmm, tell me more."

LESS EFFECTIVE QUESTIONS GET DULL ANSWERS

Some interview questions are good because they yield full, useful, accurate answers, and keys to character. Does that make other questions bad? Rather than "bad," I'd call them "less effective." Any question, no matter how offensive or clumsy, just might produce a helpful answer in spite of itself. We're talking about the form of the question encouraging success.

Less effective interview questions don't get the information you need, damage trust, and don't help you control the interview. Basically, such questions have something about them that distracts the subject from what you're after.

Less effective questions come in many forms. Subjects who are sophisticated about media know those patterns, wait for you to use them, and turn them against you to their advantage. So avoid less effective forms as far as possible.

Double Questions

First, your relatives taught you by example a type of question that smooths social situations by deliberately neutralizing the answer. I call it "hardball-softball" or a "double question." When you ask someone a question, and her facial expression tells you that you've just offended her, you immediately ask a second question before she can speak. She answers the second, safe question, and you're both off the hook. This deep instinct will get in your way, especially when you're asking tough close-in questions.

Suppose you're interviewing a CEO whose company is in trouble, and you've reached the close-in stage, ready for the hard stuff. So you ask, "What responsibility do you bear for your company's collapse? Is it really fair to blame someone?" And he answers only the second question, the softball, nattering on about fairness.

Whoa, where did that second, mushy question come from? From your mother's example. Subjects trained to handle media wait for you to throw the softball. So you remind yourself: Ask single questions.

Suitcase Questions

"The suitcase" is a series of questions, all crammed together, like this:

> Your company collapsed for a number of reasons, right? What were those factors, how many were your fault, how could you have avoided them, and what have you learned from this experience? Can you answer that?

Your subject will probably answer the next to last question ("What have you learned from this experience?") because it's the safest. Notice that this suitcase also ends with a softball: "Can you answer that?"

Leading Questions

Leading questions have a trap in them: "When did you realize that you were committing a felony?" An astute subject will spot the trap, and your interview is over. Almost anyone worth interviewing is smart enough to detect manipulation.

Assuming Questions

Some questions have an assumption built in, allowing the subject to address the assumption rather than the main thrust, like this: "Since your company's collapse was your fault, have you discussed your resignation with your board of directors?"

Biased Questions

Sometimes questions have a slant built into them, usually an offensive word or phrase. John Sawatsky calls them "triggers." They set the subject off, usually into anger, and almost always into rejection. Here's one: "Why did your company hire a *corporate wrecker* like you as its president?" And you get lots of drama but little information.

Narrow Questions Asked Too Early

This category has to do with timing as well as form. You begin a well-planned interview with a series of broad and open-ended questions to lay down a base of information and trust. You then focus in with narrow questions. Radio and television interviewers seem to lead with the narrow question. Actually, they probably didn't; they edited out the earlier ones.

Either/Or Questions

This kind of question offers the subject a fork in the road: The answer must be one of two things you've selected. But the real answer may be a third or fourth alternative, and your limiting can be offensive and reductive: "Are you likely to resign soon or get fired?"

Yes/No Questions

Listen to other people interviewing, and you'll notice that most of their questions call for a *Yes* or a *No*. These questions have the same problem as *either/or*: They limit the answer and don't engage the subject's interest. Besides, the answer to most *Yes/No* questions is "It depends."

Yes/No questions are useful during the close-out phase, when you're looking for confirmations: "Earlier, you said the board gave you six months severance, have I got that right?"

Arguing Questions

Arguing with subjects sometimes yields good results, but it damages the atmosphere of trust. Notice the rising hostility in this series:

> But didn't you just say that the company's health was your responsibility?
> *Blah, blah.*
> Well, is it, or isn't it?
> *Blah, blah.*
> So what are you going to do about it?

Arguing may destroy the relationship of trust that you established earlier.

Interrupting Questions

Interrupting is fashionable on television because viewers seem to like conflict. But breaking into the subjects' speech yields little information and makes them start thinking about ending the interview. You're there to find things out, not for personal drama. Watch this interchange:

> *Blah, blah, blah...* "But you were the president, weren't you?"
> *Blah, blah...* "What does that phrase 'in charge' mean to you?"
> *Blah...* "Why do you keep talking about others?"

You may leave that interview congratulating yourself on how tough you are, but you'll have very little in your notebook. And you won't get back in again.

EFFECTIVE QUESTIONS ARE OPEN-ENDED, ACTIVE, NEUTRAL, SIMPLE, AND SHORT.

QUESTIONS FOR MAGIC RESULTS

Some questions are so effective that I label them "magic."

1. "What happened?"
2. "Why?"
3. "Explain how X works."
4. "What can you tell me about X?"
5. "What do you remember about X?"
6. "Where can I find out more about X?"
7. "Talk about that. Tell me more."
8. "What do you expect to do about X?"
9. "What might happen next?"
10. "What does X look like when you see it?"
11. "What's important about X?"
12. "Describe your day for me."
13. "What do you mean?"
14. "How would you explain Y to Z?"
15. "What does X mean to you (or to the organization or to Y)?"
16. "How do you know that?"
17. "What am I not seeing?"

SMART PEOPLE ASK DUMB QUESTIONS

You probably hesitate to ask dumb questions for fear you'll be thought stupid. But dumb questions get at assumptions and make subjects think.

Here's a dumb question: "What's a dumb question?" A dumb question is so basic that nobody else asks it. Everybody assumes that everybody else knows the answer, or nobody thinks of the question in the first place. I find dumb questions easy to ask because I want to know the answers.

I asked one recently at a panel on the architecture of the University of Virginia. Richard Guy Wilson, a Virginia architecture specialist, was describing the restoration of the "parapets" on Pavilion Ten to an audience of architects, faculty members, and restoration specialists. During the question period, I asked what parapets are used for, and the whole audience burst out laughing. Later, I asked why they found the question funny, and they all said they either didn't know what a parapet was, or what it was for. An audience of experts sat there not knowing something that basic but afraid to ask. Several of them thanked me later.

(By the way, a parapet is a wall around a roof.)

Jennifer Stevenson asked the president of St. Petersburg Junior College to define "junior college." He replied that no one had ever asked him that, complained that every writer got it wrong, and gave a definition that opened up a whole realm of insider information she hadn't imagined.

Dumb questions have a startling effect on interview subjects. They're usually taken aback and rarely have a prepared answer. So you get a fresh, unrehearsed, and often honest reply, which leads to rich follow-up questions.

The most powerful dumb question I know is "Why?" Just ask it and smile and shut up and wait.

TAKING NOTES YOU CAN MAKE SENSE OF

What could be simpler than taking notes? You've done it for years in school without thinking about it at all. You hear the source say something you want to keep, and you write it down. Not simple at all. While you're trying to jot it down from memory, she keeps on talking, saying something even more interesting and important than what you're struggling to capture. Meanwhile, you have to listen so you can ask follow-up questions.

So you start wishing for a recorder or shorthand. Don't. Recording can make you slow and literal-minded, and shorthand tempts you to write down everything the subject says. I know only two writers who handle shorthand effectively, and both use it only to take notes, not to record everything their subjects say. Some writers invent their own small version of shorthand (* for *star*, [[[for *note*), which they mix with words.

Good notetaking means good listening, control of the interview, and a notebook full of treasure. Two factors get in your way: writing down everything the subject says and trying to get it all in quotation form.

After a terrific interview, you'll probably use five percent of what the subject said, and maybe only ten percent of that in quotation form. The best quotations usually come late in interviews, after you've established an atmosphere of trust and can ask targeted questions that get at character and depth. That's when you may need verbatim notes.

You actually want very little of the information in quotation form. Most subjects don't speak well, so you have to paraphrase them later anyway. Lots of quotations in a piece, especially long ones, make it harder to read.

You can train yourself to listen and take good notes. Record a radio interview show or a press conference from television. Try to write down everything the speakers say, then compare what you get with the recording. You'll see how much of an interview is filler and blither and not useful, and how hard it is to make sense of those notes later. Then do the exercise again with a different program, listening hard for meaning and taking notes on content, rather than the exact words. Try to collect at least one good quotation verbatim. The second method is so much easier that you'll want to perfect it, eventually practicing on live subjects. Interview your mother or a close friend; you'll be stunned by how hard she is to quote.

How much of a quotation you actually write down depends on your memory. One friend of mine never uses a recorder or a notebook. She writes down long quotations from memory later. I doubt her memory is that good. I do have a good memory, so I write down only the big words in a quotation and fill in the little ones immediately after the interview. Some writers jot down key phrases and fill in the rest later.

You can control the pace of a one-on-one interview. I always ask my sources to please talk slower so I can get down all the good stuff they're saying. They interpret that request as my being interested and careful about accuracy. (Well, I am.) You can slow things down by asking a question you don't want the answer to. Then you fill in the previous note, or jot down an observation, like "Signed pic Elie Wiesel on desk? Ask later."

When the subject says something you want verbatim, you can interject, "Oh, that's good. Can you say that again?" It'll come out clearer the second time. Variants include "Really?" "You mean X..., right?" "Did I hear you correctly, that Y...?" Use this technique sparingly so the subject doesn't notice it.

For some pieces, you may need sound or video, but even then, solid notetaking will pay off later. Good notes make sense of your recorded material quickly.

A RANT AGAINST RECORDERS

For thirty years, I've waged a campaign against tape and digital recorders. Recording can make you slow and literal-minded and a poor listener.

Effective interviewing involves creating and maintaining temporary trust between yourself and your subject. I try to turn every interview into a conversation. But the recorder reminds subjects that other people might hear what they're saying, so they go all formal and make speeches. They give guarded, safe answers. They speak oddly.

I once interviewed a star writer, with a tape recorder running between us. Suddenly, he leapt up and hit the STOP button, saying, "I can't stand for my colleagues to hear this." Of course, no one but me would ever hear that tape. The machine made him self-conscious and afraid.

Your subjects can use their recorders as weapons. You're setting up for a tough interview, and your subject lifts his big, black recorder onto his desk and pushes the REC button. He's just sent you a message: "My lawyer will listen to this, bud!" So you slap your bigger, blacker recorder onto the desk beside his, and hit your REC button. You've just replied, "So will mine, buster!" You'll get nothing useful from that session because you both poisoned the atmosphere. Expect lots of "No comment." In that situation, I would turn my recorder off and put it out of sight.

Recording encourages lazy notetaking and lazy listening. Your recorder's running and theoretically getting everything said, so you think you can relax and let it do the work. Pretty soon, you're not concentrating, and your follow-up questions get fuzzy. And when you listen to it, it may have a big surprise for you. The machine failed; your recording is blank!

A technician once videotaped a weeklong series of workshops I gave. After the first session, I suggested he listen to the tape to make sure it worked. He told me not to tell him how to do his job. On Friday, all twenty tapes had nothing on them but BZZZZZZZ.

RECORDERS ALWAYS FAIL AT THE WORST MOMENT.

Writers record conversations mostly because they're anxious to get the quotations right. However, most quotations have to be "cleaned up" a little, sometimes a lot, to make them publishable. Writers who use recorders are more likely to put long verbatim quotations in their pieces, making them less readable.

Writers often paraphrase subjects to make what they say intelligible, and having the recorded quotation available tempts the writer to quote more. Bad quotations make bad explanation; they make reading drag.

Rather than depend on the machine, teach yourself to listen intently and take good notes. Your follow-up questions will improve because you listened better. Your notebook will contain essential facts and impressions and quotations, not pages of blither.

Procrastinators try desperately to find some reason, any excuse, not to start typing. Recording can encourage you to delay. Your friendly recorder sits there waiting, singing this siren song: "Maybe you should just listen to this whole recording, just in case you missed something." Give in to that temptation, and you've just killed two, three, seven hours. That voice might even tempt you to transcribe the whole thing. Procrastinators are ingenious time wasters.

Despite all my growling above, there are times when you might use a recorder, such as in hostile interviews where lawyers might get involved later. You would need one for interviewing foreign-language speakers when you're not fluent in their tongue; later, a native speaker can help you catch nuances and check your translation. You have to record any interview that will turn into a transcript, such as "Question-and-Answer" format, or an oral history. Finally, you would record any interview with a person of historical importance. If you have the great fortune to get a session with Nelson Mandela, record it and donate it later to an archive.

Can you use recorders in ways that won't undo you? Of course. Use a small, extremely reliable machine with brand-new or freshly recharged batteries. Use it only as a backup to great listening and note taking. Write down the counter numbers of important things the subject says, and listen only to those marked items later. And always remember the temptations that accompany recording.

I get lots of flak about my crusade against recording. I'm ferocious about this subject because, as a writing coach, I constantly deal with writers hobbled by their machines. The slowest ones record everything, and then transcribe it. But, as my friend Tom Berner reminds me, "The fault lies not with the recorder, but with the person using it."

There are good ways and bad ways to use them, depending on your memory, listening and notetaking skills, intensity of the interview, and time schemes. Someone writing a book may have time to transcribe whole tapes, but someone on a short deadline doesn't.

Tom Berner told me he always uses a recorder to write his bimonthly newsletter pieces. Recording means he "can actually listen to the person and not fret about getting everything on paper. I can also frame follow-up questions rather than following my script." Later, he explains, "I download my interviews to my computer, type my modest notes, then listen to the interview and fill in the blanks. I'm listening for the salient quote, not the run-on sentence, and for the interesting fact I missed in my handwritten notes."

The key phrase here is "not fret about getting everything on paper." Many writers fail because they try to bring back everything the source said. If that's what you need, perhaps for a Q&A format, you should use a recorder, because you need to transcribe it. But in general, recording and transcribing are the downfall of procrastinators.

My friend John Sawatsky, a former investigative reporter and biographer, is the world's best teacher of interviewing. He looks for concentrated moments of news, and finds that heavy notetaking requires too much energy and takes attention away from what he calls "big themes." But, when writing news or on deadline, John "takes notes as if I didn't have the recorder." He always writes down the counter numbers of key quotations.

For fast-breaking news, he'd record and take notes, including counter numbers. He'd mark up his notes, transcribing key moments from the recording, write the first two sentences, and then dictate the piece on the phone to a rewrite man, using his notes and selected transcriptions.

Maybe I'm too snarly about transcribing as a waste of time. But notice that both Tom and John transcribe only key quotations, not the whole recording. Tom Berner is right; it's how you use your tools that counts.

MARKING UP NOTES SO YOU CAN FIND THINGS

Earlier, I talked about drowning in information. Effective gathering produces lots of data, and you need ways to manage it. Annotating your notes gives them structure, and enables you to find things. Your notebook can swamp you if you don't mark it up.

You need a marking system that works for you. My colleague Roy Clark uses the simplest system I know: He puts a check beside notes he might use. That's it. He then types only the checked notes into his computer. Roy types 140 words per minute, so it doesn't take him long. He has one principle for annotating: importance. He only marks notes he might use. Some people use a highlighter.

Other writers indicate degrees of importance, using symbols such as stars or asterisks. The more stars, the more important the note. I draw a key beside the most important notes, the size of the key indicates relative importance.

I once coached a writer who put a number grade, one to one hundred, beside every note he took, one hundred being most important. He graded each note, including those of zero importance. He kept regrading older notes as he took new ones. I asked him if his system worked for him, and he replied, "No, I think it makes me slow." He didn't know any other way to annotate his notes, so I taught him several faster ways.

> RETHINK ANY TECHNIQUE THAT MAKES YOU SLOW.

Some people code notes by subject. On a piece about a zoo, for example, they might use categories such as animals that *walk*, animals that *swim*, and animals that *fly*, abbreviated in the margin as *W*, *S*, and *F*. Then they can rapidly locate all the birds in their notes. Penguins cause problems.

Some writers, including me, figure out the parts of their piece before they start gathering, and code for the sections. Suppose I'm writing about zoo animals dying from polluted water. I might annotate like this: animals that died (D), animals that lived (L), probable causes (C), and likely solutions (S). Then I can pull all the material related to a section together quickly. Bradley Graham divided his notebook into sections by subject ahead of time and wrote each note in the relevant section. I asked him why he did that, and he said it made it easier to write in helicopters.

Some writers, especially those doing profiles, organize around quotations, so they put a *Q* in the margin beside anything quoted. Some business writers mark figures with a dollar sign ($) in the margin.

You can write notes to yourself in the notebook, but you need to distinguish them from what your subject said. I jot my initials ("DF") in the margin beside things I said or thought. If you don't understand something, put a question mark by it, so you can ask about it later. If your interview subject mentions a document you should read, you can jot "GET" or "FIND" in the margin.

You can also include notes to yourself on how to write the piece. For example, I look for beginnings and endings as I gather. When I spot something I might use, I mark it "PB" (Potential Beginning) or "PK" (Potential Kicker, or Ending).

Avoid making pejorative remarks in your notes, such as "Lying creep." Lawyers can use them against you later to prove malice. Many publications make their writers discard their notebooks to keep them out of courts; some publications require writers to keep notes for a specified period, such as the statute of limitations for libel.

Here's one page of my notes from a newsletter piece on a local investment club. I've cleaned them up so you can understand them. The sections are club (C), investments (I), and success (S).

ANNOTATION	NOTES
SPELLING?	Richard Mallison 'Dick' 96
C	Pres. Hazelwood Dr. investment club elected annually
	Start 2003, $100 each annually
C	7 members, "most engineer geezers"
I	"make sure stock is way up, then buy"
?	no-fee broker
	"hot debates" majority
I	No S[outh] A[frican] stocks
	No women, no wives, lotsa beer
S	Lost everything twice
C	Purpose: $ hide from wives, poker
I	Tech, auto, phone, ag, utilities
S,PK	"no longer speaking"
S	disbanding, 1 member—me
S, CHECK	Lost 7x$100x5-$3500
	"penny-ante thinking"
PK	"more fun than your drill press"
I	ZRB, KKT, TTP, AMV
??	Worst—insured insurance
	Best—no best

HOW TO LISTEN FOR EVERYTHING PEOPLE SAY

The key to effective interviewing is asking good follow-up questions. Most writers don't listen well, and many interviews fail because of not paying attention. Listening sharply is a skill you can learn and perfect.

Your brain is the problem. Human beings listen four times as fast as they speak, so your mind goes wandering off. Good listening involves riveting your attention.

First of all, decide that you want to hear everything the person says, whether it's interesting or not. Most human speech contains little information and merely aims at tending social relationships. Think of listening as information mining. You need to gather lots of spoken data to dig out the good stuff.

Second, while you're listening, do not think about what you're going to ask or say next. Then you're paying attention to yourself, not to your subject.

NEVER THINK ABOUT YOURSELF DURING INTERVIEWS.

Third, wait a while before evaluating the accuracy or truth of what your subject is saying. If in doubt, put a question mark beside that item in your notebook. Otherwise, you may start arguing with the subject in your head while she keeps talking. Again, you're not paying attention. Later, you can ask probing questions. And what you thought was wrong may turn out to be valid when you've heard more.

Fourth, avoid comparing yourself with the person you're listening to. Again, your brain loves to keep score and distracts you. Your subject rambles along, and you start thinking, "What a dodo. I'm a lot smarter than this guy. Why am I wasting my time with him?" And he just said, "I stole my granddaughter's trust fund," but you weren't paying attention.

Your brain can also intimidate you, like this: "Geez, this guy's smart, a lot smarter than I am. He obviously thinks I'm a dunce. Oops, was that a yawn? I'm boring him to death...." And he just said, "Global warming is voodoo economics," but you weren't paying attention.

Fifth, take good notes. Writers who take effective notes listen better by asking good follow-up questions. They're tuned up not just for the good stuff, but also for the clues to the good stuff.

LOOKING INTO EACH OTHER'S EYES

Anybody who's ever dated knows the value of eye contact in conversation. In "The Ecstasy" the poet John Donne says to his beloved, "Our eye-beams twisted, and did thread / Our eyes upon one double string."[4]

In interviews, you watch the subject's eyes for signals, and use our own eyes to keep the person engaged. But as John Sawatsky says, "It is important to maintain eye contact during the interview, which is hard while actively taking notes."

You could fire up a recorder and not take notes at all. If you have a source who pays no attention to the machine and talks normally anyway, if you can pay rapt attention and ask good follow-up questions, and if you have a recorder that never never never fails, that might be a good (but dangerous) tactic.

Where do you hold your notebook while maintaining eye contact? Some people think notetaking makes subjects nervous, so they hide it, keeping the notebook in their lap so the subject won't see them jotting. They write without looking, which means they get only a few notes on a page, and they're hard to read. The notebook also contains jottings for yourself, such as key questions and annotations, and you can't see them in your lap.

I prefer to use my notebook as a prop, letting the subject see me taking notes avidly. I create an atmosphere of intense interest. I take notes on letter-size yellow pads and write with lots of elbow. I want my subjects to see me getting their words down and asking further questions to get them absolutely right. It's part of how I build trust and turn interviews into conversations.

My subjects see me smiling and nodding and saying, "Um-hum, um-hum." They think they see me writing down their words. In fact, I may be inventorying the desk and the walls, looking for clues to character: "Bust of J Wayne? Ask."

For telephone interviewing, you can let the subject hear you typing notes. Some writers want the subject to hear them getting down every precious word, while others hide the key clicks. You can turn the click sounds on or off on most computers.

My pal Ed Miller has a tactic for riveting his attention: "I stare intently at the person's eyes while envisioning a little sign on his forehead that says 'Please listen to me!' Every time I look in their eyes, my peripheral vision 'sees' that reminder to concentrate. All I have to do to trigger this device is do what comes naturally—look at the person who's talking to me."

Like any other interviewing technique, don't overdo it. If subjects notice your tricks, they start to feel manipulated, and you lose the atmosphere of trust.

GOING "OFF THE RECORD"

(Pardon me while I get technical for a few pages. This subject is so wrapped in mythology and misunderstanding that it requires full explanation.)

Everybody knows the phrase "off the record," but few agree on what it means. I work on the assumption that everything a subject says is available for public quoting and attribution, unless the writer and the subject agree ahead of time that it's not. That's the basis of all that follows.

Writers attribute quotations to the speaker so readers can judge the validity of the information. But sometimes subjects want to reveal something without putting their names on it. They might fear being fired or punished for revealing secrets. The off-the-record process allows writers to grant them that privilege, although it harms the readers' understanding and reduces the writer's credibility. So, in general, writers use the technique sparingly, only to protect the source and because the information has compelling public importance.

I'm talking about agreements you make with the source. Several technical terms govern sourcing: "off the record," "not for attribution," and "on background." Casually used, "off the record" usually means that the writer may quote statements but not attribute them to the source, in other words, "not for attribution." Others think that "off the record" means the writer may not quote or attribute the statement, but can use it to obtain the same information elsewhere. A strict definition would say that the writer cannot use the information at all, even to follow it up; this version is often called "on background."

Unless a publication you write for has specific definitions of these terms, I recommend the following. When a subject asks to "go off the record," *i.e.*, say something without attribution, you reply: "By 'off the record,' you mean I can use this information, even quote it, as long as I don't put your name on it? We call that 'not for attribution.' Okay?" If the subject agrees, you write, "not for attribution" in your notes, and record the time. If the subject disagrees, negotiate what "off the record" means, and what you can do with the information. Either way, you continue to take notes on what's said. As soon as possible, get the subject to agree that you're back on the record, record the time, and write in your notes, "on the record." Years later, perhaps in court, you can document exactly what was and was not on the record, if you kept your notes.

> CONSISTENT NOTETAKING MAY SAVE YOU IN COURT.

Here's a magic technique to get off-the-record stuff back onto the record, so you can use it fully. Near the end of an interview, during the CLOSE OUT stage, try something like this. "I'd like to use some of the things you said while we were off the record. Could we review them and make sure we agree?" The subject agrees. Then read some fairly innocuous thing said in confidence, and ask if you can use it. The subject agrees. Then read some less innocent thing said in confidence, and ask if you can use it. The subject agrees. Then ask if you can use that part about the axe murder. The subject agrees. Be ready with follow-up questions. Slow and easy, not scary.

This trick succeeds about half the time. Why does it work? Subjects tell you something in confidence because they're afraid of you, or not sure what you'll do with it. Later in the interview, particularly after hard questions, if you've created an atmosphere of trust, they worry less and will reconsider passages.

What if the subject tells you something terrific, and then announces it's off the record? You don't accept that condition; you negotiate. You might also ask why the subject wants the information off the record. If you play hard-ass ("You said it, bud, and it's goin' in this piece!"), the interview is over, and you can't ask follow-up questions.

> EVERYTHING IS ON THE RECORD UNLESS YOU BOTH AGREE THAT IT'S NOT.

There are also legal and ethical aspects of this process. Off-the-record agreements, even oral ones, are legal contracts between the subject and the publishing organization, not between the subject and the writer. Be prepared to identify your anonymous sources to your editors.

I believe professional writers have an ethical obligation to protect unsophisticated subjects with a warning. A shrewd interviewer can get an innocent person to say almost anything, but that doesn't mean you should publish it. The warning might go like this: "Your mother will read this. Are you sure you want to say in public that she has three husbands?" Sometimes being ethical can cost you good material, but you can live with yourself later.

Finally, never violate off-the-record agreements, which are promises based on trust. You won't get to talk to that subject again, and that subject will no longer talk to me or any other writer. We're all in this game together.

YOU CAN'T SEE ON THE PHONE

Interviewing on the phone is harder than face-to-face. You can't see your subjects, they can't see you, and they can bail out more easily when you start to close in. So you need some special techniques.

Because you're not present, you can't pick up cues from facial expressions or body language. Your subject may be talking perfectly calmly, but you don't see her doodling scowling faces. And she can't see you smiling and nodding, apparently writing down all the fascinating things she's saying. You can't ask about things you might notice in the scene, such as that dartboard of Dick Cheney's face, which you can't see.

Telephone interviews tend to be shorter, so you need to know what you're after, plan your questions ahead, and manage the time. I always make up a list of key questions to ask at the right moments. Resist the temptation to use a list of questions as a script, asking them in sequence. The key to great interviewing is listening hard to follow-up answers and adjusting your questions.

You have less time for chat to create an atmosphere and relax your subject. You'll spend less time asking factual questions that lay down a base for harder questions to follow. So you need a little more preparation to get things underway quickly and focus on essentials.

You can use time efficiently by keeping your questions short, clear, simple, and to the point. You're interviewing to find out what the subject knows, not to hear yourself talk. Direct the flow of topics, not letting the subject wander. Interrupt rambling politely but firmly, saying, "Hmm, that's really interesting. Now, let's talk about...." You can also sharpen the language and guide the flow by paraphrasing back what your subject says: "What I hear you saying is...." or "Do you mean...?"

Not being present makes confirming facts harder; you can't share documents easily. And you won't hear as well on the phone. So you double-check orally by reading back spellings and numbers, for example: "You mentioned Jane Jones, spelled 'J-A-N-E-J-O-N-E-S,' right?" You'll feel stupid spelling out "J-A-N-E-J-O-N-E-S," but then your subject replies, "Oh no, it's 'J-A-Y-N-E-J-O-H-N-E-S.'"

Sometimes a subject wants to end the call before you're through, so you turn it into an interruption. Ask for a time to call back. If the subject hangs up on you, here's a technique from the great police reporter, Edna Buchanan: Count to thirty, call back, and say, "I'm sorry. We were cut off."

At the end of a call, thank your subject and create a channel to talk with her again. Ask if you can call back to check things; request a home number and perhaps an e-mail address. Then say, "If you think of anything you'd like to add, give me a call; here's my number." And thank her again.

These phone techniques apply equally well to all interviews, whether you're there or not.

YOUR BUSINESS CARD STASH

Business cards are tools for writers, with probably more information per square inch than any other medium. You need your own, and you should collect them.

Ask everyone you interview or talk with for a business card and give them one in return. They contain important information, and reveal messages and images that suggest the character of the owner and the organization. My first business card from the Poynter Institute had raised gold lettering. Get the message?

Study the card immediately, and ask if everything on it is correct. Sounds like an obnoxious question, but often, the answer is "No." The commonest errors are the title and the e-mail address, which tend to change.

Now you have the person's full name, full title, full spelling of the organization, its address and logo, its phone number and the source's, as well as cell numbers, the e-mail address, maybe a fax number, and, if you're really lucky, the home phone. Some business cards even have the owner's picture. A treasure trove.

Some writers staple business cards into their notes, very efficient and accurate storage. Others have files of business cards, organized by name, subject, business, city, somehow. Several writers I know keep business cards in no order at all, usually in a drawer, and pull them out at random to get ideas. I write notes on business cards to remind me who the people were and anything distinctive about them. I correct any errors.

Why would you give a source *your* card? It helps to establish your image as a professional. It allows the subject to call you the next day when she figures out what she really wanted to say. And it gives her a way to find you later when she wants to tip you off or hire you to write something for her.

VACUUMING THE SCENE

Someday you'll be writing a piece about an event, maybe a trade show or a conference, and you'll notice a person walking in front of you, gathering anything with a picture, logo, map, diagram, or list on it. That's one of my students, who is "vacuuming the scene."

All that swag has two audiences and two purposes. It helps the writer make the piece visual, and it helps graphics colleagues with the visuals.

Most writers can't sketch and forget their camera, so they have trouble taking notes on visual things, such as the layout of rooms, details of machines, arrangements of objects, or the colors of food. If you don't take notes on things, you'll have trouble recalling them later when you need them. Visual materials spark your memory, and allow precise description. And if you're working online, you need original objects for illustration, not just downloaded video, which may or may not fit.

Sometimes you can't take objects with you, but you can shoot a photo. You'll recognize food writers in a restaurant; they take pictures of their dishes.

You don't necessarily need a good copy of a document if you're only using it for notetaking, so make a photocopy. Ask people sitting nearby at a conference if you can get it copied. Here's a little secret: Most people sitting behind tables in conference hotels want you to carry off their stuff so they don't have to lug it back to their office.

You also bring things back for graphic artists to turn into visuals. My colleague Pegie Stark Adam taught me not to worry about the condition of materials; artists can do wonders with almost anything. Matchbook with a coffee stain on it, no problem. Half a map, no sweat. Picture torn out of a magazine, okay. Just bring it all back.

If possible, brainstorm with the graphics people, explaining what you want to say and how. They don't think like you, so they'll come up with terrific ideas. Think for a moment about trying to describe the uniform of a Vatican Swiss guard in words alone. It's a piece of cake with a photo or a drawing. Photographers and graphic artists can save you and your readers many detail-oriented paragraphs.

So vacuum the scene and lug it all back. Such riches will make your pieces deeper, and editors and artists will adore you.

WRITING WHILE IT HAPPENS

Here's the fastest technique in this book. You write a continuous narrative on-site to capture a developing event, such as a problematic surgery or a chef preparing a tricky dessert. You draft action paragraphs as events unfold, without worrying much about significance until later. You can't know until the end what's really important for the outcome. So running copy is like taking notes, only in a more finished form. Blogging continuously from an event is a form of running copy. The technique works best when you can predict the overall shape, actors, and conventions of the event, such as a beauty contest.

Themes develop as you go along, and you can revise key paragraphs during breaks in the action. If beginnings or endings or key sentences pop into your head, just type them in. You can select or revise or delete them later. Some writers take separate notes, while others simply type notes into the running copy.

When the event ends, you may want some reactions from the actors, and it's easy to poke them into your existing text. Then you make final decisions about beginnings and endings and structure, do a quick revision, and you're done. Although I'm emphasizing speed here, these techniques work well for handling a lot of fairly predictable information seen from a limited vantage point.

Sounds easy, doesn't it? The key word in that previous paragraph is *predictable*. Sometimes the event is running smoothly on rails, and you know exactly how it'll all turn out, and you start revising toward that end. And suddenly the patient dies. That's unfortunate and sad, but you don't have to write from scratch. You reselect what you've written, recast the order, compose a new beginning and ending, maybe grab a few final reactions. That's why prewritten paragraphs pay off.

In a related technique, you compose running copy and file it as fast as you type it via an electronic hookup, such as e-mail. An editor receives and edits each bit as it comes in, awaiting the writer's final decisions. In some cases, the editor actually writes the piece from what you send.

Trying to get things out as fast as possible risks mistakes because of a lack of proper editing. Copy editors may not have time to check facts outside the narrative. You might write from memory that this is the first woman so honored in forty-seven years, when she's actually the third. Blogging and Twitter and Facebook share this hazard: no editors.

Now you're thinking, "I don't write about events, so running copy is irrelevant for me." But try it, even on a piece you don't submit. You'll be surprised how it improves your normal note taking and speedy decision making. And you'll know how to do it in a pinch. You never know when the earth will shake beneath your feet.

ENOUGH ALREADY

How do you know when you have enough? When do you stop gathering materials, organize what you want to say, and start typing? Well, you need a test, otherwise you might just keep gathering and not leave enough time for the DRAFT and REVISE stages. Here are some tests to help determine whether you're ready for the next step:

- You never have enough, but you have to type anyway. So stop.
- You have enough when you have good answers to all your questions. I like this test because I do it this way. I write down questions I have to answer, and add questions as I learn more. When I have the right questions and full answers, I've got enough. But this test won't work for you if you can't think up questions ahead of time.
- You have enough when you can fairly represent all sides of an issue you're writing about. This is an especially good test for political writing. But don't cripple yourself by chasing too many sides.
- You have enough when you can prove your thesis. Also common in political writing, this test is not a good one unless you also try to disprove your thesis.
- You have enough when you can't think of anybody else to talk to. A bad test, because you can always think of somebody else to call. This test destroys procrastinators.
- You have enough when you can explain what you've got in two minutes to smart people who don't know the subject, and they understand it. (It's called "Telling it to Mother." If you're reading this, you had a smart mother.)
- You have enough when you're tired of it, bored to tears, fed up. This terrible test afflicts feature writers, researchers doing large projects,

and book authors. It comes too late; you want to type while you still love the subject, when you're hot.

- For visual thinkers, you have enough when you can imagine the sections of your piece as boxes, and those boxes are full of the information needed for each one. This test works for me because I think in pictures.
- You have enough when you have a beginning, middle, and end, as well as the information needed to fill in between them. A good test because it considers both form and content.
- You have enough when you can answer any question your editor might ask you. This paranoid test leads to compulsive overgathering. It also suggests you suffer from a bullying editor.
- You have enough when you can fill the space. A bad test. Writers are in the explanation business, not space filling.
- Some writers have enough when they can fill the holes in a draft. They stop midway in their gathering, write a quick draft, see what's missing, and then find material to fill the gaps. This method sounds slow, but some of the fastest writers I know use it. It works better if you don't revise the draft until it's filled.
- Many writers say "their gut tells them" when they have enough. A bad test, because most writers fear they've missed something or got something wrong. If you wait for your gut to tell you that you got everything and it's all accurate, you'll wait forever.
- You have enough when you reach your deadline. A bad test, because it means you're going to turn the piece in late. The deadline is the time you must turn in your piece, not the time to start typing. To make it a good test, calculate tasks against the time left to deadline. If it's 2:00 P.M., and your deadline is 5:00, and you're an hour's drive from the office and you need one hour to type your piece, you can gather from 2:00 to 3:00, drive until 4:00, and have an hour to type. Remember to figure in a little extra time for the unknown.

You can combine tests. For example, I have enough when I can answer my questions, see full boxes, and have an ending in mind. If you don't have a test for enough, you'll always start organizing and typing late. So pick the tests that might work for you.

That's the GATHER stage, and now on to ORGANIZE.

six

STAGE THREE: WHAT TO SAY AND HOW

One of the horrors of the writer's life is sitting at your keyboard not knowing what to say. After you read this chapter, it will never happen to you again.

Having gathered enough materials, you can now ORGANIZE them. About half of the problems I deal with as a writing coach happen in the ORGANIZE stage, mostly because many writers just skip it. They have no concept of organizing what they write. Many think they don't have time to figure out what to say and how, and that makes them slow.

Many students are taught to end the GATHER stage by asking, "What's my beginning?" No organizing at all, no questions about content or what the piece is about. Just try to come up with that first sentence without knowing what you want to say.

About half of all writers begin typing without thinking about content or form, in a slow process I call "scribbling," which has four steps:

1. What's my beginning?
2. Backing up the beginning
3. What else have I got?
4. What have I left out?

The first step usually begins with some variety of the question, "What's my beginning?" Writers have been taught that without a perfect, terrific first sentence, readers won't read them. They see the beginning as a hook. But research shows that readers enter a package in this order: photo, title, photo caption, beginning. In that fourth position, beginnings aren't hooks.

But writers believe they are, so they try to come up with a perfect sentence when they have no idea what they want to say or how. Obviously, that's hard to do and often takes a lot of time and produces a lot of agony. The time it takes to come up with a hook ranges from five minutes to a month. The longer it takes, the more anxiety grows.

Finally, the writer types something on the screen that's good enough to get him going, and polishes it until it's perfect, like this:

> CODES: ~~Strikethroughs~~ = Deletions.
> Underlining = Additions.

> ~~Have you noticed that wren in your bird feeder is bullying the other birds?~~
> ~~The wren in your bird feeder is a bully.~~
> The wren, despite being the smallest North American bird, is a bully in your feeder.

He likes that third version, so he shifts to the second step, "Backing up the beginning," trying to prove it's true. He types the second sentence:

> This smallest of North American birds (except for hummingbirds) makes up for his lack of size by aggressive behavior.

Now the beginning is wrong, so he fixes it:

> The wren ~~despite being the smallest North American bird~~ is a bully in your feeder.

Then he has to revise his second sentence:

> This smallest of North American birds ~~(except for hummingbirds)~~ makes up for his lack of size by aggressive behavior.

The beginning is still not perfect, so he fixes it again:

> The wren ~~is a bully~~ bullies everybody else in your bird feeder.

Then he writes the third sentence, still not knowing what he wants to say or how, still backing up the beginning, producing this sequence:

> The wren bullies everybody else in your bird feeder.

> This smallest of North American birds makes up for lack of size by aggressive behavior.
> Tail flicking up, he elbows his way in, pushing even larger birds aside.

Not bad, but wrens don't have elbows, so the new sentence needs revision:

> Tail flicking up, he ~~elbows his way in, pushing~~ pushes even larger birds aside.

Now the first two sentences need revision, again:

> The wren bullies ~~everybody else~~ all the other birds in your ~~bird~~ feeder.
> This smallest of ~~North~~ American birds makes up for ~~lack of~~ his size by ~~aggressive behavior~~ sheer pushiness.

And so on. I call this process "down and up." Everything the writer writes down makes something above it wrong or unsatisfactory or imperfect, and he thinks he has to fix it before he can write the next sentence.

There are several assumptions here, all of them wrong:

- You must write the piece in the order the readers will read it. Wrong.
- Everything must be perfect. Wrong.
- Anything not perfect must be fixed immediately. Wrong.

He continues down and up throughout the rest of the draft, constantly trying to make the top perfect. In a piece with twenty-five sentences, he may rewrite the beginning twenty-five times. And it gets worse, not better; denser, not clearer; longer, not shorter and punchier.

Stage three asks, "What else have I got?" He writes this the same way as the first two, but now there's more text above that keeps getting imperfect. Nevertheless, he trudges along, down and up, down and up, wearing himself out, making the piece harder to read. He still doesn't know what he wants to say, or how.

The final stage, "What have I left out," happens when the writer is tired, fed up, and running out of time. You can spot a writer who's in this step because he's flipping through notes frantically and swearing at himself. "Dammit, how could you leave that out?!" So he types, "Male wrens may make as many as four nests, hoping to attract as many females as possible," and sticks it in somewhere, and it causes problems above and below, requiring not only down and up, but also down and down.

Then he turns in the piece, late and messy.

What's wrong with scribbling? It does get the piece written eventually. But it's the slowest and hardest way to do it, and the most damaging to confidence. It makes writers give up and apply to law school. And the resulting piece is heavy and dense, full of qualifiers, poorly written, and the second half is barely revised because the writer ran out of steam.

I estimate that half the world's writers suffer from scribbling. You can write like that if you enjoy agony, but there are easier ways. And the first is to organize your pieces. There are many ways to do that, and this chapter explains some of them.

DEEPER INTO PLANNERS AND PLUNGERS

I discussed "planners and plungers" earlier in the book. Human beings divide into two types: PLANNERS and PLUNGERS. Planners figure out what to do, and then they do it. Plungers figure things out by doing them. Planners plan and execute their plan; plungers organize by acting.

Imagine a buffet lunch. Planners walk around the whole table, looking at all the food, decide what they want, and then pick up a plate. Plungers grab a plate and select what looks good to them. Planners plan their meal; plungers dive into the food, making decisions as they go along.

I'll use navigation as an example. My wife, Joan, and I are going to drive somewhere, and I have the wheel. I'm a planner, so I look at a map and plan my route. If Joan, a plunger, has the wheel, she will start in the general direction and correct as she goes along. We both get to the same place at the same time.

How will we drive to the same place the second time? I have the wheel, so I look at the map *again* and go the way I went the first time. Planners are rigid. How will my plunger wife navigate the second time? She starts in a different direction and corrects until she arrives. Plungers like variety. Again, we both get there at the same time, but we thought it out in different ways.

Unsure whether you're a planner or a plunger? Don't decide yet. There's more to come.

This distinction applies to writers as well. Planners write plans and follow them. Plungers just start typing and organize toward the end. Planners plan, and execute their plan. Plungers plunge in, and write by discovery.

As a planner, I always write a plan before I type, but it's not the classical multilayered outline you hated in school:

I. Writing is hard.
  A. Everything must be spelled right.
  B. Everything must be grammatically correct.
  C. Everything must please the teacher.
II. Writing is boring.
  A. Everything must be neutral.
  B. Nothing can annoy anybody.
  C. The teacher must agree with everything you say.
III. Writing is good for you.
  A. It teaches discipline.
  B. It teaches you to obey teachers.
  C. You should learn Latin.

What's wrong with that? Nothing. It's a great way to analyze something already written, but it's not a great way to plan something, unless you're a total control freak. I dislike outlines so much that I call them "plans."

I write columns with a beginning, a few sections, and an ending. My simple plan consists of a few words, just labels for the parts and their order. Here's my plan for a recent column on reinventing yourself after a buyout:

REINVENT YOURSELF
1. NO GUILT
2. INVENTORY SKILLS
3. WANT NOW?
4. NEW SKILLS
ENDING: GET HELP

Then I follow my plan, but not necessarily in order. I write the beginning last.

How would plungers write that column? They would type a lot of units: sentences, paragraphs, sections, just stuff. Then they rearrange the bits and pieces into sections that make sense, and write transitions between the parts. Some write the beginning first, some later, some last. Plungers figure out what they want to say by typing it; then they rearrange it to make sense to themselves and their readers.

Both planners and plungers, if they use methods suitable to them, can write at the same speed and the same quality. You can't tell planners from plungers by reading what they write. You have to ask them about their writing process and how they think.

Here's the problem for plungers: The world of writing is ruled by planners. Most writing teachers are planners. Most writing gurus are planners. All nuns are planners. All editors are planners. So how do plungers get along in a world dominated by planners? Simple, they pretend to be planners.

Okay, plungers, back to your youth. Suppose you're a plunger in sixth-grade English class in early September. The assignment: Write five hundred words titled "My Summer Vacation," and turn it in with your outline. Plungers, remember how you did that? You wrote and finished five hundred words and *then* outlined them, what I call a "back outline." And the nun thought you were a planner like her, and gave you an A, and that's why you're a writer today.

If you've decided you're a plunger, come out of the closet. It's okay. There's nothing wrong with you. About a third of the writers I know are plungers and proud of it.

What's the dark side of planners and plungers? Planners are rigid; they'll follow a bad plan even when they realize it isn't working. I usually make a mess of planning part three of my columns and type it anyway. Plungers write a lot to figure out what they want to say, so they write long and cut back, which makes them inherently slow.

Both are helped by a good "debriefing," i.e., talking to someone just before they type, about what they intend to say and how. If the debriefer doesn't understand the plan, neither does the planner. So the plan gets rethought before typing. With a plunger, the debriefer listens for things that have nothing to do with the piece, and they don't get typed. Either way saves time and effort.

Plungers can also save time by drafting without revising, otherwise they cut things they've already revised. So for a plunger, the fast sequence would be type, cut, rearrange, revise.

Few writers are pure planners or plungers. For instance, I plan nonfiction and plunge fiction; I outline columns, but start novels without a plot. Some people plan short and plunge long, and vice versa. Some plunge when they're afraid, and plan when they're not. Some plan the top, and plunge the rest. Whatever works for you, but make sure you plan or plunge based on your strengths, not habit or ignorance. In general, people who plan their lives write better using planner methods, and people who plunge through life feel more comfortable plunging their writing. The trick is to know lots of ways to do things and to choose the combinations that work best for you.

So, are you a planner or a plunger?

STACKING A FEW BLOCKS

Your readers will understand you if you write in forms that serve their needs, not yours. What form would you write in for maximum power and understanding? Here's a scheme based on 2,500 years of practical research.

1. A beginning, middle, and end.
2. The middle contains the information, divided by subject into sections, in logical order.
3. The beginning predicts the form and content of the middle.
4. The ending gives a sense of closure.
5. The sooner readers know what the piece is about and why they should read it, the better they will understand.

BEGINNING
PART 1
PART 2
PART 3
ENDING

I call this form the "stack of blocks" because the middle consists of a sequence of subject-related blocks or sections, framed by a beginning and an ending. One section follows another based on what readers need. If they need Part One to understand Part Two, then Part One comes first.

How many sections can you have? Not many, preferably no more than seven, and better three. The human attention span is about seven things, so we break material up into smaller related units.

You design a stack of blocks by clumping material on similar subjects into sections, and then stacking the sections in logical order, framed by a beginning and ending.

Here's a short stack with only one middle block, opened by a beginning and closed by an ending:

> **[BEGINNING]** With Halloween rapidly approaching, the question arises: What wine goes with candy? Food writer Kara Newman suggests in *Wine Enthusiast* online that, like pairing desserts with wine, you should match wine to flavors, "such as chocolate and caramel, fruit and spice, custard and vanilla—that you're as likely to find in your trick-or-treat bag as on any fussy restaurant menu."
>
> **[ONE BLOCK]** She recommends port to pair with chocolate, "but pour anything in the red wine family, such as banyuls (a sweet red wine from France) or shiraz alongside handfuls of M&Ms, pint-sized candy bars or other chocolate Halloween treats. Baby Ruth, Snickers or other nutty candy bars in your bag? Select a sherry or Madeira to complement rich nut flavors."
>
> **[ENDING]** (Last year a neighbor who accompanied his kids was standing in the background holding an empty wine glass, which I filled with some cab. That's my idea of adult trick-or-treating.)[5]

Every chapter in this book is a stack of blocks, or individual sections each treating one set of related techniques. The whole book is a stack of blocks, a series of chapters, each based on one step in the writing process, framed by an introduction and closing apparatus. The thinking behind the stack of blocks works at every level and length.

Next up, some info about forms.

THE INFERNAL PYRAMID

First, a bad one I hope you'll never use but must understand.

The so-called "inverted pyramid" is the commonest form for newspaper stories worldwide. Most journalists learn it, and it remains a template in reporters' and editors' heads. I've aimed this book at nonfiction writers who are not journalists, but you need to understand the inverted pyramid because some of your editors may think in it. I've tried to avoid newspaper terminology throughout this book, but I use it in this section because avoiding it would prove awkward. As you will see, I hope you never write pieces in this form, because your readers won't understand it.

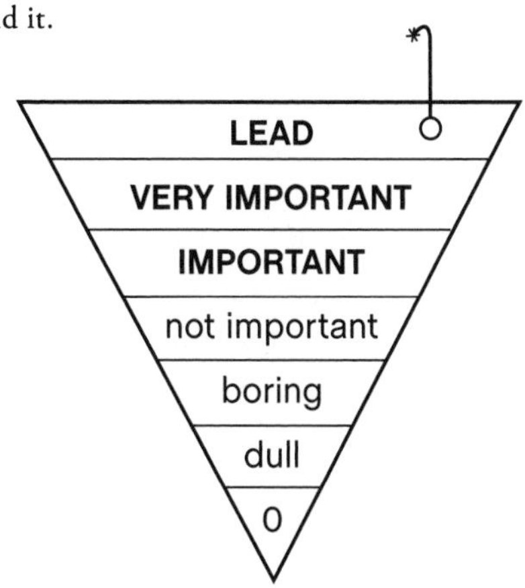

The structure works like this. The story begins with a "lead" or "lede," conceived as a hook to get the reader interested in the subject. Ideally the lead tells what the piece is about, but sometimes it involves a fetching anecdote. The next few paragraphs try to prove the lead is true and amplify it. Subsequent paragraphs add detail and context. The most important and interesting material goes at the top, and the less important and less interesting appears as the text unrolls down. Eventually the piece simply peters out. Sometimes it just stops, in crudely edited newspapers, even in midsentence.

If you read newspapers, you've read lots of stories in this form. Unfortunately they have a fatal flaw: All serious research shows that readers don't understand them.[6]

Journalists regard background and context as not new and therefore boring, so they put them in the second half of the piece, the part less interesting *to them*. But readers can't understand the top of the piece without background and context. So readers give up and never reach the second half, which contains the information they need.

Journalists spend less time on the part of the piece they value least, the second half. So it often ends up poorly written and unrevised. Many editors used to be reporters, and share the same prejudice. They often neglect to edit the second half, or even read it.

See what I mean about writing for your readers' needs, not yours?

The second flaw is thinking of leads as hooks. Readers enter a package in this order: photo, headline, caption, lead. Something in the fourth position cannot hook anybody. Later in this chapter, you'll learn how to use this sequence effectively.

Why does such a self-defeating form still exist, especially today with the press under huge stress? It suits the convenience of overworked editors. If the piece is too long, they can cut it from the bottom without reading it. The piece then lacks an ending and makes even less sense. Many reporters write inverted pyramids because it's the only form they know.

If you write inverted pyramids, your readers will not understand you. And readers who don't understand you, won't read you anymore.

> THE INVERTED PYRAMID IS THE WORST WAY TO EXPLAIN SOMETHING IN WORDS.

Why do you need to know this form since (I hope) you would never write such a monster? Many editors, including magazine editors, come from journalism and retain the inverted-pyramid template in their heads. Something in the second half will strike them as "too good to be this low in the story," so they "move it up." Or they may push the context further down because they don't find it interesting. These moves can destroy the structure of your piece and make it harder to read. If you don't understand their inverted-pyramid thinking, you'll think their changes don't make sense. Actually, they don't, because writing in a form your readers can't understand doesn't make sense.

FILLING THE CHAMPAGNE GLASS

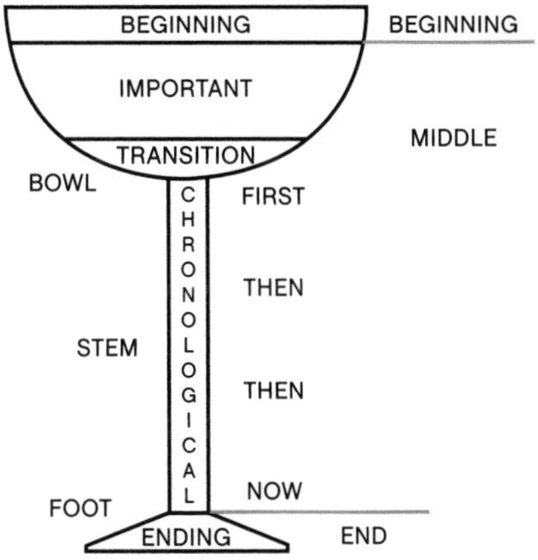

You can explain some things better by treating them twice, once descriptively and then chronologically. The "champagne glass" form has the traditional beginning, telling the readers what the piece is about and why it's important, and the traditional ending, giving a sense of closure. The middle has two sections divided by a clear transition. The first section treats the subject descriptively and analytically, and then transitions to a second section in narrative chronological form. This form works best to straighten out a complex series of events, such as a year-long debate over health care, perfecting an invention, or a complicated rescue of miners.

Here's my favorite champagne glass, from the *St. Petersburg Times*: "Firefighters Rescue Manatee From Crab Trap" by Christina K. Cosdon. (By the way, a manatee is a marine mammal resembling a walrus, about ten feet long and weighing one thousand pounds as an adult. It must surface to breathe every two minutes.)

> SAFETY HARBOR – Struggling to free itself from a crab trap rope wrapped around its neck and body, a young manatee was rescued by two city firefighters.
>
> The men worked nearly an hour to calm the 10-foot-long mammal before freeing it Thursday.
>
> "With anything that big and powerful, you could get hurt if you got in its way," said Safety Harbor Fire Capt.

Max Shimer, who estimated the animal's weight at 600 pounds. Shimer and firefighter-paramedic Ray Duke freed the manatee.

"We knew they are gentle creatures and wouldn't hurt us on purpose. But we didn't know if this one was injured or how it would react to us. We just played it by ear," Shimer said.

The rescue operation began shortly after 8 A.M. when the struggling manatee was spotted by Bill Pleso, the city building maintenance foreman. He was making his daily inspection of the municipal pier when he saw the animal about 150 yards north of the pier.

"I could see he was tangled in a crab trap," Pleso said later. "He was dragging two buoys with him."

Pleso, who said he regularly sees manatees around the pier, radioed City Hall for help. The Florida Marine Patrol was called, as were the Florida Game and Fresh Water Fish Commission and Sea World. The two agencies and Sea World are involved in the state's mammal rescue and rehabilitation program.

Fire Chief Jay Stout said his men agreed to attempt the rescue when he learned it would be several hours before the Sea World team would arrive. Since no one knew if the mammal was injured, Stout said he felt the rush was necessary.

Shimer and Duke got into a boat and paddled up to the manatee. "It was frightened at first, but gradually it seemed to sense we weren't going to hurt it," said Shimer. It did not appear injured.

For nearly an hour, the men reached out to calm the manatee each time it surfaced to breathe. Finally, Duke reached into the water, held the rope as close to the animal's neck as he could and cut through the rope with a pocket knife.

When the rope fell away and the manatee was free, "about five other manatees, all much larger, suddenly appeared out of nowhere," Shimer said. "They came up to

> the surface and rubbed faces and noses. It was a pretty neat experience."[7]

The beginning tells what the piece is about: "a young manatee was rescued by two city firefighters." Then the first half of the middle details the creature's plight and the rescue. Halfway through the middle, the tale starts to unfold in chronological order: "The rescue operation began shortly after 8 A.M. . . ."

The narrative ends with Shimer's terrific quotation. In traditional inverted-pyramid thinking, that quotation is too good to come at the end. A literal-minded, inverted-pyramid editor might move it up, weakening its power in the most emphatic position, the ending.

Champagne-glass pieces are inherently long, and they're hard to shorten. You would choose this form because the second, chronological telling helps the reader understand complex events. But you have to gather enough material to tell it twice.

TELLING DEEP STORIES

Think about all the stories you've heard in your life. They aren't just fun tales of spiders talking to pigs, good witches fighting evil witches, or elderly kings struggling with their daughters. They tell you how the human beings and our world work.

I grew up in the American South in a storytelling culture. My relatives would tell stories to explain things, so even the children would understand them. Many tales warned against marrying strangers from scary, godforsaken places like New York.

To explain things clearly, you connect the unknown to what your audience already knows. Stories draw on common human knowledge and experience, and link those knowns to the unknown, or the old to the new.

A story consists of actors performing actions in time for reasons, or a voice revealing actions by actors. That voice is the storyteller, and all stories have one. Writers call the storyteller "the *persona*," to distinguish it from the author.

The storytelling voice, the *persona*, is an artifact, a device created and controlled by the author. (The second half of this book will show you how to create your own voice.) Your *persona* allows you to escape the trap of sincerity; you don't have to believe or mean what your *persona* says. Your *persona* is a fiction, even when you're writing nonfiction. When Joan Baez sings, "I am a *man* of constant sorrow," her *persona* is male, while the singer remains a woman.

In stories, actors perform actions. Writers use various devices to characterize the actors, to make them seem like real human beings to the readers. Characters aren't necessarily human; some are monsters or talking cats. The primary devices for characterization are description, action, and speech.

Human beings become experts at judging character, not just by *what* people say, but also *how* they say it. As you read quotations or dialogue, you make judgments about the speakers. Here's Johnny Moore, who witnessed the Wright brothers' first flight: "They done it, they done it, damned if they ain't flew."[8] That quotation, just eleven words, conjures up Johnny for you.

I didn't describe Johnny, but you pictured him speaking, perhaps with his mouth gaping. Notice how that little detail enriched the image. You may have imagined a landscape surrounding Johnny, perhaps one that included the Wright brothers' plane. Description works best when you don't tell readers too much, allowing a few details to help them create their own version of the character.

Action yields more power than description, so set the actors in motion, *i.e.*, let them interact with each other. What they do and how they do it reveals their characters, and also makes up the plot, or a sequence of motivated actions. Storytelling is the most powerful form of explanation, the most fun to read and to write.

LEAPING INTO THE MIDDLE

Classical epics begin telling their stories *in medias res*, in the middle of things. Homer's *Odyssey* starts like this:

> Sing to me of the man, Muse, the man of twists and turns
> driven time and again off course, once he had plundered
> the hallowed heights of Troy....
> Launch out on his story, Muse, daughter of Zeus,
> start from where you will—sing for our time too.[9]

The Trojan War lasted ten years, and readers find Odysseus in the middle of a second ten years struggling to return to his wife, Penelope. The muse begins this retelling at that point.

Why begin there, instead of at the beginning of the war? Each story defines the actions it covers, and the storyteller chooses where in that action to begin. Where you start determines what you have to explain to your readers.

Starting at the beginning of the action, a perfectly valid way of telling a story, involves all sorts of background. Memoirs of World War II flyers tend to start with recruitment and training, taking a long time to get into the air. Starting in the middle, at a high point in the action, hurls the readers into the plot. The telling starts fast and stays that way. I once began a novel like this: "Bombs away!"

Homer and his audiences had the advantage of knowing the plots and details of their traditional stories. Our audiences need background, and you supply it just before the readers need it through flashbacks, references, and digressions. The Russian dramatist Anton Chekhov advised tearing a story in half and starting in the middle.

You can use this technique in nonfiction as well as epics and plays. My friend Wilbur Landry told me his secret for explaining complex political events in a short space: "Start as close to the end of the action as possible, and stop as soon as you can."

Here's an example from *The New York Times* of a quick start from the middle:

> In Washington, Representative Joe Wilson of South Carolina was sharply criticized by both Democrats and his fellow Republicans for shouting "You lie!" during President Obama's health care address on Wednesday. But here in his strongly Republican Congressional district on Thursday, he was celebrated by many of his constituents for his outburst. [10]

Readers find themselves right in the middle of the action because the author gets it onstage in two clear sentences. Notice the effect of a more leisurely approach:

> Since the earliest origins of deliberative bodies, members of the audience have expressed their disapproval, sometimes politely and sometimes not. In Parliament, legislators heckle each other mercilessly. In our more polite Congress, senators and representatives jab at each other now and then, but

> nobody, nobody calls the President of the United States a liar to his face in public. But on Wednesday night....

Starting slowly has its uses, but it creates the expectation in the readers of longer explaining. Try this fast start:

> "You lie!" shouted Rep. Joe Wilson at the President, and the entire Congress turned toward him and scowled.

Very dramatic, but it assumes readers know what happened, as in the Homeric epics. Writers must balance the immediacy of starting in the middle with the potential for confusing readers. Confused readers tend to stop reading. They feel dopey and assume they'll stay confused, and so they decide to read something else. The trick to the fast start *in medias res* is a first paragraph that orients readers quickly, gives them the basic information they need, and pulls them into the action. If your first sentence is "Bombs away," you need an airplane, a target, and a bombardier in the next sentence.

SPREADING THE OREOS

Your readers' interest and energy begin to sag about halfway through any piece. They start thinking about stopping. You need to lift their spirits and expectations. So you put something wonderful just before the sag, a little bit that will refresh them, a reward for reading that far. I call these little gifts "gold coins" or "goodies" or "Oreos."

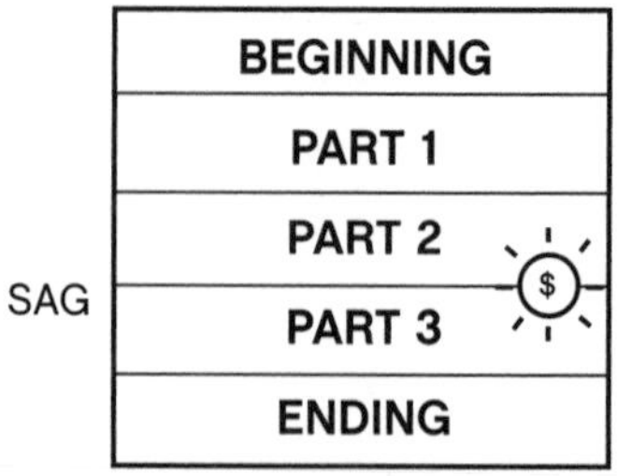

Suppose you're a witch, and you want to lure two children from one side of the forest into your hovel on the other side. You open a box of Oreo cookies, spreading them out, one every fifty feet along the path. The children find the first Oreo, share it, and spot the second one just up the path. They eat that one, and another, and so on, until they end up in your oven.

That's how you draw your readers all the way through a piece to the ending, by spreading the goodies. Inverted-pyramid thinking would put the whole box of cookies at the beginning, and the children/readers would eat it there and never read beyond your second paragraph. You space the rewards to keep readers salivating.

A gold coin is simply something readers will enjoy, such as a terrific quotation, a striking new character, a wonderful sentence, a telling detail, or an amusing anecdote. Quotations work especially well as gold coins, such as my mother-in-law, Dorothy Baker's, announcement that she intended "to turn over a clean breast." She also swore never "to count my bridges before I burn them." A new character, saved until later, can perk up the narrative, such as Ruby Thewes, played by Renée Zellweger, in the movie version of *Cold Mountain*.

In general, you avoid startling sentences because they momentarily stop the reader. But that striking quality is exactly what you want in a gold coin. For example, here's a wonderful sentence from Adam Nicolson's *Seize the Fire*: "A man-of-war would sail with a breeze so slight it could just be felt on the windward side of a licked finger."[11] I wish I'd written that sentence.

Telling details are especially golden. When World War II broke out in 1939, the staff of the Louvre Museum scrambled to crate and hide their art treasures from the Nazis. In *The Rape of Europa*, Lynn Nicholas gives this ironic detail: "One curator was amazed to find her packers, recruited from two department stores, the Bazar de l'Hôtel and the Samaritaine, dressed in long mauve tights, striped caps, and flowing tunics, as if they had just stepped out of the fourteenth- and fifteenth-century Italian pictures they were about to wrap."[12] And a splendid sentence too.

Here's the ultimate anecdotal gold coin, known to writers as "the Chicken Test." It comes in the middle of an immense, very technical series in the *Seattle Times* by Peter Rinearson on the design of the Boeing 757 airliner. Engineers are testing the strength of the windshield:

> Boeing is a little touchy about the subject of chicken tests, and points out they are required by the FAA. Here's what happens:
>
> A live 4-pound chicken is anesthetized and placed in a flimsy plastic bag to reduce aerodynamic drag. The bagged bird is put in a compressed-air gun.

> The bird is fired at the jetliner window at 360 knots and the window must withstand the impact. It is said to be a very messy test.
>
> The inch-thick glass, which includes two layers of plastic, needn't come out unscathed. But it must not puncture. The test is repeated under various circumstances—the window is cooled by liquid nitrogen, or the chicken is fired into the center of the window or at its edge.
>
> "We give Boeing an option," Berven joked. "They can either use a 4-pound chicken at 200 miles an hour or a 200-pound chicken at 4 miles an hour."[13]

No matter how long or difficult a piece is, if you reach that anecdote, you will not stop reading.

JOTTING DOWN SECTIONS

Readers understand the middle of a piece best if you section it, *i.e.*, organize it into groups of material related by subject matter, putting those sections into logical order. How do you determine the sections? One way is by rearranged jotting.

You ask yourself, "What are the important things here? What does my reader have to know?" You jot down those things (perhaps ten of them) as separate sentences or just notes. Then you ask which of those jots are sections, which are parts of sections, and which have nothing to do with this piece. Then you rearrange them to make sense. The example below comes from a piece about my family's financial strategies in a recession:

JOTTING

Retirement savings down 30%
Wife strategy: convert to cash
My strategy: ride it out
B. Madoff
Money managers smarter
Hard to time upturn
Preserve capital
Treasury incompetent
Advice several sources
Patience & courage

Quick tactical moves of funds
Diversification
Cash hurt by inflation

I rearranged those jottings into sections:

BEGINNING: Retirement savings lost 30%, what to do
WIFE'S STRATEGY, CONVERT TO CASH
  Preserve capital
  Quick tactical moves of funds
MY STRATEGY, RIDE IT OUT
  Money managers smarter than I am
  Cash hurt by inflation
  Difficult to time market upturn
OLD WISDOM STILL TRUE
  Advice from several sources
  Diversification
ENDING
  Patience and courage
DELETE: Bernard Madoff, Treasury incompetent

A little rejiggering and revision turned that sectioned list into a plan for drafting.

LEAVING OUT CHARACTERS

Too many characters confuse your readers and make pieces hard to read. And all new characters you introduce require apparatus to identify them. You select characters ruthlessly to keep from jamming up storytelling and explanation. How do you choose characters, people, and names to include?

"Characters" are persons (or creatures) that you develop enough so readers experience them as real. "People" remain flat and undeveloped; they're bit players or part of the scenery. "Names" often appear in attributions of facts or quotations. In terms of jamming up the piece, place names also count. The more names, the harder the piece is to read.

You include characters because readers need them to understand what you're talking about. The cast would include the main actors in an action, plus minor players required for explanation.

Some people, usually commentators, appear in a piece because they supply context, such as a key quotation or explanation, although they don't participate in the action. Writers try to identify them lightly. And you should always ask yourself if readers really need that context.

A lot of pieces get cluttered because writers believe they have to quote everybody they talk with, both as a courtesy to those sources and to show they gathered widely. You don't owe subjects a mention, and readers judge pieces by quality, not by the number of named sources.

YOU DON'T HAVE TO QUOTE EVERYONE YOU INTERVIEW.

But sometimes you do include a person, or quote somebody, for purely political reasons. You massage them by naming them. If your regular sources are people you also write about, quote them enough to keep them happy and talking to you. Keep 'em short.

You don't include characters because you like them or because they deliver a delicious quotation that has nothing to do with what you're writing about. That's a good test of rigor: Can you chop a great but irrelevant quotation and the person who said it? Theodore Roethke said, "Any fool can take a bad line out of a poem; it takes a real pro to throw out a good line."

It helps to discard characters and people and names before you type. Once you've put them in, you're less likely to take them out.

WRITING UP AND DOWN YOUR SPINE

Danish radio disc jockeys taught me a trick they call "the motor." They tie an hour-long music program together by repeating a word or image or theme to unify the broadcast. That thread keeps the listeners attached, segment by segment. The same trick works in writing, but I call it "the spine."

David John Marotta, a Charlottesville financial advisor, recently asked in a column in *The Daily Progress*, "What does a (financial) woman want?" He begins by saying that women need retirement planning, and his third paragraph quotes the singer Sophie Tucker:

> From birth to age 18, a girl needs good parents. From 18 to 35, she needs good looks. From 35 to 55, she needs a good

> personality. From 55 on, she needs good cash. I'm saving my money.[14]

Marotta then walks through a typical woman's financial life, from teaching her daughters how to handle money to living in retirement, citing each of Tucker's stages and adding material from her own entertainment, business, and philanthropic careers. The piece ends with Sophie saying, "I've been rich and I've been poor—and believe me, rich is better."

Sophie's life is the spine, which appears in different forms: the idea of stages, her careers, and two other quotations. The chronology is fun to read, and the readers stay with it to the end. They identify with Sophie, who leads them through.

The 2008 movie, *The Curious Case of Benjamin Button*, has two spines. The larger spine is the life Benjamin lives backward, and the smaller one is a minor character who keeps popping up and telling Benjamin how lightning hit him seven times. Sometimes in longer works, each of the parts has a separate spine.

This book you're reading has a spine. I keep telling you in one form or another: "Use techniques that work for you." The second half has an additional spine: "Create your own voice from the devices that create the *persona* you want to represent you."

All pieces don't necessarily have a spine, but those that have one entice readers all the way to the end.

PATHS INTO THE TOP

Many writers try to come up with a great beginning to hook their readers. But research shows that readers enter the top of a piece in this order:

PHOTO > TITLE > PHOTO CAPTION > TEXT

If the package includes pull-out quotations, sidebars, graphics, or boxes, some readers may enter through any of them. Ten percent of readers skip the caption, but the sequence is always the same: photo(s), title (or headline), caption (or cutline), text. The only person who reads the first sentence first is the one who wrote it.

Now you're thinking, "Nonsense, I don't read that way. Nobody does." But all research confirms this pattern, which I call "the path."

Notice where the beginning of the text falls in that sequence: fourth, last. Something in a fourth position isn't a hook. The photo is the hook, and the headline (or title) does a little hooking. Captions bridge but don't hook. Some pieces run without a photo and a caption, and the title or headline does the hooking. Even then, the beginning is too late in the sequence to serve as a hook.

Now it gets more complicated. Whatever the reader reads first sets expectations. Readers immediately begin to predict what comes next, the content of the whole piece, and the likelihood of their understanding it. If their expectations are met, they feel smart and guided, and keep reading. If their expectations fail, they feel stupid and don't trust you and stop reading.

Readers scan the photo and title first, and those two (not the beginning) set the expectations. To actively manage the success of your piece, you need to get involved in everything above the beginning of your text, *i.e.*, photo, title, caption (places where writers don't normally tread).

First, help the photographer. That relationship succeeds when you work as equals. If possible, gather information with the photographer present, trading suggestions and discussing what you find and how you might use it. Failing that, make sure the photographer knows ahead of time what the piece is likely to be about, its content, and style. If you can, help the person who chooses the photos to select the pictures that best bring the readers into your piece. Remember that photographers choose aesthetically (color, composition, focus), while you want the best predictor. After the piece appears, thank photographers for their help and good work.

Second, always suggest titles (or headlines). An editor or copy editor will finish them, but may not think about the title as a predictor. I suggest titles with every piece I write, often half a dozen of them. No editor has ever published a single title I wrote; I'm not good at writing them. However, my pieces usually have great titles because my suggestions supply editors with key words and ideas.

Third, volunteer to write photo captions, or submit ideas for them anyway. Captions bridge between the photo and title into the text, often providing an enticing piece of information for the reader.

Let's look at two examples of path thinking. The first involves a funny story about a nest full of ducklings that hatched on the second-floor façade of a bank. The fledglings leaped toward the sidewalk, where a banker caught each one, saving its life. The photo shows the banker catching the ducklings, but it doesn't show the name of the bank or its logo.[15] We can compensate by manipulating other parts of the path. Our headline could read, "Banker Rescues Fledglings in Mid-Air." (I told you I'm not a whiz at headlines.) The caption could read, "Joel Armstrong, a senior loan officer at Sterling Savings Bank in Spokane, snags a mallard duckling on its maiden flight." (Not so hot at captions either.) The caption supplies the name of the hero and his bank. The photo, headline, and caption work together to deliver the reader with enough intriguing information to read your wonderful beginning, which comes next.

Sometimes path thinking gets us out of tricky situations. *The New York Times* published a photo showing two soldiers staring at the sky.[16] The caption read: "American troops from a bomb-detection unit on duty in Wardak Province, Afghanistan, watched passing aircraft on Monday." The caption saves readers from distraction, wondering throughout the piece what the soldiers are looking at.

A WONDERING READER IS NOT PAYING ATTENTION.

If the beginning doesn't hook readers, what does it do, and how do you write it? I talk about writing beginnings in the DRAFT chapter.

BOXING THE EXTRA STUFF

Would you like to have a little more space for your text? Moving some information into a box or sidebar creates room in the main body. Instead of cluttering up a profile with details of the subject's resume, you can put it in a sidebar and devote the text to capturing the person. Some types of information, such as lists, can be easier to read in a box than in paragraphs.

Boxes allow readers who want more information to get it when they want it, and return to the main text. For instance, you can put a whole document in the box and quote bits from it in the main text. A printed box is the equivalent of an online link, although linking has no space limitations.

Most writers assume that readers read the main text first and boxes later; why else would we call them <u>side</u>bars, as in *be<u>side</u>* or *a<u>side</u>*? Readers are more likely to read the box first, so the contents of that box must make sense to readers who have not read the main text. Readers are more likely to understand the box if it starts with a headline or caption.

Some people read only the box, so it must be able to stand alone. Readers should not have to read multiple parts to understand any other part of a package. Readers tend to sample boxes and not read them straight through. The secret is to keep boxes simple, perhaps using more than one.

Charts, graphs, and graphics may be read first, and must make sense without reading the body text. A photo will always be read first and must not depend on the main text. Careful labeling and wording solve these difficult problems of clarity.

You can put signals or references in the main text that point to the box or to other apparatus, like this: "(See box, below)." You can duplicate some of the information in the main text and the box so each makes sense.

WHAT MIGHT GO IN A BOX

- Resume
- More numbers
- URLs
- Information sources
- Restaurant addresses

Many publications assume that editors will break out boxes from the writer's submitted text. But you want to do it yourself to make sure it comes out right. If you don't know how, ask friendly editors to teach you. You'll save them time later.

WRITING IN AN EMERGENCY

Some people think that all writing is "emergency writing." They're correct in describing their own work that way, if their clumsy, slow methods turn every piece into a last-minute disaster.

But everyone struggles with a writing emergency now and then. If you have twenty minutes to knock out eight hundred words that announce the new widget, how do you do it? Several ways, depending on how you think and how you work.

I'm a planner, meaning I write a plan and follow it. I also type badly. So I'll spend the first two minutes deciding what to say and how to say it, typically by answering two magic questions: "What's this about?" and "What are the parts of this piece?" Now I have a plan: the beginning and the parts. The answer to "What's this about?" creates my beginning, usually one paragraph. Then I draft the hardest part first, followed by the rest. An ending will usually pop into my head while I'm typing. I draft a little slower than usual, because I have less time to revise and need a cleaner draft as a base. I take a one-minute break, read aloud, and then revise. In an emergency, I can knock out eight hundred words in about eighteen minutes, depending on how much I know about the subject.

Why does this work for me? I use methods that produce organized thinking about structure from the beginning, and then I slow down my drafting to minimize typos that need correcting.

Suppose you're not a planner, but a plunger, meaning you type to decide what you want to say. The paragraphs come out in no particular order until you glimpse a pattern, then you type some more, but in a more directed focus. Then you use the block-move function to rearrange things to make sense. Plungers tend to write long and cut back, which makes them slow.

In an emergency, plungers might first decide what the sections are and then type only paragraphs that will fit into those parts, resisting the urge to digress into interesting bits. They would not revise as they draft, because they'll probably cut some things later. When they've typed enough, they would cut, rearrange, and then revise the whole thing.

Finally, there's another emergency method, regardless of whether you're a planner or a plunger, but it's not for the faint of heart. You type with the screen off. You ask yourself out loud, "What do I want to say?" Then you turn the screen off and type at top speed. You watch your fingers to make sure they don't shift off the correct key range. When you realize you just typed the ending, turn the screen back on. Here's a shocker: The piece will be terrific, and you probably won't have to revise much, if any.

Why does this work? You can't criticize what you can't see, and criticizing yourself while drafting slows you down. And you may type better when you don't watch the screen. My bad typing makes me feel stupid and distracts me. When I use the screen-off technique, I don't make typos. Well, not many, mostly numbers. I'm not kidding; try it.

I wrote this section in twenty-two minutes, without an emergency.

And that's the ORGANIZE stage. Next comes the two typing steps, DRAFT and REVISE.

seven

STAGE FOUR: GETTING IT DOWN

You've finally reached the typing stages of the writing process. And here's a question for you: When does the writing actually begin? When you start to type? No. Effective writing is more than putting letters on a screen. It begins in the IDEA stage, proceeds through the GATHER and ORGANIZE stages, and delivers the thinking and information behind the words.

In the DRAFT stage, you type a rough version of the whole text; then you finish the piece in the next stage, REVISION. Get it down, and then get it right.

In this chapter, I'll talk about typing text on a word processor, although I'm sure many of you use the old media, sometimes to the point of obsession. Use whatever works for you.

I know a lot of writers, sometimes including me, who still draft on lined pads. They type the finished piece eventually and submit it. I spent half my working life writing in longhand on yellow legal pads, then cutting and stapling pieces of the draft until it made sense. For some writers, longhand drafting amounts to a ritual, and because it works, they keep doing it that way. That's fine if it works for them.

A historian I know cannot compose at all without ten Ticonderoga No. 2 pencils, perfectly sharpened, and a Mead yellow pad. My former colleague, the Icelandic scholar Robert Kellogg, would place two lined pads side by side. He would write a sentence on the left-hand pad, revise it to perfection, and then copy it onto the right-hand pad. He kept that up until he'd written the whole piece. Sounds slow, right? But I once saw him write a ten-page scholarly talk that way in an eight-hour overnighter. And he read it to an audience of critical medievalists two hours later.

Even in this computer age, many writers stick with typewriters, sometimes manual ones. My wife, Joan, considered our Smith Corona electric typewriter an improvement over our manual Olivetti, although she complained that it kept humming at her, a tune she heard as "Hurry up, hurry up."

Word processors have distinct advantages over all previous devices.

- Easy revision
- Search and replace
- Automatic correction and spell checking
- Multiple printings and versions
- Integration of visuals and sound
- Direct publication in electronic form, such as e-books

If you don't use a word processor, you should learn how. Sooner than you think, all publication will be digital. And it's so much faster and easier. My former colleague, the poet Louis Simpson, sniffed, "I don't process words. I write them." Even he came around.

Many writers draft and revise at the same time, which makes them slow, as you may remember from our discussion of scribbling, above. The fastest way is to type the whole draft with no revision, and then revise it once. You can revise it some more, of course, but this method turns out solid drafts that need less revision.

GET IT DOWN, THEN GET IT RIGHT.

WHAT TO TYPE FIRST

Where in your text should you begin typing? At the top, of course, and then write your way to the bottom. Actually, that's an assumption that comes from habit or from the idea that you have to have a perfect first sentence to write the rest, which is also an assumption.

You can start typing anywhere, whether you're writing a novel or a short article. You should start wherever works best for you, and it may vary from day to day, piece to piece.

You can start at the beginning, type through the middle, and finish at the ending. The majority of writers do it that way, because they don't know any other way. If you develop an argument or a plot by just typing it, rather than planning it, straight through may help you. Many fiction writers compose chronologically, but there are other ways.

My colleague Roy Clark dreads the start of typing, saying he "likes to have written." So he begins with whatever's easiest, just to get going. He says it's "all downhill from there." I tend to start with the hardest part, usually the core of an argument, because for me, it just pours out from there. See how you choose techniques that suit you?

Some writers begin with what they know best. By the time they get that part written, they've figured out how to handle the part they know least. I've never met any writers who start with what they know least.

Some writers organize by typing a draft of what they do know, and read it over to discover holes in their knowledge. Then they do some more gathering to fill the gaps, and rewrite the draft. This technique works best if you draft fast, without revising; otherwise, it tends to be slow.

One writer invented a method he called "from-through-to." He thought of the ending ("to") as a target he shot at from the beginning ("from"). So he wrote the ending, the beginning, and the middle in that order.

Some people, sometimes including me, write the framework and then fill it in. I often write the answer to the question "What's this about?" then the first sentence of each section, and finally the ending. Then I poke in the rest. My friend Frank Caperton came up through the ranks as a copy editor and did his best work in big type. Later, he had to write a weekly column, so he would write a headline and the subheads, and then the stuff in between.

If you're a plunger and figure out what to say by typing it, it doesn't matter where you start. You just write a lot of paragraphs or even chapters until you think you've got it all down; then you rearrange it to make sense. Again, it's faster if you don't revise until you cut and rearrange.

Writers who work for both online and print at the same time often write an online brief first. After the short version, they have a better idea of what they want to say in print.

I know what you're thinking: "Some of these methods are just nuts; nobody would do it that way." But real writers use these techniques. I've tried most of them myself at one time or another. I started typing this section in the second paragraph.

So do it your way. To discover your way, try different ways.

VOMITING UP A DRAFT

Sometimes you don't know what you want to say, and all the organizing tricks fail. You need what Calvin Trillin named a "vomit draft." You just type whatever falls out of your fingers. Don't worry about clarity, don't worry about spelling, don't even type sentences. Just type. Some people turn off the screen, and let the words gush out. Keep that up until you run out of steam. Stop and take a break. When you come back, there will be ideas on those pages—unformed and ragged ones, but ideas nonetheless. You'll see what your head was thinking about.

Roy Clark organizes pieces using this method, which he calls a "barf draft." He types two screenfuls of junk, prints it out, and uses a Magic Marker to circle useful things. I've watched him doing it, and he mumbles, "Oh, that's good," and "Hey, I didn't know I think that."

Sounds slow and bizarre, doesn't it? But not for some people. Maybe not for you.

> IDIOSYNCRASY IS GOOD WHEN IT WORKS FOR YOU.

QUESTIONS PLUS ANSWERS EQUAL A DRAFT

While writing this book as a blog, I accidentally invented a new technique, which I call "Q&A drafting." I just fell into it on bad days, when I had trouble deciding what I wanted to say and what order to put it in. I typed questions and answered them, mostly one paragraph at a time, although some answers sprawled for a screenful or two. Then I rearranged the paragraphs and later revised the questions into statements.

Many discussions in this book start with questions, a technique I had seldom used. But I found that this Q&A format sounds conversational and invites readers to think with me, which is part of my voice.

Unexpectedly, the technique broadened into a way to organize. I wrote down a series of questions, sorted them into logical order, and treated the list as a plan. Then I drafted the answers and rewrote the questions. It turned out to be a relatively fast way to draft, even on good days. Once you start fooling around with techniques, they turn into new techniques.

IMAGINING REAL READERS

Usually it's not a good idea to write with an actual, specific reader in mind, except in proposals, letters, and e-mail. You may not spell things out that your targeted reader already knows, but your other readers don't. You should assume that anything you write will reach readers you didn't anticipate, especially if you're writing for the Internet.

Most authors write for a specific person: themselves. Remember the theme of this book: *writing your own way.* What could be more egocentric than that?

I'm not talking about who will actually read your pieces, but who's in your head as you write them. Here are some audiences you might imagine:

- Yourself, when you're taking notes or writing a diary entry
- One person, or a few, perhaps in a business letter to your department head, who may share it with other staffers
- A specialized group, such as the twenty-seven other scholars in the world who study Anglo-Saxon riddles
- Your editor, or critics
- General readers, the hardest audience of all to picture

You imagine the audience to figure out what they already know and what you have to explain. You assume that you know what they know, but you really don't. We assume that what's in our heads is in our audience's heads. Wrong.

Suppose you're right about what your pictured reader knows, but except for personal letters or e-mails, the audience is usually larger. Your specific targeting may exclude the rest of the audience.

AUDIENCES IS ALWAYS PLURAL.

If you're afraid of the person you picture, such as a grumpy editor or nasty critics, you're likely to write generic mush that won't offend anyone. Many writers try to leave out anything their editor might question. They avoid the imagined conflict by writing as blandly as possible. Then they wonder why their writing is boring.

Picturing how your readers will react may also make you write nothing at all. Classical scholars live in a culture of savage criticism of any tiny error; some get so intimidated that they never publish anything. I know writers who want to publish their memoirs, but they're waiting for their parents to die first. They imagine how their mother will react when she reads the part about how she didn't know how to write a check (as mine didn't), or how their father will be offended when they tell how he terrified the family trying to pass every other car on the road (as mine did). So many writers don't ever start their autobiography. After all, your parents may outlive you.

WELCOME, READER, I'LL BE YOUR GUIDE

First, a digression. Some readers may have noticed that, except in the earlier discussion of the Inverted Pyramid, I avoid the word *lead* or *lede*, the journalistic term for the beginning of a piece. This term has many associations that confuse clear thinking about form. *Lead* signifies the hook that lures readers into reading a piece, and many journalists believe that their stories live or die depending on a perfect lead. Their lead becomes the essence of the reporter's professional soul, like a dog's private tail. Some newspaper contracts specify that no editor can change a lead without the writer's permission. All of this mystical thinking, in my opinion, gets in the way of clear writing. So I use the somewhat awkward term *beginning* rather than *lead* in this book. End digression.

What's going on in your readers' heads as they start to read your piece? They make predictions about content: Is this something they want and need to know? They predict if they'll understand your prose; if not, they feel stupid and drop out. They estimate how long the piece will be and whether they have time for it now. They start imagining a personality speaking to them from the page, the *persona* or voice.

All of this subconscious calculation happens as the reader takes the path from photo, title, caption to text. By the time she finishes your first sentence, she has a fairly clear picture of what to expect, fairly clear if all elements are crafted well and fit together to lead readers in.

I like to imagine a piece of writing as a journey through unknown territory. Readers need a map and a guide. All those devices at the top add up to a map, and the beginning introduces the *persona* as a guide. As readers start to read the text, they start judging the voice to see if they trust it. If the *persona* talking to them seems reliable, they keep reading. You've established "Authority." But if they don't trust the persona, or voice, they don't expect skilled guidance, and they drop out.

READERS BAIL OUT IF THEY DON'T TRUST THE GUIDE.

What establishes your authority? Clarity and assurance. If the voice of the beginning speaks clearly and firmly, readers expect to continue to understand it. Readers predict they won't get lost.

Readers are not up to speed on your voice at the beginning, so start simply. Don't write sentences like this:

> In an effort to disarm recent allegations of ordering the torture of prisoners in murky foreign settings, members of the former Bush administration, including some at the very top, who have kept silent on the subject until recently, have begun, in ways that suggest a coordinated campaign, to use friendly cable-news and talk-radio shows to create the illusion of widespread foiling of sinister plots.

We call that "a suitcase," too much stuff crammed into too small a bag that won't quite close, even if you sit on it. The readers expect the whole piece to read like that, so they go read something else.

For maximum clarity, begin with simple sentences with simple structures to ease your readers in. You don't have to *tell* readers everything you know in the first paragraph. Rather, *predict* the whole piece, the whole journey, and readers will follow you if they expect to continue understanding.

You achieve power by certainty of tone. Simple, clear sentences imply you know what you're talking about. Saving qualifiers until later simplifies early statements. Use lots of strong verbs and few adverbs, and all the devices of clarity you'll find later in this book.

I think of myself as saying to my reader at the top: "This is a tricky journey. I've been there. You haven't. Take my hand, and we won't get lost. Okay? Here we go. First, let's look at...."

WRITING THE TOP AT THE BOTTOM

I usually write the beginning, the opening paragraph, last. So do about five percent of the writers I know. They thought they were nuts until they heard me talk about it. They're also among the fastest writers I know.

I want a solid beginning to introduce the subject matter, set my readers' expectations, and establish my authority as a good guide through the journey of the piece. I find it hard to write such a terrific beginning for a text I have yet to imagine. So I write the text first, and then the beginning.

Good beginnings mirror the language of the text, and I find that simply typing the piece creates a beginning before I reach the bottom. Sometimes I write bits and pieces (the way I wrote this book) and let them fall together. By that time, a beginning will appear in my head, and I type it.

Sometimes a terrific beginning pops into my head as I'm composing the text, and I just type it in wherever I am. I avoid the distracting temptation to polish it on the spot. I move it up later during revision. By the time I type to the bottom, an even better beginning often shows up.

My procedure may sound like nonsense to you, but I know how it works. I'm typing the body text, and my brain is watching key words appear on the screen. Those words call up other words and phrases, and my head creates a beginning for me.

Here's the good news: A beginning invented from an existing body text seldom needs revision. Maybe a little buffing, but no heavy reworking. It hasn't been revised over and over as you wrote the rest.

The best writers of beginnings often have a head full of openings when they sit down to type. As they gather materials, they stay tuned for beginnings, and they write them in their notebook. I mark potential beginnings (*PB*) and potential endings (*PK*) in the margin. On a good day, I may organize with five possible beginnings and a couple of endings already in play. So I've already done a lot of thinking about the beginning before I start drafting.

THE FASTEST WRITERS THINK ABOUT FORM ALL THE TIME.

QUESTIONING YOUR WAY IN

Is it okay to start with a question? Yes, but like all techniques, it depends on how you use it.

I just opened this section with a question, and it drew you immediately into the topic. What's wrong with that? Some people object that writers *answer* questions rather than *asking* them, which is pretentious nonsense.

Question beginnings engage your readers, and, done simply, start you off with a conversational tone. Readers will expect you to answer the question quickly, and get impatient if you don't, which makes it important for you to get to the point. They're the easiest kind of beginnings to write.

Question beginnings have one drawback: They're addictive, especially when you feel low. It's Monday, and you've got post-weekend blues, so you get yourself going with a question beginning. On Tuesday, you think you're coming down with the flu, so you just slide in with a question. That night, your dog Stumpy dies, so you get through Wednesday with a question opener. And on Thursday.... Question beginnings are so easy, they can become a crutch.

The best opening for your readers answers the question "What's this about?" right away. How do you figure that out? Ask and answer a question that strikes at the heart of the matter, like this:

What's this about?

Well, is it patriotic to save money in a consumer-spending crisis?

Bingo.

Type the question as a draft beginning, then answer it, and develop the topic. When you revise, delete the question and buff up the answer. You'll have a terrific beginning in record time.

THE TOP STORY

An anecdotal beginning starts a piece with a person in a short vignette or story. Business writers who found their subject matter boring invented the anecdotal beginning to hook readers. First, you tell the anecdote, then what the piece is about, and follow with the rest of the text.

Readers begin a piece by predicting its subject. If their prediction comes true, they keep reading. If not, they feel confused, and drop out. Anecdotal beginnings predict that the piece will be about the person featured at the top. Here's an example:

> Carole Blizzo stands in line at her local Commonwealth Bank for 45 minutes, finally reaching Harold Peterson, who calls himself her "relationship banker." She's unemployed, six months behind on her adjustable mortgage, and desperate to find a way to keep her home. Peterson smiles, until he learns what she wants, and then he says, over and over, "I'm sorry, but...."
>
> The Obama administration's Mortgage Relief Program was supposed to help nine million Americans like Carole, but....

Readers will predict the piece is about Carole, and they want to know what happens to her. But it never mentions Carole again; she's just the hook.

Readers resent this kind of "bait-and-switch" tactic, and that resentment can mean they stop reading a piece they may need to read.

On the other hand, Carole might serve as the spine of the piece, weaving in and out of the data and analysis. Then the anecdotal beginning is functional and unifies the piece, helping readers understand by providing someone they can identify with.

Besides confusing readers, an anecdotal beginning can also turn into "a writing job." If you consider your subject matter boring and think you need a tricky beginning to get somebody, anybody, to read it, you're likely to overwrite.

Anecdotal beginnings also tempt copy editors to write anecdotal titles or headlines on top of them. The headline is supposed to tell readers what the piece is about. If the beginning and the headline don't tip the readers off, they get hit twice with confusing signals.

Can you make anecdotal beginnings effective? Sure, pick an anecdote that directly concerns the subject, put an informative headline on it, keep it short and simple, and continue the main character throughout the piece. Better, don't write anecdotal beginnings. Start with a solid headline, write a short beginning that tells the reader what the piece is about, and follow with a brief, relevant anecdote that introduces a character readers want to know about.

> DON'T TRICK YOUR READERS; TELL THEM STORIES.

CRACKING NUT GRAPHS

The "nut graph" is usually defined as a sentence or paragraph at the top that tells the reader what the piece is about. The term and technique originated as the second half of anecdotal beginnings, which unfortunately delay the readers' understanding of what pieces are about, and make them harder to follow. A good beginning serves readers by telling them the subject immediately.

Nut graphs have three functions:

1) they tell what the piece is about
2) they explain a key fact readers need to understand
3) they tell why the piece is important

The first kind of nut graph tells what the piece is about, and by now, you know that's the key to clarity. When the piece is very complex, and the beginning is unavoidably confusing, as some are, you can use a nut graph early to snap the reader into focus. In a long piece, a nut graph can introduce a new section, telling what the next part is about. And when you're about to explain something really difficult, a nut graph can steady your readers before the hard trudging to come. Here's an example: "So many mortgages are failing that bankers are considering a type of reduction procedure called a 'cram down,' rarely used, seldom successful, and difficult to understand."

Some publications use the term "nut graph" for information that readers have to know in order to understand the piece, such as that manatees are marine mammals that have to surface to breathe every two minutes or so. This essential information must come early enough to be effective.

> TELL READERS WHAT THEY NEED TO KNOW BEFORE THEY REALIZE THEY NEED IT.

A third kind of nut graph tells readers at the very beginning why the piece is important and why they should read it. Here's an example: "The proposed budget reductions will eliminate the teaching of music for your children." I call this type of nut graph "the so-what."

TALKING TO YOUR SCREEN

Some writers, including me, draft by speaking to the screen. With my bad typing, I need a way to produce a cleaner draft. The secret is typing only good sentences, or not typing bad sentences.

I speak a sentence aloud. If it's what I want to say and how, I type it. If not, I speak a better version. If it's what I want, I type it. And so on, until I've spoken and typed the whole piece. You can see that dictation is also a form of thinking on the fly.

This method sounds slow, but for me, it's faster than fixing bad sentences. One side benefit: my prose sounds conversational because it resulted from a monologue with the screen.

A friend of mine lived two hours away from his office as a university dean. He dictated mystery novels into a tape recorder in his car four hours a day, two hours in and two hours out. His private secretary typed up the tapes triple-spaced, and he revised the draft into a finished typescript, which she also typed. He dictated and published a novel every two years.

Some writers use dictation software. You speak into a microphone, and your computer turns your speech into text on the screen. Half the fun is the howlers it comes up with: "Hour farther hoe heart in heaven, Howard bee thigh name." (Okay, I made that up.) It works well for writers who have Repetitive Stress Injury (RSI), or otherwise damaged hands.

Some writers just sit down at a terminal and blast it out, apparently typing perfect copy at supersonic speed. Their colleagues look on with envy. How do they do that? Why don't they struggle like everybody else?

Here's their secret: They're not *composing* as they type. They're dictating from memory. They composed and revised the whole piece earlier in their heads, and then dictated it to the screen. If you look closely, you'll probably see their lips moving.

"What a great technique," you say to yourself. "I'd love to compose that fast." Wait, there's a prerequisite: you have to have that good a memory. See what I mean about you can only use techniques you're qualified for?

TURNING YOUR SCREEN OFF

Now here's an interesting experiment that will convince you that you can draft without revising. I don't recommend it as a way to compose but as a demonstration for yourself that you only do once.

Wait until you're about to write something with little at stake. Decide in general what you want to say, or write a plan. Note the time, and turn the screen off, or cover it up so you can't see it. Then type the piece as fast as you can. You have to watch your fingers to make sure they're aligned correctly on the keys, so you don't end up with gibberish. When you think you've typed the whole thing, stop, turn the screen back on, and note the time.

You will have typed this draft faster than you've ever written before, quicker than you've ever imagined. And I'll wager that what you wrote will be better than what you normally turn in.

How can that be? You couldn't see the screen, and your internal critic couldn't either. So he couldn't criticize what you were writing and distract you. He couldn't damage your confidence and make you slow and timid. He couldn't make you keep revising although you were just typing a draft.

You will have just succeeded in drafting without revising.

Writing coach Bruce DeSilva says, "One of the worst traps a writer falls into is revising as he goes.... On pieces that take several days, the tendency is to start each writing session by revising what you've already done before creating anything new. As a result, the beginning of a long piece might be rewritten ten times and the bottom only once, creating uneven work."

An easier version of drafting without revising involves leaving blanks in the text to be filled in, either later, in the DRAFT stage or in the REVISION stage. Again, the idea is to get it down, then get it right. Maybe we should call this technique "Get it down, then fill it out."

Here's an example about Admiral Nimitz arriving to award the Medal of Honor:

> [[DATE?]]
> Four senior naval officers stepped tentatively into the hospital room. "Commander Fixx, I'm Admiral Nimitz," said the tallest one, extending his hand. "Let me introduce XXXX."

In this case, I'm not sure of the date, so I leave a blank. I know the names of the other three officers, but not their exact ranks, so I simply type XXXX. Using consistent codes, such as XXXX or double brackets around the blanks, makes it easy to find them later with the search function.

You can also specify what's missing in the blank, such as [[SELLER'S HUSBAND'S NAME?]]. Some writers leave messages to themselves in the blank, such as [[IS THIS CORRECT?]]. Many coaches and editors use coded blanks to send queries to writers inside the text, such as [[CHECK SPELLING IN FRENCH]] or [[CONVERT TO GRAMS?]]. I use ALL CAPS to make the insertions easier to spot during revision.

Wouldn't it be quicker just to find the information as you need it and type it in? Maybe, but you'll lose the flow of rapid drafting. And you might get distracted and come back an hour or so later. Undisciplined and disciplined writers need different techniques.

One caution: At the end of revision, check that you've filled all the blanks and eliminated all the codes. You don't want your editor or reader to see something like [[WHERE DID I FIND THIS?]].

JUST LET LOOSE

Most writing advice comes from planners, who tell you to decide what to say and then say it. Eleventh-grade English teachers demand detailed outlines before students put down a word. Most manuals on how to write novels prescribe creating a chapter outline and character biographies first. Plan, then execute. But plungers don't do it that way, and some of the best stuff comes unplanned. The secret is to relax and let it come.

A decade ago, I started writing novels. I'm a dedicated planner but suddenly found myself writing fiction without a plot. I worried that I might have a brain tumor. And I really fretted when my characters started acting on their own. A pilot in my third novel suddenly committed a murder, which he'd clearly planned ahead of time without consulting me. Hey, this was my story, not his.

My novelist son, Jason, advised me to relax my inner control freak, and follow the characters when they took off on their own. If what they did or said panned out, I could develop it. If it didn't, I still controlled the Delete key.

One night in a Washington, D.C., hotel room, I woke up at 1:00 A.M., typed nonstop for an hour, and went back to sleep. The next morning, I found a chapter on my screen that I hadn't planned or imagined. It was better than what I'd written before. Strangest of all, it had no typos. Who wrote it? The crew in my head.

In her book, *Naked, Drunk, and Writing*, Adair Lara uses exercises, questions, and prompts to bring about what she calls "epiphanies," or breakthroughs in thinking. For example, you keep asking yourself why you did something and writing down the answers. "Your fingers can type things you didn't know were in your head," she says.[17] Screenwriter Larry Gelbart said, "I need to write to find out what I'm thinking."[18]

Chip Scanlan of the Poynter Institute conducts an exercise where participants write a short piece, then toss it out and write it again, and toss it out and write it again. On my fourth version, I astonished myself with this beginning: "I'm glad my father died." I didn't know that until it popped out on my screen.

In a less-structured version of this technique, turn the screen off and just type. (Watch your fingers so you don't type gibberish.) Don't think, just type. And the staff in your head will tell you what you're thinking about.

Letting go helps with form as well as content. Sometimes you can't come up with a structure, things just won't jell, or everything seems equally important (or unimportant). So you just type sentences, lots of sentences about your subject. Don't worry about how they go together.

After a while, clumps will emerge. As food writer Michael Ruhlman puts it, "Telling the story generates the shape."[19]

If I can suppress my inner control freak, so can you, when you need to.

WRITE SHORT

Outside of Phyllis Peacock's class, I've never met anyone who was taught how to write short. I had to teach myself to write short as a naval communicator. Here's how.

For adults, writing short is a lot harder than writing long. You may remember the famous quip by Mark Twain (or Blaise Pascal): "I apologize for writing you a long letter. I didn't have time to write you a short one." Writing short effectively takes more knowledge, thinking, and design.

How long is short? Brevity involves more than actual length. A piece can read short or long, regardless of how much space it occupies. I believe short means it seems short to readers as they read it.

The secret is selection, not compression. You write short by leaving things out, not by mashing things in. So short writing begins with simplifying, *i.e.*, adjusting the number of subjects and details to the amount of space available.

For most professional writers, editors assign the space, usually based on their publication format or their estimate of the piece's importance. Important subjects tend to get more space.

How do you figure out how much space you need? I ask myself how much explanation my readers require. If they need no explanation, the piece is short, and that's the default. If they need some explanation, the piece is a little longer. If they need a lot of explanation, the space is even larger. If they need an enormous amount of explanation, I write a series or a book. The trick is to match your space to your readers' attention span.

You need to know how much space you have before you type, unless you're writing a book. Writers who have a length in mind write that length or a little more, about 110 percent. Writers without a specified length write long, both in space and time, and tend to turn in drafts rather than finished pieces.

If you work with an editor, always negotiate a length before you draft. Nice editors will sometimes say, "Oh, just write as much as you want," thus sabotaging you into writing long, late, and drafty. Insist on a length. If they don't give you one, set your own.

Here are some techniques for writing short.

First, open with the essence of the piece, jumping to the action and avoiding introductions. You find that essence by asking, "What's this about?" or "What's my point?" Then type the answer as your first sentence. You may revise it later, but at least you've started with the heart of the matter.

Describing actions makes reading seem quick, so get to actors and action as fast as possible, pulling your readers in and along. If you're telling a story, they want to know what happens and how it comes out.

Quotations are wonderful, and everyone loves them, but they slow things down and take up a lot of space. Every character you introduce requires at least name and title to get on the stage. So select the characters, and speakers, and quotations rigorously. Everything has to justify its space in short writing. (Actually, everything has to justify its space in *all* writing.)

Background and context can take up a lot of room. Ask yourself what your readers already know, and how little you have to explain. Provide background in bits, parts of sentences, rather than in blocks.

Attributing facts lets readers judge their validity. You maintain their trust by clearly indicating where each fact comes from. Attribution clutters the piece, so limit the number of sources you have to include and acknowledge. Sometimes you can save space with "umbrella attribution." For example, starting a section: "Jones introduced the members of the cast."

You can't simplify what you don't understand, so short writing requires deeper gathering. You don't have room for a lot of qualifiers and nuance.

See why short writing is harder? You don't have as much space for devices that build authority and interest.

You also don't have room for showy style, so you make every sentence add to the readers' knowledge and understanding. You don't have room for transitions, so don't write them; readers will bridge the gaps themselves. Finally, write an ending to cement the piece in the reader's memory. Even in very short writing, you need to close the loop so readers remember what you said.

Common sense would tell you that you don't have room for visuals in short writing, but they can save space. Push complex information into graphics, pictures, blurbs, at-a-glance boxes, sidebars, captions, and titles. One photo describing a pasta shape can save you from having to write one hard paragraph.

The "look" of a piece can make it seem shorter or longer to readers. Large blocks of type, long paragraphs, wide margins, and multipage layout can make a short piece look long. Things that look long to readers make them start calculating how long it will take them to read it.

All these principles of writing short apply just as well to long writing. The trick is to make long writing read short, no matter how long it is.

TWITTERING NDR 140 LTRS

Jon Winokur invited me to contribute to his Twitter feed, "@AdviceTo Writers." I decided to write a tweet to help writers who stall while drafting, or even worse, become paralyzed by writer's block. I advise them never to think of themselves with their fingers touching keys, unless they're writing autobiography. Otherwise they're off the subject while they're typing. When you think about yourself while writing, your internal critic can grab the chance to wipe out your confidence. He screams things like this:

> What a stupid sentence!
> If you publish this, people will laugh at you!
> You're no good!

Notice the sequence: from a rough sentence to worthlessness. If you let him keep that up, you'll give up in despair, maybe even leave our profession to sell insurance.

So how do I say all that in 140 characters and spaces? Actually, 132 because I have to leave room for six letters (D-O-N-F-R-Y) and two spaces. Here's my first try:

> Never think about yourself with your fingers on the keys, unless you're writing autobiography or a memoir. Otherwise you're off the subject. DON FRY.

Jon said that was too long (148) and shortened it:

> Nvr think about yrself wth yr fingers on the keys, unless yr writing autobiography or a memoir. Otherwise yr off the subject. DON FRY.

That's 133. But I like words too much to abbreviate them, so I tried this version:

> Never think about yourself with your fingers on the keys, unless you're writing autobiography. DON FRY.

Much shorter, 102, but I've left out the internal critic. So I deleted "unless you're writing autobiography or a memoir" to make room for the monster. Then I tried a telegraphic, guru-ish version:

> Never think of yourself with your fingers on the keys. DON FRY.

A count of 62, but I've lost the reason for not thinking about yourself.

I could gain a little room by giving up "fingers on the keys," but the visual image makes the advice memorable. And I can't give up the monster because every writer struggles with one. So here's the next version:

> Avoid thinking about yourself with your fingers on the keys, or your internal critic will start talking about failure. DON FRY.

126, but flat and clumsy. Let's streamline the sentence:

> Thinking about yourself with your fingers on the keys starts your internal critic whispering about failure. DON FRY.

115 and better, but your Internal Critic is always there. He doesn't "start," and he never "whispers." Mine snarls. One more try:

> Thinking about yourself with your fingers on the keys lets your internal critic rave about failure. DON FRY.

107, bingo, done.

Notice what I didn't do. I didn't get there by shaving a letter, a syllable, or a word here and there. When I finally got to what I wanted to say, the character count worked. If it had too many words, I revised what I wanted to say or how to say it. Chop chunks, not letters. These techniques work for any kind of short writing or attempt to shorten writing.

> ACHIEVE BREVITY BY SELECTION, NOT BY COMPRESSION.

GETTING GOING AGAIN

You're typing along, and the phone rings, and five minutes (or three hours) later, you're about to resume. How do you get your momentum back? Here are some tricks. Some will work for you, and some work for other writers.

1. When the phone rings, stop in the middle of the sentence you're typing before you answer. When you restart, the rhythm and meaning of the partial sentence will propel you forward.

2. When you restart, read aloud what you've already written from the top of the unit you're in: chapter, section, paragraph. Reading aloud will get you back into the swing, but don't stop to fix things because that will bounce you out of the flow. This technique works best if what you read out loud is short.

3. My friend Steve Lovelady would inspire himself by typing a few paragraphs of someone else's writing that he admired. He said he liked to see admirable sentences emerging from the top of his typewriter. Then he would type more admirable sentences.

4. You may need to refresh your grasp of details, especially after a long time lapse, by reviewing your notes for that section. This technique is especially helpful to those who close their notes and write from memory, as well as writers with lots of notes, like book authors.

5. Here's the most extreme technique: Erase from the top of the unit and start typing from there. This method only works for decisive fast typists.

6. I restart by asking my favorite question: "What's this about?" I ask it about every half hour throughout the writing process anyway, and it refocuses me after a break.

> HIT THE "SAVE" KEY EVERY TIME YOUR PHONE RINGS.

JUMPING OVER THE BOUNDARIES

Your readers are aware of the boundaries in your text, and they think about quitting reading just before every one. What's a boundary? The end of a paragraph, section, or chapter; the "jump" from one page to another; the bottom of the screen where they have to scroll or click "Next."

How do you keep your audience reading across boundaries? Well, obviously, by writing brilliantly. Frankly, I'm not brilliant and maybe you're not either, but here are some techniques that encourage readers to jump over hurdles.

First, write with authority. From the beginning, readers size up the voice speaking to them from the text and decide whether they trust it or not. They're less interested in whether they like you or not. If they trust you as a reliable guide throughout the piece, they will probably read all of it.

You create such authority at the start by telling readers immediately what the piece is about and why they should read it. You write as clearly as possible so your readers think, "I understand this; I trust this guide." You start off writing a little simpler than you might usually write, just to ease readers in at the top.

You maintain authority by retaining your voice of assurance and clarity all the way through, but especially just before the boundaries. Readers who wonder, "How did I get here?" or "Where are we going?" are about to bid you *adieu*.

Readers who start wondering also start thinking about leaving. So you supply what they need to know just before they need to know it. Otherwise, they feel dumb or shaky, and they depart.

In a longer piece, you put either a cliff hanger or a gold coin just before each major boundary, such as a jump to another page. A cliff hanger, named after a technique early movie serials used to get viewers to watch the next segment, is a bit of suspense. Television dramas use the same technique. The scantily clad heroine clings to a branch over a thousand-foot drop. Can she hang on until the fully clothed hero arrives?!

Here's a cliff hanger: "The finger pointing at him wasn't a finger. It was a .357 Magnum." Here's another: "Margaret looked at her fiancé as the minister asked, 'Do you take this man to be your lawfully wedded husband?' and thought, 'Do I?'"

A gold coin can also keep readers moving. It's an intriguing anecdote, a fascinating new character, a clever turn of phrase, or a funny bit. Gold coins refresh and reward the readers, and make them predict that more gold coins lie ahead. Here's one in quotation form from my local paper, *The Daily Progress*, about a wild fox that bit two students and carried off a sweater. "There's also no way to be sure that a fox that's trapped in the area is the fox that was acting aggressive," said Ed Clark, "unless it's wearing the sweater."[20]

GUIDE YOUR READERS ALL THE WAY TO THE BOTTOM.

ENDING WITH AN ENDING

Your readers can remember what they've read in general outline if you give them a sense of closure. Without a sense of ending, readers can't remember much of anything you said, except maybe the funny bits. So endings aren't decorative, but functional. They can take many forms.

1. **Simply stopping** leaves readers with no sense of closure.

   EXAMPLE: Pomegranates will also attract songbirds to your feeder.

2. **Ending with a piece of context** too boring to put anywhere else does not give closure.

   EXAMPLE: Pine saplings are especially valued for their fast growth.

3. **Trailing off** in poetic language for a movielike finish can prove memorable.

   EXAMPLE: The Juangs plodded on, toward a sunset bright with napalm.

4. **A quotation** needs to be relevant and sound like an ending.

   EXAMPLE: "Readers remember what they read last," said Don Fry, "but you have to lure them to the bottom."

5. **A telling anecdote** must be relevant and short.

   EXAMPLE: John recalls the day his wife left him. His father Sam waved good-bye as she drove away, and said, "Son, treat her like she's dead."

6. **An information block** or link helps interested readers find out more.
   EXAMPLE: For further information, go to www.savethe peccary.org.

7. **Pointing to the future** suggests ways readers can act on the information.

   EXAMPLE: You can sit tight on your nest egg, you can lose it by getting back in too early, or you can watch and wait. Just don't bury it in the backyard.

8. **Forward spin** points to what will happen next.
   EXAMPLE: BP will test the oil well cap on Tuesday, while the Gulf holds its breath.

9. **A call for action**, common for opinion pieces, gives readers a way to participate.

   EXAMPLE: If you don't like the new chancellor's decision, here's his phone number: 555-555-5555.

10. **Echoing the beginning**, which classicists call "ring composition," repeats a word or image or idea from the beginning to give a sense of closure and unity.

    EXAMPLE BEGINNING: Sarah Palin's supposed appeal to red-meat hunters never happened.

    ENDING: A roof over your head perhaps counts more than moose on the supper table.

11. **A returning character**, usually from an anecdotal beginning, closes the loop.

    EXAMPLE: Meanwhile, Janice still has nowhere to sleep and no hope.

12. **Answering a question** posed at the beginning gives a sense of completion.

    EXAMPLE: So to survive an airliner crash, sit over the wing, keep your seatbelt fastened, and get out fast.

13. **A twist sideways** can introduce a new and often ironic note.
    EXAMPLE: These techniques may prevent your employees from burning out. But to make them work, you may have to deal first with your own burnout.

14. **Restating your point** cements complex arguments into readers' memories.

    EXAMPLE: No matter how tempting derivatives look, investing in core businesses lets you sleep at night.

15. **A summary** cements long and complex material in the readers' memory.

    EXAMPLE: So who runs the world? People who can read, write, think, and talk.

16. **"Stopping at now"** ends a piece organized chronologically at the end of the action.

    EXAMPLE: Serve with Ruffino Serelle Vin Santo del Chianti for a great finish to a perfect meal.

17. **Stopping at the destination** closes a piece organized as a journey.

    EXAMPLE: The Marines, despite their wounds, fell to their knees and kissed the tarmac of Andrews Air Force Base.

18. **An epilogue** tells what happened to the characters later, and how their stories continue.

    EXAMPLE: Harold became the model father he always wanted.
    Clarice served a ten-year sentence for child abuse.
    Little Hal wrote his bestseller, *How to Divorce Your Parents*.

19. **Zooming to a detail** lets a small thing represent larger issues, a device called "synecdoche."

    EXAMPLE: "Some will always be poor, and some will always be rich," sighed the archbishop, offering his golden ring to be kissed.

20. **Return to normality** lets readers down slowly after horrendous events.

    EXAMPLE: Carla's restaurant has reopened. The waitresses still fold the napkins into little birds. And regulars still order "my usual."

And that's just a sampling of ways you can end a piece.

I speak also of "a sense of an ending," which has to do with sound. Consider this ending of a highly technical article on memory by Alessandro Treves:

> In general, one deals with internal representations (of behaviorally relevant objects, of a syntactic structure), which can be provisionally labeled by appropriately defined symbols σ, even though their relationship to the underlying neural activity variables {ri} is yet to be determined. The grand goal of elucidating this relationship is a fascinating challenge for cognitive neurosciences, and for the science of memory.[21]

Notice how the voice changes in that last sentence from the scientific jargon above it to an elevated, enthusiastic, and slightly florid style, creating the sense of closure.

The power of endings also applies to sections, so here's my ending to this section:

Which ending technique should you choose? You select the one that helps your reader understand and remember what you've just said.

CHILLING OUT

Writing involves intense thinking, strategies and tactics, memory, and self-control, all at the same time. This intensity tires you out, your head seems too full of information, and you can't see anything but detail and problems. Time to cool off.

During the GATHER phase, you might interview numerous people, perhaps even hundreds for a book. You digest written sources and scour the Internet. Your hard drive fills up, and you sit amid piles of paper. And suddenly, you can't imagine anything but more of the same. Time to cool off.

Cooling off involves getting away from what you're doing so that when you return to it, you can see it fresh. Ideally you get as far as possible from what's overpowering you. Oddly enough, some writers cool off by drinking hot beverages, such as coffee or tea. One music reviewer I knew cooled off by getting drunk, a bad tactic that made him miss deadlines. Some take a walk, call a friend, get a massage, or eat ice cream. I cool off by eating a carrot, which I don't like, but it's low calorie. The trick is to get away and not think about what you're immersed in. You un-immerse yourself temporarily.

How long you cool off depends on you and the project. Some people cool off for a few minutes, and some book authors let things sit for a year or so. I had to avoid this book manuscript for two months before I could see it again. But make sure you're really cooling off and not just procrastinating.

In the DRAFT stage, you add typing to all the intense mental work described above. You need to cool off when everything you're typing sounds alike. If you suddenly ask yourself, "How did I get here?" you're drowning and should stop. If you decide you're bored with what you're writing, you should either take an extra-long break or type as fast as possible and just finish the beast.

My poor typing wears me out. I cool off about every four paragraphs unless I suddenly "get up on the step" and just blaze away, in which case

I don't want to cool off. I sometimes start typing, shift into a trance, and come to after a while with a finished draft on my screen. I wish that happened more often.

You should always cool off between the DRAFT and REVISE stages. Take a long break, maybe ten minutes or the lunch hour or a year, depending on how long you need to get your head clear and fresh to revise.

The symptoms in the REVISE stage resemble those in the DRAFT stage. If you keep revising the same thing and it doesn't get better, take a break. Pick a unit, such as a section or a certain number of paragraphs, and force yourself to take a break after revising each unit. Sometimes I revise for a set span of time, such as one hour.

Some writers, especially perfectionists, let a revised, finished piece sit for a while, and then give it one more pass. If you get a better finish that way, it's a good technique. If that second revision leads to a third, fourth, or twentieth, you need to ask if you're making it better. In most cases, excessive revision makes prose stiffer. That's why I recommend one draft and one revision as a default.

(Two paragraphs back, I drew a blank. I couldn't think of any reason to cool off during the REVISE stage. Nothing came into my head, and nothing fell out of my fingers. So I recognized that I had entered what I call the "brainless zone," a period when nothing is going to happen at the keyboard. So I went to the grocery store and bought broccoli crowns and Band-Aids. When I came back, I had things to say, although I hadn't rehearsed them on the trip. Your brain can do the heavy lifting for you while you distract yourself.)

WHEN YOU FEEL BRAIN-DEAD,
CHILL OUT.

A ROOM OF YOUR OWN

All my best ideas occur in the shower, and I compose my best sentences in my head while driving. Essentially I create a kind of quiet zone. Writers tend to frazzle themselves chasing information, and you need ways to slow things down so you can think and plan and compose. Slowing down speeds you up overall.

Sam Stanton wrote about agriculture in California, which involved long drives back to the office to type. He would plan his piece at 70 miles per hour by asking himself questions aloud and then just "steering until the lead formed on the windshield."

California Zen has nothing to do with this technique. The secret is shedding distractions so you can see larger patterns. The chief distractions are life clutter, fear of failure, and drowning in detail. These problems happen whether you work in an office or in a car or alone.

An editor friend of mine wears a red baseball cap when she wants total seclusion to write, which she does right in the middle of her six demanding writers. They temporarily respect her privacy, and then deluge her when she takes the cap off. She allows them to interrupt only if the building's on fire. Not being spoken to isolates her in a boisterous writing pit. She's one of the fastest writers I know.

Many writers use headphones to seclude themselves while writing, but the effectiveness of this technique depends on the equipment, the sound (or lack of sound), and you. For example, listening to music isolates some people and distracts others. I prefer classical music but have discovered that with Bach, I keep paying attention to the music, but not with Mozart.

You can also use headphones that delete sound rather than convey it. Some people wear headphones, but don't plug them in. Noise-canceling headphones sample the racket around you and generate the opposite sound wave to suppress it. You hear only a slight hiss and a little of the room noise. You can also wear ear protectors, pads that cover your ears and shut out everything. Some writers put a white noise machine on their desks.

In a busy office, you can create a temporary quiet zone simply by holding the phone to your head and moving your lips; no one will interrupt you.

Gathering information almost always involves sitting around. In a library, you can plan what you're going to write while you wait for your book orders to arrive. If you're reviewing a restaurant, you can think between courses. You can jot down ideas during ceremonial parts of an event, while the minister pins medals on new Eagle Scouts. Interviewers can think in waiting rooms, after they've surveyed the walls for clues to their subject's personality.

You can create a moving or a static quiet zone. At the Poynter Institute, we improved meetings by walking around together. You can wander up and down a hall, or sit in your car. A friend of mine thinks in a bathroom stall; in public places, it's better if you don't talk to yourself aloud.

KILLING THE BABIES

This happens to every writer sooner or later. You're in the middle of the GATHER stage, perhaps in an interview, and suddenly the speaker delivers a delicious quotation. It's clear, grammatical, witty, short, and not obscene. A prize-winner if ever you've heard one. Unfortunately, it has nothing to do with what you're writing.

How do writers deal with this situation? They want to include that quotation, no matter what, so they stick it in down near the bottom of their piece. Since it doesn't fit their subject matter, they warp the entire text just to jam it in. To avoid such wreckage, you have to leave the wonderful quotation on the cutting room floor.

I call this technique "killing the babies." George Orwell (or Arthur Quiller-Couch) called it "murdering your darlings." These violent terms capture how much it hurts to leave out something you love so much.

THE SECRET OF GOOD WRITING IS LEAVING OUT, NOT PUTTING IN.

The term "killing the babies" comes from a coaching session I had with a monthly magazine writer who turned in five times as much copy as her editors had room for. She wrote brilliant profiles. Each featured one man. I asked her the secret of her powerful portraits. She said she spent twenty-four hours a day for a whole week with each subject, and they'd fall in love temporarily. "I get everything in his head," she said, "all in beautiful quotes." She took so many notes that she had to write them on 3 x 5-inch cards, one quotation per card. She pointed to a huge stack on her desk, and said, "That's why I write so long, because I can't bear not to put all those quotes in. Help me."

I replied, "Could you divide those cards into two stacks: one, fabulous, super-duper quotations; and the other, not quite so fabulous, merely great ones?"

"Yes," she said, "that would be easy."

"Good," said I, "and then you could put the 'merely great' cards away in your file cabinet, and write from the other pile alone."

"Great!" she exulted. "Then I could keep them. I wouldn't have to kill my babies!"

Hear the metaphor? She and her source fall in love, producing these fabulous quotation-babies. To her, not including all of them in her profile was tantamount to murder. And that's how painful leaving wonderful things out can feel.

So how do you kill the babies? I use the magic question, "What's this about?" as a sword. Faced with a great but irrelevant quotation, I ask myself if it helps my reader understand what the piece is about. If the answer is no, *adios* baby.

Here's a way to soften your grief. Write the wonderful, unused quotation on a 3 x 5-inch card, along with the name and phone number of the speaker. Drop it in your "future file" as a prompt for ideas. Then you can keep it.

Of course, killing the babies also applies to terrific characters, anecdotes, sentences, and turns of phrase that must die.

ESCAPING WRITER'S BLOCK

You've probably experienced writer's block at one time or another, although some people never do. It's the inability to write at all, as opposed to being temporarily stuck somewhere in the writing process, usually in the DRAFT stage.

Some people deny there's such a thing as writer's block, but I've been there several times and I guarantee you it's real and painful. You feel like you have nothing to say or that your writing is hopelessly inept or that everything you've ever written is junk, or all of the above. Once into writer's block, you can't see any way out; you're doomed. Your literary career is over. You might have to sell dental supplies or work as a tunnel guard.

If you get depressed enough, you might take the easy way out: plagiarism. Plagiarism (from the Latin *plagiarius* 'kidnapper') is a form of stealing and occurs when a writer submits somebody else's work as their own. Resist this urge. Plagiarism isn't just dishonest; it's fatal to careers. Sooner or later, you'll get caught, especially in our age of universal search capabilities. Then you're a pariah.

What causes writer's block? You can see from the list of symptoms above that it's a failure of confidence. You just suddenly feel like you can't do it anymore, and when you sit down to type, nothing happens. As a writing coach, I've helped a lot of writers, including Julia Child and myself, dig their way out of writer's block. Here's how to save yourself without a coach.

Since failure of confidence causes writer's block, restoring confidence pulls you out of it. You think about something you're written in the past that really worked, that people praised, that you were proud of. Then you recall the whole history of that piece, how you did it, beginning with the idea, all the way through publication. Then you ask yourself what worked in that piece and that process, and how you made it work.

And you say to yourself, "I could do it then, so I can do it now." And then you type something, anything, without judging it. And praise yourself and start writing again.

How do you prevent blockage in the first place? One way to think about writer's block is to see it as your internal critic's way of finally shutting you down. The internal critic keeps punching the failure button. Jon Favreau, President Obama's chief speechwriter, said, "If you start thinking about what's at stake, it can get paralyzing."[22] When you think about what's at stake, you're thinking about failing. At the deepest level, you're thinking about yourself. Yourself failing.

Of course, you cannot *not* think about something. But you can think about *something else.*

So you never think of yourself with your fingers on the keys, unless you're writing about yourself. Otherwise, you're off the subject. You think about the subject you're trying to write, not about yourself writing it or not writing it. Say things like this out loud:

- TYPE!
- Type it to the end. (I use this one a lot.)
- What do I want to say here?
- This is just a draft.

If all else fails, turn the screen off and just type.

GAGGING YOUR INTERNAL CRITIC

I keep talking about your internal critic. Now it's time to tackle him face to face.

All writers are phonies, and all writers know it. How do you know it? A voice inside your head keeps saying so while you type.

You didn't know that other writers suffered from that voice, did you? Stick with me, and I'll show you that you're not as odd as you think, and I'll show you ways to deal with your inner weirdness.

The mildest form of the internal critic asks, "Are you sure about that?" A good question for REVISION, but it slows up the DRAFT stage. It leads to a slow slide of confidence, like this: "You might be wrong about that last sentence. Or maybe just that first part's a little shaky. Or maybe you got the emphasis just a little wrong. Remember the last time you screwed up?" Confidence starts to drain, and you trudge along. Or quit.

Most internal critics are imaginary, but some are real people, including reviewers, English teachers, editors, even mothers. As you type, you might imagine your editor's reaction, inevitably negative: "He'll hate this. He hates all my stuff. What if he asks me how I know this? What if he calls me 'a little college snot' again?" And your internal critic cripples you.

At the other extreme, consider my internal critic. He screams at me sentence by sentence: "That sentence sucks! The one before it is worse! If you print this drivel, everybody will laugh at you! Stop typing! GIVE UP WRITING!"

Your internal critic damages your confidence sentence by sentence. He distracts you into thinking about yourself instead of what you're trying to say. And that's the problem.

It's okay to think you're a phony; everyone is in his own ways. But you need to shut your internal critic up while you're drafting and train him to say helpful things during REVISION.

Here's how. You need a mantra, a saying that shifts your attention away from yourself failing at the keyboard back to what you're trying to say. Whenever you realize you're thinking about yourself with your fingers on the keys, speak the mantra. Or simply repeat the mantra as you compose. (Here's mine: "Keep typing!") Other writers have found the following mantras helpful:

- "It's the content, stupid." (from the Clinton era)
- "Nobody will see this draft but me."
- "Get it down, then get it right."
- "Shut up, Mother!" (or "Editor!" or "Sister Snarlissima!").

Yes, I am suggesting that you talk to yourself while you compose. Your internal critic shouts at you as you type, and you can talk back, calmly.

One stage later, in REVISION, you want your internal critic to change her tone. No longer can she sneer, "You're no good." You want her to say things like, "That sentence is merely good; give it one more try." She might even concede, "Hey, this is almost not bad."

UNSTICKING YOURSELF

You're typing along, and suddenly you're not typing along. Nothing is falling out of your fingers into the keys. You're not caught in writer's block; you're just temporarily stuck. How can you unjam yourself?

It helps to know where you are in the writing process:

IDEA • GATHER • ORGANIZE • DRAFT • REVISE

If you are in the GATHER stage, and your notes don't add up and no patterns arise, ask yourself "What's wrong?" Perhaps you don't know what you're after. You need to back up to the IDEA stage and ask developing questions, such as "What is this likely to be about?" or "Who are the actors?"

Or if you're in the ORGANIZE stage, but you can't type a plan or a point statement, or even a list of important things, once again ask, "What's wrong?" You can't organize because you haven't gathered the right materials, so you back up one step.

Or you might be in the DRAFT stage, and the next sentence won't come. What's wrong? You don't know what you want to say or how. So you back up to the ORGANIZE stage and ask focusing questions: "What's this about? What are my main points? What do I need to tell my readers?"

Or you're revising, and you keep redoing sentences that just won't land. What's wrong? You're trying to say something you don't believe or can't prove. In this case, you back up two stages and reorganize with focusing questions. You may even need to do a little more gathering. Then ask, "What do I *really* want to say?"

PROBLEMS USUALLY LIE ONE STEP BACK IN YOUR PROCESS.

Asking yourself why you're stuck tends not to work, because now you're thinking about yourself failing instead of about what you want to say. Remember the basic principle for staying unstuck: Never think about yourself with your fingers touching the keys.

You can always take a break, as long as you don't turn it into one more distraction. For example, don't read e-mail, Facebook, or Twitter.

My food-writer friend Russ Parsons has his own method for getting back underway. "When I get stuck, I mean really stuck, sometimes I'll jump ahead to the next section, one I know I have a good plan for, and start from there. That kind of unlocks the gears." Some writers jump out of a jam into an easy part. And I know of a few writers who just type whatever falls out of their fingers until it turns into sentences.

UNBLURRING THE CHARACTERS

Characters make reading interesting, but at a certain point, every new person you add to a piece makes it heavier, more confusing, and harder to read. The shorter the piece, the more difficulty each new character causes. So you select the people to include ruthlessly; they must justify their weight. And you use techniques that make the characters work.

First of all, you avoid what I call "blurs of names," too many characters introduced too close together. Read this passage, from John Gardner's novel *The Secret Generations*, and see if you can make sense of the cast:

> So it was with General Sir William Arthur Railton VC KCB DSO—known to all within the family simply as The General.
>
> The entire family had spent the Christmas of 1910 at Redhill, as was the custom. The General's younger brother, Giles, had been there with his naval officer son, Andrew, who brought his wife, Charlotte, and their three sons—Caspar, and the twins, Rupert and Ramillies. Giles' second son, Malcolm, had traveled from Ireland with his recent wife, Bridget; while Marie—Giles' only daughter—had come with her French husband, Marcel Grenot, from Paris, together with their two children, Paul and Denise.
>
> The General's own two sons were present—Charles, the younger, with his oddly dowdy wife, Mildred, and their daughter, Mary Anne; and John, the Member of Parliament, proud with his young second wife, Sara, and the son of his first, tragic, marriage—James.[23]

Could you follow that hurricane of names? Of course not, and Gardner makes it worse in the next two paragraphs:

> It was the happiest of holidays, for this was a special time at Redhill, and the General was in excellent spirits.
>
> On the Tuesday after Christmas they had gone their separate ways, leaving the General to celebrate the New Year at the Manor with his staff—Porter, his old servant; Cook; her daughter, Vera the head maid; the two undermaids; Natter the groom; Billy Crook the odd-job boy and the others.

Those 224 words contain twenty-four personal names and three place names. Luckily for readers, Gardner didn't name the "two undermaids" or "the others." This passage occurs early in the novel, and later, many of these characters appear under nicknames, titles, code names, and aliases. Readers don't stand a chance of following the plot.

So you introduce characters slowly and separately, developing details so readers can picture them. When characters reappear after some time, you give readers a clue to remember who they were. If Natter walks in later, you remind readers that he's the groom. See, you've already forgotten.

Short pieces tend to focus on fewer players, surrounded by names in attributions to the quotations. Again, you select without pity. The shorter the piece, the more ruthless you have to be. Every character, every name, every quotation must justify its space.

PLEASE SPELL MY NAME RIGHT

Senator Edward Kenedy dominated our political lives for the forty-seven years he served in the Senate. All of the most important social legislation had his stamp on it. Even people who opposed him miss him.

Of course, you noticed that I misspelled "Kennedy" in that first sentence. And as you read through the rest of the paragraph, you kept thinking about my mistake. By the end of it, you started to doubt my authority as a writer.

Nothing damages your credibility like misspelling a name. It sends editors into shock, plunges copy editors into apoplexy, and makes your readers wonder about everything else you're saying.

My last name is spelled "F-R-Y," not "F-R-Y-E," as some people who have written about me spelled it. It irks me when they get it wrong and makes me less likely to talk with them again. My name isn't as important as "K-E-N-N-E-D-Y," but people who know me might wonder about writers who spell it wrong.

Names must be spelled correctly in order to identify the right person. In 1965, an engineering honorary society at UC Berkeley sent out hundreds of letters inviting students to join. They were told to respond to Donald L. Fry, the president, and the letter gave his phone number. Unfortunately, my name, Donald K. Fry, came earlier in the Berkeley phone book, and my telephone number appeared in the letter. My wife, Joan, told the last hundred callers to put their invitation in a paper bag and scream like a chicken.

If you write about Donald Zapolia Fry, the [fictional] serial rapist who's just been arrested, I want you to get that middle name right. I don't want neighbors at my door with torches and pitchforks.

How do you spell names right?

First of all, you would ask me how I spell my name. Stupid, you think, until I reply, "F-R-Y, no E." Same with "J-O-N S-M-Y-T-H-E" or "M-E-R-R-Y G-R-E-N-E." If in doubt later, call the person, or send an e-mail. You'll feel dopey, but you'll get it right. Your source will regard you as careful and may thank you, as I will.

Phone directories are fairly reliable, depending on the size of the city. In my little town of Charlottesville with forty thousand souls, my wife and I are spelled correctly as "Fry, Donald & Joan," and there's a "Fry, Donald J." Sometimes the problem is deciding which person is the one you want; in one town in Massachusetts, half the population is named "Pelletier." Don't assume; call.

You should request a business card, and ask if everything on it is correct. Usually it's not.

You obtain their annual report, and (yes) ask if the spelling's correct.

You can search for them on Google, which gets problematic. Searching for "Don Fry," I came up eighth out of about 10,500,000 hits, among a slew of realtors, wrestlers, and civic leaders. "Don Frye" yielded about 699,000 hits, mostly for a famous street fighter, with lots of gritty photos. "Donald K. Fry" brought me up first out of about 683,000, but that's my professional name as a medievalist, not as a writing coach, where I'm "Don Fry." You might not connect the two without a lot of reading.

You could look up my blog: www.donfry.wordpress.com. Most blogs have a bio somewhere, and you'd expect authors to spell their own names right, wouldn't you? Don't assume it. Blogs can be sloppy.

If your publication has an archive of previous articles (called a "Clip File"), you can look up the spelling there. Conscientious organizations update their clip files when they print corrections, but you can't depend on it.

ALWAYS ASSUME ARCHIVES HAVE ERRORS.

Your spell-checker may or may not help you. (Actually, mine caught "Kenedy.") It'll endorse "Fry" because that's a word in its dictionary.

You can spell a name correctly, and then misspell it somewhere else in the same piece, so compare them for consistency. Don't forget to check names in photo captions, on maps and diagrams, and in back-of-the-book lists. At the Poynter Institute, I edited the annual catalog; one year, I managed to misspell the name of a member of our advisory board four different ways in the apparatus.

TELLING SO YOU CAN SHOW

Many writing guides advise, "Show, don't tell." Bad advice. You tell readers *about* things, but you show things *to* them. I can tell you that my mother couldn't cook her way out of a paper bag, or I can show you:

> My mother boiled everything for eight hours, vegetables, fruits, meats, destroying all food value and flavor. She used no herbs or spices, except salt, lots of salt. Everything she cooked turned gray. When I was 18, I was served rare roast beef at a banquet. I turned to my companions and asked, "What's this?" I didn't recognize it as food, much less meat.

You need a combination of showing and telling; essentially, telling frames the showing.

David Finkel described the aftermath of the 1989 San Francisco earthquake, focusing on one family in Los Gatos, beginning like this:

> Patty Hermann is leading the way through her house. The kitchen is bad—cracked walls, broken dishes. The dining room is bad, too—more cracks, plaster everywhere. Then comes the living room, the room that two days after the earthquake, Hermann won't go in.
>
> In this room, there is no longer an outside wall. There is only a wide hole where the wall was, and a sagging, unsupported roof. There is also a TV set, still plugged in, still tuned to the channel showing the World Series, but Patty Hermann is too afraid to retrieve it.
>
> "We are working up our nerve," Mark Hermann, Patty's husband, says.
>
> "Sickening, isn't it?" says Patty. "It was," she adds, "a spectacular house."[24]

Finkel shows readers the devastation and the family's reaction to it, with a little telling: "The kitchen is bad—cracked walls, broken dishes. The dining room is bad, too." Patty tells us, "It was … a spectacular house." Finkel follows her statement with a little telling of his own, making a transition into context: "It was, indeed, and it is no more. Instead, it is unsalvageable. It is the most severely damaged structure in Los Gatos, and, in its own way, it illustrates how there wasn't one earthquake in northern California Tuesday, but two."

Later, he returns to showing: "the cafe next door with the pink napkins still folded on the plates," and the family camped out on their lawn because they're afraid of their trees.

Showing has more power than telling, as David Finkel shows you above: "The kitchen is bad" versus "cracked walls, broken dishes." Showing hits readers harder.

How do you achieve such power? First, you look for patterns that you can tell, and details that will show those patterns, and you write them in your notes. You might jot, "Shoes too small." But then you'd look for what made you draw that conclusion: "Wincing each step." You might note that a chef's a bully, and put down: "Screaming idiot, throwing bacon, smacked *sous chef* with ladle." If your notes only say, "Chef bully," you have to remember what made you think that.

Then you use specific details to create images, active verbs to capture action, and quotations to convey character. In REVISION, you recast long spells of telling with showing. But you can't do that unless you GATHER what you need to show in the first place.

DETAIL CREATES EMOTION

Writing about emotion worries writers because it's so easy to lapse into sentimentality. The secret is restraint at every level. Whatever moved you, artfully described, will move your readers.

Above, I explained how showing has more power than telling. Showing allows precision that telling lacks. The vocabulary of description is huge; the diction of human emotion is limited and limiting.

The first step is to get yourself out of the way. If you narrate in the first person, sooner or later you'll start adding adjectives and adverbs about your own feelings. If you show what you saw and heard, rather than what you felt, you make readers respond in ways that mean more to them.

Think for a moment about horror tales and movies. The least effective ones, the least scary, show you the monster over and over in close-ups, lots of fangs and claws and red eyes and bloody slobber. The really scary ones never show the whole monster, except for maybe a shadow, a shape, or one arm ripped off at the shoulder. Readers make up their own monster out of what they're afraid of.

Showing works best with a little framing and small details. Set the scene and then zoom in on a few telling details. A telling detail conveys meaning and impact to readers, like that "one arm ripped off at the shoulder" I just mentioned. Beowulf tore it off Grendel, who is never fully described in the poem.

Where do you find telling details in real life as opposed to epics? They're all around you. You look for them while you GATHER, and you can mark them in your notebook margin. (I use "TD."). You won't put detail in a piece unless you get it into your notes. If you don't capture it in the notebook, you might not see it in the first place. Some writers see more and better than others because they're tuned up to look for key details.

Because writers worry about emotion, they tend to find other people to talk about it. They end up telling a lot and showing little. What people say can also be a telling detail, and needs the same rigorous selection and omission.

Storytelling conveys emotion best because it involves detail and speech and action. As V.S. Naipaul puts it, "Great subjects are illuminated best by small dramas."[25]

Restraint is the key to writing about emotion. And it helps to have a good editor to keep you from flying over the edge.

WRITING SENTENCES FOR READERS

You learned in school that the structure of a sentence defines what it means; that's called "grammar." But nobody taught you how to arrange the sentence so your readers could understand it easily.

An English sentence has two anchors: the SUBJECT and the VERB. The sooner the readers get to the subject and verb, the more likely they are to understand. So here's the first secret of clear sentences: Keep the subject and verb together, as close to the beginning as possible. Check out this diagram:

<[LEFT BRANCH] SUBJECT + VERB [RIGHT BRANCH]>

The left branch includes anything that comes before the subject, and the right branch is everything that follows the verb. Anything you put in the left branch delays the reader in getting to the subject, and hurts clarity. Anything you put between the subject and the verb delays the reader in getting to the verb, and injures understanding.

So, for maximum clarity, start the sentence with the subject, put the verb next to it, and add other stuff to the right.

This pattern doesn't mean that every sentence should start with the subject. It means that you pay a penalty in clarity if you start with anything but the subject. The longer and more complicated the left branch, the higher the penalty you pay, and the less your reader understands. Try to read this example:

> Wearing a burnt-tangerine windowpane-checked linen and cashmere blazer, beige suede trousers, brown Gucci boots, a shirt unbuttoned low on the chest, a leather-thong necklace, and with a gold ring in the shape of an alligator coiling on his finger, Mr. Solomon, accidentally observed admiring his appearance in a pier mirror inside the front door, greeted his guest in the drawing room and led him upstairs to a rooftop garden for a talk, his golden retriever, River, at his side.[26]

You had to wait thirty-nine words for the subject ("Mr. Solomon") and then thirteen more for the verb ("greeted"). You drowned trying to get through that sentence, and so would your readers.

Which leads us to the next technique: Don't insert things inside other things; put them end to end.

In the dreadful sentence above, the author inserts "accidentally observed admiring his appearance in a pier mirror inside the front door" inside the unit of the subject and verb, damaging both.

Consider this sentence:

> The one bill that would take apart the old, employer-based model without resorting to a government-run solution, a bipartisan proposal from the Democratic senator Ron Wyden and the Republican senator Bob Bennett, has been largely ignored in Congress.[27]

By the time the readers get to the verb ("has been"), they forget the subject ("bill"). Actually, that sentence would make perfect sense if spoken, because the speaker's voice would punctuate it. But in prose, with no speaker, you might have to read it two or three times to puzzle it out.

It's easier to write clear sentences in the first place if you picture actions. Start with the actor (subject), put the action (verb) next to it, then add things end to end to the right. I call this pattern a "simple sentence," as in simple to read.

PUNCTUATING FOR READERS, NOT GRAMMARIANS

Columnist Bryan McKenzie wrote a tongue-in-cheek piece confessing his inability to use commas:

> The truth is, I've never figured out when to use that little squiggle that looks like a fallen quote mark.... Everything I write has at least one comma out of place. At one point, I just started sprink,ling the ,dang things through,out the ,sentence and letting the, editor sort it all out.[28]

Writers have trouble with commas (and other punctuation) because they think of them in terms of rules to please teachers, stuff you can forget about as soon as school's out. I don't punctuate for my eleventh-grade English teacher or even for editors. I punctuate for my readers, because I want them to understand my sentences.

Here's the problem. Your readers have never seen your sentences before. To read them, much less understand them, readers have to break them up into parts, into units of meaning. Punctuation shows them the breaks, and leads them through the units. I think of sentences as journeys, with punctuation as road signs to guide my readers. Road signs have two functions: They tell you what to do, and what comes next.

Why did I put a comma in that last sentence between the phrase "what to do" and the phrase "and what comes next?" No grammar rule demands that comma. I put it there to show you, my reader, the units.

I'm an eccentric punctuator, as you've probably noticed. So I offer a contrarian primer on commas. I'll start with an easy one, punctuating a series. *The Associated Press Stylebook* says:

> Use commas to separate elements in a series, but do not put a comma before the conjunction in a simple series.... Put a comma before the concluding conjunction in a series,

> however, if an integral element of the series requires a conjunction.... Use a comma before the concluding conjunction in a complex series of phrases.[29]

Confused? Of course you are, just as you were in school. American newspapers dislike punctuation, and nobody ever accused their *Stylebook* of being reader friendly.

Here's how to make it simple. Always put a comma between items in a series, including one before the conjunction *and* or *or*. Here's the pattern: **X, Y, and Z**. Your readers will interpret the commas as separators; then the road sign, *and* tells them the next item ends the series.

If you don't use the final comma, you can end up with a mess like this: "Their restaurant serves bacon, toast, ham and eggs and fish and chips." Or this: "Rain crushed the cages, floods drowned deer and monkeys and alligators swam away."

Not using the comma before the conjunction consistently can cause misreading, as in this example from Edwin T. Layton's *"And I Was There." Pearl Harbor and Midway—Breaking the Secrets*:

> They were soon boasting that without the efforts of the Negat cryptanalysts in Washington, Midway and the Hawaiian Islands would have been captured by the Japanese.[30]

Punctuated that way, you're likely to read the sentence to say that the cryptanalysts were in Washington, Midway, and the Hawaiian Islands, rather than that Midway and Hawaii were threatened. You can solve the problem by avoiding the series, like this:

> They were soon boasting that without the efforts in Washington of the Negat cryptanalysts, Midway and the Hawaiian Islands would have been captured by the Japanese.

Despite what I've said above, you should follow the punctuation style of any organization you write for, just to stay on the right side of your friends, your copy editors.

We use commas to separate clauses. Let's make up a song verse:

> So now if you leave me,
> That will really grieve me,
> But you'll never see me again.

It's one sentence with three clauses. We call that first line a "dependent" clause, because it can't exist alone as a sentence. It depends on other parts of the sentence. The second and third lines are "independent" clauses, because each one can stand alone.

Commas separate and link things at the same time. Here commas divvy up the sentence, so the reader can see the parts. The comma after the first line tells the reader that the first (dependent) clause has ended, and predicts that another clause will follow. The second and third (independent) clauses are separated and linked by a comma followed by the conjunction "but." See how commas act as road signs, telling readers when one part of the journey ends, and what to expect in the next part?

> So now if you leave me,
> That will really grieve me,
> But you'll never see me again.

A heavy punctuator, like me, might put a comma after "So now" to separate the introductory phrase for the reader: "So now, if you leave me,..." But remember that readers can take commas as pauses, so a comma after "So now" might hurt the rhythm. Sometimes, but rarely, we might put a comma between a complex subject and its verb, like this: "A comma after 'So now,' might hurt the rhythm."

Our made-up verse would make sense without any commas, although sentences without punctuation are harder and slower to read: "So now if you leave me that will really grieve me but you'll never see me again."

Sometimes unpunctuated clauses crash into each other, like this: "The restaurant served ham and eggs and biscuits and gravy never appeared on the menu." The reader doesn't know where to split the clauses. Did the restaurant serve ham and eggs and biscuits, but never gravy? Or did it never serve eggs and biscuits and gravy? Or did it serve ham and eggs, but never biscuits and gravy? Commas create meaning and help readers understand.

Try this one: "Although the restaurant served ham and eggs biscuits and gravy never appeared on the menu." The reader crashes into the combination "eggs biscuits" because the writer failed to separate the opening dependent clause ("Although the restaurant served ham and eggs") from the independent clause that followed.

Here's an example from Frank McCourt's *'Tis: A Memoir*:

> Sometimes when I peel my banana people from Park Avenue with sensitive noses will sniff and whisper to each other.[31]

The reader stumbles over the combination "banana people" due to the missing comma that belongs after the opening dependent clause.

You can join two independent clauses with a comma in less formal writing: "The chef loved ham and eggs, his wife hated biscuits and gravy." In more formal writing, you might use a semicolon: "The chef loved ham and eggs; his wife hated biscuits and gravy." As a third option, you could break the sentence into two: "The chef loved ham and eggs. His wife hated biscuits and gravy."

Notice the different lengths of the pause in the middle of those sentences depending on which punctuation you choose. With a comma, short. Semicolon, longer. Period, even longer. You might decide which to use on the basis of rhythm.

DASHES CONFUSE READERS

I've waged a twenty-five-year campaign against the dash, and I want you to join me. What's wrong with the dash? A reader coming upon a punctuation mark asks two questions unconsciously: What does this mean, and what comes next? So let's test some punctuation marks against these two questions:

> A **period** [.] means the sentence has ended, and a new, not necessarily related sentence begins next.
>
> A **semicolon** [;] means the clause has ended, and a new, related clause begins next.
>
> A **colon** [:] means a list follows, and then the list begins, although it might have one only item.
>
> **Ellipsis** […] means something is left out, and the sentence will resume.
>
> An **open quotation mark** ["] means a quotation begins and will end with a close quotation mark ["].

An **open parenthesis** [( ] means an insertion has begun, and will end with a close parenthesis [ )].

A **dash** [—] means, well, you don't know, and you have no clue what comes next.

The dash is an ambiguous road sign, and readers don't know what to do or expect. Most readers interpret a dash as an open parenthesis and wait for the closing parenthesis. But the writer may have meant it as a pause, or just used it out of habit. The reader ends up confused.

CONFUSED READERS STOP TRUSTING YOU, AND MAY STOP READING.

There's one situation where I might consider using a dash, because there's no other punctuation mark to cover it. I like to indicate in quotations how the speaker spoke, and the dash is the only punctuation mark I know to indicate a pause. I can't use ellipsis because the reader will interpret it as something left out and wonder what that something was.

Okay, I know you love the dash, and I don't expect to win this campaign against it. So here's a technique to minimize the damage. If you draft a sentence that contains dashes, in revision, ask if another punctuation mark might be clearer to the reader. If you want maximum clarity for your readers, choose clear signs.

AVOID THE DASH.

DO *THAT* AND *WHICH* MATTER?

This book is not a guide to usage, but I want to talk about *that* and *which* to make a point about formality. The distinction between *that* and *which* beginning a subordinate clause is easier to write than explain. Take these two sentences:

This is the ball that Beckham kicked for the winning goal.

A soccer ball, which doesn't cost much, is worth a lot after Beckham wins the game with it.

In each case, the thing referred to ("the antecedent") is *ball.* The relative clause that follows refers to the antecedent *ball,* and either limits it or not. In the first example, *ball* refers to a specific ball, because the clause "that Beckham kicked" limits the reference to that ball. In the second example, *ball* refers to soccer balls in general, because the clause "which doesn't cost much" does not limit it to a specific ball.

Traditionally these are called "restrictive" and "nonrestrictive" clauses, or "essential" and "nonessential." Clauses that limit the antecedent begin with *that,* and clauses that do not limit the antecedent begin with *which.*

Nonlimiting clauses are usually surrounded with commas. Strunk and White explain nonlimiting clauses as parenthetical, and therefore set them off with commas. One test works like this. Draft the sentence, then put commas around the relative clause. If the sentence works when you read it, leave it alone. Otherwise, delete the commas. I'll test the first example above: "This is the ball, that Beckham kicked for the winning goal." It doesn't make sense, so we delete the comma.

When talking informally, you would more likely use *which* for both cases. Distinguishing *that* from *which* reminds readers of schoolteacher grammarians and makes prose sound more "correct," and therefore more formal. I don't think about this kind of distinction in terms of right and wrong, but as a device for creating voice. It depends on your audience and what sort of person you're trying to sound like.

LISTS OF STUFF IN A SMALL SPACE

You can use lists to pack a lot of easy-to-grasp information in a short space. At the simplest level, you can save space by using phrases rather than writing in sentence form. You can also save room by reducing the "white space" around things, although some lists prove more legible by using bullets to increase white space.

Here's my favorite list, a masterpiece by Patricia McLaughlin explaining the plight of modern women:

> The first handbook of the Girl Scouts of America, published in 1913, was a self-help book of amazing scope. It told girls how to stop a runaway horse, splint a broken leg, prevent frostbite, recognize poisonous snakes, start a fire, tie knots, send a message in Morse code or by semaphore, tie up a

> burglar with 8 inches of cord, tell time by the stars, discourage mice, prevent consumption, rescue a person who has fallen through the ice, exercise to develop strength, scrub and polish floors, read a map, patch a hole in a dress, cure a ham, take a pulse, test milk for butterfat content, clean wire window screens, play various games, be observant, sew on buttons properly, poach eggs, use sour milk to bleach linen, make a "really good rice pudding," bathe a baby, put a child's stockings on, stop a nosebleed, remove a cinder from an eye, put out a fire, rescue a person drowning and give artificial respiration.[32]

Ladies and Gentlemen, meet Superwoman. Look how much information you absorbed easily in just one paragraph. Lists have some hierarchy; the first and last items are more memorable, simply by position. But everything in the middle is equal, creating the possibility for ironic pairing. For example, "make a 'really good rice pudding'" has the same value as "tie up a burglar with 8 inches of cord." (Actually, I've always needed at least two feet of cord to bind criminals.)

Lists can appear in the paragraph form above, but they're easier to read with bullets:

The first handbook of the Girl Scouts … told girls

- how to stop a runaway horse
- splint a broken leg
- prevent frostbite
- recognize poisonous snakes
- start a fire
- tie knots….

Long paragraphs look dense and intimidate the reader. Of course, a bulleted list as long as the original Girl Scout paragraph above might run awkwardly over several pages.

Lists are used to put a lot of information in a small space, but the density can make the paragraphs hard to read, as in this example:

> Understanding nutrition is very important. But why does it have to be so complicated?

> High carb, low, carb, no carb. Good carbs, bad carbs. Simple carbs, complex carbs. High fat, low fat; saturated fat, trans fat; polys and monos. Antioxidants, vitamins, minerals. Soluble fiber, insoluble fiber. Serum cholesterol, dietary cholesterol.
>
> Who can keep all that stuff straight?[33]

Of course, that list is about confusion, which it illustrates. Whatever clarity it has results from opposing pairs.

Some lists convey impressions rather than material to be recalled. This passage from Malcolm Gladwell's *Blink* gives us a window into the thinking of experts by using their terminology, but it's too dense to remember:

> Jam experts, though, don't have the same problem when it comes to explaining their feelings about jam. Expert food tasters are taught a very specific vocabulary, which allows them to describe precisely their reactions to specific foods. Mayonnaise, for example, is supposed to be evaluated along six dimensions of appearance (color, color intensity, chroma, shine, lumpiness, and bubbles), ten dimensions of texture (adhesiveness to lips, firmness, denseness, and so on), and fourteen dimensions of flavor, split among three subgroups—aromatics (eggy, mustardy, and so forth); basic tastes (salty, sour, and sweet); and chemical-feeling factors (burn, pungent, astringent).[34]

Readers could remember some of those terms as they taste mayonnaise but would probably have to study the passage to recall the structures.

Short bulleted lists work best. Long lists work better with numbered items, although numbers imply hierarchy. Bulleted lists have benefits for the reader:

- Lots of information in a small space
- Parallels easily apparent
- Lighter pages because of the white space
- Quicker reading of phrases rather than full sentences

That's much easier to read than this paragraph version:

> Bulleted lists have benefits for the reader: lots of information in a small space, parallels easily apparent, lighter

> pages because of the white space, and quicker reading of phrases rather than full sentences.

Here's another example:

> While he is not raising money for libraries, Mr. Bradbury still writes for a few hours every morning ('I can't tell you' is the answer to any questions on his latest book); reads George Bernard Shaw; receives visitors including reporters, filmmakers, friends and children of friends; and watches movies on his giant flat-screen television.[35]

Here Jennifer Steinhauer uses semicolons rather than commas to divide the items in series, because some of the items have internal punctuation. You could use bullets to make that list easier to read. But bullets are more formal and carry connotations of technical material, unsuitable here for the informality of Ray Bradbury's activities. They also require more space. Writers balance clarity against formality.

This selection from Annie Proulx's *The Shipping News* captures the variety and wacky ordinariness of life in a seaside village with a pell-mell rush of terms found in newspaper advertisements.

> He had never seen so many ads. They went down both sides of the pages like descending stairs and the news was squeezed into the vase-shaped space between. Crude ads with a few lines of type dead center. Don't Pay Anything Until January! No Down Payment! No Interest! As though these exhortations were freshly coined phrases for vinyl siding, rubber stamps, life insurance, folk music festivals, bank services, rope ladders, cargo nets, marine hardware, ship's laundry services, davits, rock band entertainment at the Snowball Lounge, clocks, firewood, tax return services, floor jacks, cut flowers, truck mufflers, tombstones, boilers, brass tacks, curling irons, jogging pants, snowmobiles, Party Night at Seal Flipper Lounge with Arthur the Accordion Ace, used snowmobiles, fried chicken, a smelting derby, T-shirts, oil rig maintenance, gas barbecue grills, wieners, flights to Goose Bay, Chinese restaurant specials, dry bulk transport services, a

> glass of wine with the pork chop special at the Norse Sunset Lounge, retraining program for fishermen, VCR repairs, heavy equipment operator training, tires, rifles, love seats, frozen corn, jelly powder, dancing at Uncle Demmy's Bar, kerosene lanterns, hull repairs, hatches, tea bags, beer, lumber planing, magnetic brooms, hearing aids.
>
> He figured the ad space. *Gammy Bird* [the newspaper] had to be making money. And somebody was one hell of a salesman.[36]

The breathless pace is dizzying, but the writing is clear, although no one would expect to remember all the details.

SAME SOUNDS IN SYNC

Alliteration is front rhyme. The initial sounds rhyme, as in "fancy feet," instead of the final sounds, as in "neat feet." Consonants alliterate only with themselves ("faulty feet"), while any vowel can alliterate with any other vowel ("itchy arches").

I'm talking about sounds, not letters. So "happy herbs" does not alliterate (in American English anyway), but "erotic herbs" does. "Pneumatic knees" alliterates, but "persistent pneumonia" does not.

Alliteration links words, creating extra meanings. It makes phrases jump off the screen or page, and can cement them into the readers' memory: "Don't do dashes."

It works unless it's overdone, as in William Safire's famous phrase coined for Vice President Spiro Agnew: "nattering nabobs of negativism." In stretching for two words to alliterate with "negativism," Safire nose-dived archly into archaic nonsense.

Here's a sentence I wish I had written, from Adam Nicolson's *Seize the Fire*:

> The ship was a place of yelling, the guns roaring, the blocks and tackles with which they were hauled out through the gunports and manoeuvred to bear on the enemy, screaming and squealing like pigs on the point of slaughter.[37]

Nicolson alliterates *screaming* and *squealing* and *slaughter*, tying those terrifying words together; and they in turn frame *pigs* and *point*. Lord Nelson's enemies didn't stand a chance.

MUDDLES IN MIDDLES

Readers have to struggle through sentences with jammed middles. The problem is not only too much information in too little space, but also delaying what the reader needs to know.

Sometimes the jam happens between the subject and the verb, the anchors of a sentence, as in this example from Lisa Jardine's *On a Grander Scale: The Outstanding Life of Sir Christopher Wren*:

> In 1668, the Earl of Clarendon fell, and Pratt, whose reputation had been irrevocably linked to his patron's since the unfortunate timing of the completion of Clarendon House in Piccadilly at the very moment when many Londoners lost all their worldly goods (and their property) in the Great Fire, took retirement.[38]

Forty words intrude between the subject *Pratt* and the verb *took*. Easily solved with two sentences, and nothing separating subject and verb:

> Pratt's reputation had been irrevocably linked to his patron's since the unfortunate timing of the completion of Clarendon House in Piccadilly, at the very moment when many Londoners lost all their worldly goods (and their property) in the Great Fire. In 1668, the Earl of Clarendon fell, and Pratt took retirement.

Sometimes attribution and dependent clauses get in the way as in this example:

> Bats are mammals, but the species now afflicted by white-nose syndrome are cave-hibernating bats, and when the bats lapse into their hibernation torpor, said David S. Blehert, a microbiologist with the United States Geological Survey in Madison, Wis., their core body temperature drops down to just a couple of degrees above cave conditions, as low as 44 degrees.[39]

This sentence has three independent clauses, with a dependent clause ("and when … torpor") plus a fourteen-word attribution in the middle. The reader can't tell if Dr. Blehert said all three independent clauses or just the third one. Better to get the speaker on the stage and then let him talk.

In the following example, the middle gets jammed up with titles and names:

> Authorities do not suspect foul play in the recent disappearance of Sweet Briar College professor Eleanor Salotto, the college's president, Jo Ellen Parker, said in an e-mail to students and staff on Monday.[40]

Readers will confuse the professor with the college president because of the jam of five names and titles in the middle twelve words.

Sometimes extraneous facts slow things down and clutter up the middle, as in this example:

> Dorothy (played by Judy Garland in the 1939 movie), backed up by the Tin Man (Jack Haley) and the Scarecrow (Ray Bolger), slaps the paw of the Cowardly Lion (Bert Lahr) for frightening her dog Toto and says, "It's bad enough picking on a straw man, but when you go around picking on poor little dogs...."[41]

The inserted movie-star names keep delaying the verb and the action, and complicating the list. They add nothing to the reader's understanding. Luckily, the author left out the name of the dog playing Toto.

Sometimes parenthetical asides, such as this one in V.A. Kove's *Telling Images: Chaucer and the Imagery of Narrative*, cause readers to lose the beginning of a thought by the time they get to the end of it:

> I made some notes on it, not because it reminded me of anything in Chaucer—the research I was in fact beginning—nor as a seed for the major research project it would become—it was years before I recognized that—but because I did not want to lose the details of this image.[42]

Those four dashes create a feeling of hesitation and a tone of uncertainty.

Sometimes the middle gets cluttered with flashy junk:

> Editors could still accommodate a degree of financial risk in their acquiring, and so it came to be that Reif Larsen, a

> 28-year-old graduate of Brown and Columbia, with his explorer's name and brief history promoting a Botswanan marimba band, ignited the spending impulse of the publishing world, producing such a fire that he extracted a reported $1 million for his first novel, *The Selected Works of T. S. Spivet*, a book in which each page seems a vitrine constructed to exhibit the author's discursive, magpie imagination.[43]

This reviewer was evidently trying to compete with "the author's discursive, magpie imagination," while her editors snoozed.

Many of those sentences fail by trying to show off. In writing, we always have to balance readability against voice.

IMPORTANT STUFF IN IMPORTANT PLACES

Here's a little device that will make your prose pop. In any unit of writing (sentence, paragraph, section, the whole piece), different positions have differing degrees of emphasis, or memorability. Readers remember what you put in emphatic positions. This scheme is called "2-no-1" because whatever comes *last* has most power, whatever comes *first* has next most power, and anything in the *middle* has no power by emphasis.

NEXT MOST EMPHATIC (#2)
not emphatic (no)
MOST EMPHATIC (#1)

Consider this pair of sentences:

> "My cat Templeton finds me adorable," Don said.
>
> "My cat, Templeton," Don said, "finds me adorable."

By moving the attribution ("Don said") from the final (most emphatic) position to the middle (not emphatic) position, the emphasis shifts to the word *adorable*.

You can also de-emphasize something, even hide it, by burying it in the middle of a paragraph. Watch this politician's voting record vanish in the middle:

> The candidate wanted voters to see him as a populist friend of the working man. But he voted seventeen times against measures to raise the minimum wage. His stump speech always concluded, "Vote for me, vote for yourself, vote for Joe Sixpack."

Or you can emphasize his voting record by putting it at the end:

> The candidate wanted voters to see him as a populist friend of the working man. His stump speech always concluded: "Vote for me, vote for yourself, vote for Joe Sixpack." But on measures to raise the minimum wage, seventeen times he voted no.

In this second version, we used the emphatic end of the paragraph to highlight the candidate's actual voting record, and we changed the end of the final sentence to close with "no." Double emphasis, double hit.

The 2-no-1 template also applies to sections. Readers can remember what a section said better if it's framed cleverly, a memorable beginning of the first paragraph, and a memorable ending of the last one, perhaps mirroring the beginning, as in this review:

> Jacques Pepin's newest *Cooking Techniques* video teaches expert knifework and then applies it to prepping vegetables.
>
> **[Several paragraphs]**
>
> Add this video to your collection. Your vegetables will thank you, and you'll still have all ten fingers.

At the next level, whole pieces have a beginning, middle, and end. Memorable pieces have a strong beginning and a strong ending, often echoing each other. Whatever you begin with and whatever you end with will stick in your readers' heads. So you choose what you want them to remember and put it in these memorable positions.

Suppose you're writing a piece that includes the opinions of different people. You give each of them fair amounts of space, but you'd really like to endorse one of them without saying so. Let that person speak last, and readers will remember most what she said.

Here's a problem. If you want readers to remember what you end with, you have to write the piece so compellingly that they read all the way to that ending. I talked about how to lure readers to the bottom in an earlier section on "gold coins."

That phrase "gold coins" sits at the end of the previous sentence, the end of its paragraph, and the end of this section. How emphatic can you get?

LITTLE THINGS AND BIG IDEAS

Specific detail engages your readers and moves their emotions. But you can't write everything at that level; you need some abstractions to frame the details. The linguist S.I. Hayakawa invented a useful scheme to describe the interaction between the specific and the abstract, called "The Ladder of Abstraction."[44] It involves a vertical spectrum from specifics at the bottom to abstraction at the top. Here's an example using my cat; scan the diagram from the bottom up.

<<ABSTRACT>>
IDEA IN THE MIND OF GOD
THING
CREATURE
ANIMAL
MAMMAL
FELINE
CAT
SHORT-HAIRED CAT
SIAMESE CAT
TORTOISE-POINT SIAMESE CAT
DON FRY'S TORTOISE-POINT SIAMESE CAT "THEBESY"
<<SPECIFIC>>

My cat, Thebesy, occupies the bottom rung of this ladder because only one Thebesy exists. I could go into smaller detail, such as her pointy ear tips or her habit of hiding dead lizards under the rug, but she remains unique. As I move up the ladder, she starts to get abstract, reaching a Platonic ideal at the top. Writers try to stay near the bottom of the ladder to keep their readers engaged, but we move up and down, as I do in the following piece:

> Our beloved cat, Andromache, died, so my wife, Joan, and I wanted to replace her immediately. A local breeder, Joan Bernstein, showed us a "Tortoise-Point," a variant of Siamese we'd never heard of. One look at Thebesy, who'd just rolled over onto her back, and we were hooked. Ms. Bernstein also gave us Thebesy's grandmother Cairo to sweeten the deal.

I start partway up the ladder with "our beloved cat" and move down to Thebesy playing on a rug. I could go higher up the ladder to capture an abstraction like "pet," or further up to "companionship."

Why don't writers stay at the most attractive end of the spectrum, the specific bottom? Some writers avoid the foot of the ladder to prevent mistakes. If I tell you my cat is named "Thebesy," you might worry about misspelling such a queer name, and leave it out. So you call her a "Tortoise-Point Siamese," but you've never heard the term "Tortoise-Point," so you leave that out. Keep up that kind of timid thinking, and you'll end up calling her a "pet." When you find yourself thinking defensively, say to yourself, "Go down the ladder."

Sometimes you don't know enough to be specific, and you can't find out. Take this example: "An object pierced the windshield of the Volvo S-60 and struck Harold Panko in the right temple before ricocheting out the passenger window." We climb up the ladder to "object," because police haven't found it yet. But don't give up too fast; keep looking for the specific.

MIND THE GAP

For maximum understanding, writers organize material into sections, each containing related subject matter, and arranged in logical order. *Transition* comes from Latin, "across + go." Transitions lead readers from the end of one section to the beginning of the next. They provide bridges and keep readers moving forward.

My teachers taught me to write "seamless transitions" between sections so readers wouldn't notice them. But you want readers to be aware of the structure and to know which section they're reading. You tell them at the beginning what the piece contains, and as you change sections, you mark their new subjects. In other words, you keep reminding them of the map so they'll feel guided. (See what I mean about escaping your teachers?)

See if you can spot the transition in the middle of a two-part column, organized around two paradoxes about torture:

> This is why torture is at its heart a political scandal and why its resolution lies in destroying the thing done, not the people who did it. It is this idea of torture that must be destroyed: torture as a badge worn proudly to prove oneself willing to 'do anything' to protect the country. That leads to the second paradox of torture: Even after all we know, the political task at hand—the first task, without which none of the others, including prosecutions, can follow—remains one of full and patient and relentless revelation of what was done and what it cost the country, authoritative revelation undertaken by respected people of both parties whose words will be heard and believed.[45]

Garbled sentences, yes. The author has buried the transition ("That leads to the second paradox of torture") in the middle of a paragraph, where readers won't notice or recall it. Remember that the beginning and end of a unit, such as a paragraph, are emphatic, but readers seldom notice or remember anything from the middle.

So how do you make effective transitions? They can be as simple as a word or phrase beginning the next section: "Meanwhile...," "On the other hand...," "Before Noah's Flood...," "Third...," or "After your soufflé flops...." You can make them as long as a short paragraph or as short as a sentence, like this: "But official American definitions of torture may not have much valence offshore."

You can write effective transitions that take up no space at all. You make the last sentence of a section sound like an ending and the first sentence of the next section sound like a beginning. Here's an example:

> ....So Jane swore off the male of the species forever.

[SECTION BREAK]
Looking around for something to do instead, she picked up her wicked pen....

HEADING ONWARD

Subheads serve as bait to entice your readers into the next section. Subheads enhance the power of transitions in drawing readers across boundaries. Readers see subheads approaching in their peripheral vision as they read down, and they start thinking about whether they want to keep reading. Subheads should point forward, across the boundary to the next part.

You could think of them as cliff hangers. Notice how I introduce each new technique in this book with a subhead to entice you to keep reading.

I mostly write for publications and websites that don't use subheads. I include them in my submissions anyway to make sure my editors understand my structure. It's okay with me if they don't print them.

TRANSITIONS HELP YOUR READERS SEE YOUR STRUCTURE.

ACTIVE ACTS, PASSIVE DOESN'T

Some books on writing advise that "the passive voice should be avoided." Bad advice. Both active and passive voices have their uses.

Clauses can have one of two "voices." In the ACTIVE voice, the subject acts. In the PASSIVE voice, the subject is acted upon.

ACTIVE: "Hannah wrote a best-selling cookbook."

PASSIVE: "The best-selling cookbook was written by Hannah."

In the active sentence above, the subject (Hannah, the author) acts, writing the book. In the passive version, the subject (the cookbook) receives the action, gets written.

Active sentences have more power. First, because they're usually shorter and punchier; second, because they emphasize the actor acting; and third, because the reader knows the agent, who did what. You choose the active or passive voice depending on what you want to emphasize. Take these two examples:

> **ACTIVE:** An unidentified donor gave the Rare Book School $500,000 yesterday.
>
> **PASSIVE:** The Rare Book School was given $500,000 by an unidentified donor yesterday.

The active sentence emphasizes the actor, the donor giving, while the passive one emphasizes the recipient of the action, the Rare Book School. Which you choose depends on the situation, what you know, what you want to feature, and what you want to say. If you wanted to reveal the name of the donor and honor her, you would probably choose the active voice: "Ms. Sophie Incunable gave our Rare Book School $500,000 yesterday."

Passive sentences are longer because they need some form of the auxiliary verb "to be," and they have a phrase at the end starting with "by," followed by the agent, the person or thing that performed the action ("by an unidentified donor").

Passive sentences can have sinister uses. If you leave off the agent phrase, the reader doesn't know who did what. Remember President George H. W. Bush's explanation of the Iran-Contra scandal: "Mistakes were made." Agents were hidden.

That's why the passive is the favorite construction of bureaucrats. They can avoid blame by hiding their actions, as in this passive sentence: "Huge merit raises were voted for members of the executive board," as opposed to this active one: "The executive board voted itself huge merit raises."

During World War II, the Allies were about to invade Normandy. General Dwight Eisenhower realized that if the operation failed, he would have little time to write a communiqué saying so. So he drafted this first version: "Our landings in the Cherbourg-Havre area have failed to gain a satisfactory foothold and the troops have been withdrawn." Then he changed the second clause to read: "....I have withdrawn the troops." In this second version, he takes responsibility for the withdrawal, for his failure. Fortunately for him and the world, the invasion succeeded. Choosing the active voice took courage, and this wise bureaucrat knew the difference.

Sometimes you choose the passive because you don't know the agent. Take this sentence: "Eighteen minutes of the Oval Office tape were erased." Who did it? We may never know. Writers are in the business of revealing knowledge, not hiding ignorance, so you would only use that construction after exhausting all other means. Otherwise, you leave your readers wondering. Even better, tell your readers that you don't know.

For maximum power, use the active voice as much as possible, keeping the passive in reserve for special emphasis. The relative mix of active and passive is one of the devices that create voice, which I'll discuss in the second half of this book.

WRITING ON THE EDGE

Writing with "edge" is easier to do than to define. You manipulate your voice, slanting it toward a particular personality. That *persona* is a fiction, an adopted pose, not the real you. But you'll find it easier to write edgy if you're an edgy person, as I am.

I could define edgy as "writing with attitude," as opposed to *objectivity* or *neutrality* or *evenness*. That attitude tends towards smartness, even "smart-ass-ness," to make up a word. It involves sophistication, even worldliness beyond the normal and the daily. It usually includes wit bordering on wickedness. The smartiness implies a sense of superiority, even snobbishness, and so on to arrogance and downright meanness. That last spectrum could describe the range of restaurant critics and book reviewers, specialties noted for edgy writing.

Let's look at this example how David Brooks begins a review of two new restaurants:

> The great thing about being in Washington, D.C., at the dawn of an administration is that there are so many new backs to stab. Every four or eight years, fresh faces come in from all over America, and some old faces come back after having piled up mountains of private-sector cash. All of us who live here permanently have to figure out how we can welcome these people, how we can befriend them, help them, and then suck them dry before sending them back to the miserable little places from whence they came.[46]

This edgy voice assumes the point of view of the Washington insiders, superior to the newcomers and to everybody else. But this piece appeared in *Food & Wine*, not in *The Washington Post*. The reader (you) is not included among the superiors. This voice is talking down to you, while mocking others. And that's the paradox of edgy writing, its tricky stance toward readers.

Look at some of Brooks's edgy techniques: First, he plays positive language against negative: "the great thing" and "dawn of an administration" against "backs to stab." "Welcome these people... befriend... help" versus "suck them dry." Juxtaposed phrases interact in the readers' heads.

Brooks uses "slant vision," violating expected points of view to show his readers a new and surprising way to look at things. The paragraph begins with newcomers to be welcomed and ends with them exiled to "their miserable little places." Notice the closing phrase "from whence they came," archaic language asserting old superiority.

Brooks uses irony, saying the opposite of what you mean, to show readers his slant vision. You're not sure he means it (he just might), and his ambiguity makes you wonder whose side you're on. His witty phrasing makes you see it from his side, even joining with him against targets that include you. He's also satirizing the snotty attitude of people who live inside the Beltway, as opposed to the newbies.

He uses exaggeration to show you the insiders' point of view, while parodying it: "... some old faces come back after having piled up mountains of private-sector cash." And all this heavy lifting occurs in a three-sentence opening paragraph on top of a restaurant review.

You run two risks in writing edgy: overdoing it and being misunderstood. It's hard to know how far to go, how sharp you want to get on the spectrum from kidding to killing. Edgy drafts tend to get edgier because they're so much fun to write. You need a good editor to help you write edgy. Clark Hoyt says, "The problem with being edgy is that, sometimes, you fall over the edge."[47]

You have to assume when writing edgy, especially satire, that many in your audience will take it straight. Your edgy *persona* is not really you, but a lot of your readers won't make that distinction. Many people still think Jonathan Swift advocated eating Irish babies.[48]

SCRUBBING UP THE QUOTATIONS

(Fasten your seat belt. Here comes the most controversial part of this book.)

With quotations, you have four choices: paraphrased, cleaned up, fragmentary, or verbatim. Verbatim quoting is difficult and rare, because most sources don't speak clearly. Mostly sources say things in conversation, and writers have to convert what they say to make it work in prose.

In conversation, the audience is present with the speaker, so you can use informal grammar, pronouns, and gestures, both physical and vocal. In conversation, I can point to a member of my audience and say, "He's the one to lead us out of this mess." If you see "the one" I pointed to, no problem, but if you're not present, you have to guess which male I meant. Or I might have said, "Our leader," as I pointed him out. My audience gets it, but people who aren't there will be confused by the sentence fragment. And I might have rolled my eyes as I spoke and pointed, but only the audience knew I was mocking him.

In prose, the audience is not present but reading, and you have to do things like turn gestures into description, substitute nouns for pronouns, and use more formal grammar. Most quotations have to be changed a little, sometimes a lot, so readers can understand them. Verbatim quoting seldom happens, despite the usually false assumption that everything between quotation marks is exactly as spoken.

Take fillers, for example. Writers routinely delete fillers such as *well, um,* and *you know.* They're a form of oral punctuation, and people generally don't notice them in conversation. But these words jump off the page or screen if you leave them in, especially if you leave a lot of them in. Sometimes you leave in one or two, especially "you know," just to keep the quotation sounding conversational. But if readers notice them, you lose the effect.

Writers routinely and silently clean up quotations, correcting grammatical errors and deleting profanity. Your source says to you, "That goddamn pack of thieves up there, you know, are in bed with 'em." Problems: swearing, subject-verb disagreement, unclear references, and an unspecified dialect pronoun (*'em*). So the quotation will probably get cleaned up into something like this: "That pack of thieves up there [in Washington] is in bed with [the health-care industry]." And your editor will question the sexual slang of "in bed with." The messed-with quotation is still a mess. So what to do?

First and foremost, you can paraphrase it. In general, if you can write it better than the source said it, you probably should. Two principles: You have to get the meaning right, and your readers have to be able to understand it. So it might come out like this: "Smith charged that Congress is colluding with the health-care companies." We just traded an entertaining quotation for clarity. Writing is a constant balancing act.

Or you can clean it up a little, taking out the filler and the swearing, correcting the grammar, and framing it to clarify the groups involved. And it comes out like this: "Smith criticized both the Congress and the health-care industry: 'That pack of thieves up there is in bed with them.'" Writers often make grammatical changes silently (*are* to *is*) because telling readers how the quotation was changed might distract them.

Or you can shrink the quotation to a couple of fragments, like this: "Smith said that Congress, 'that pack of thieves,' is 'in bed with' the health-care industry." You gain in clarity, but the quotation's hard to read, and partial quotations invite readers to wonder what you left out.

Or you could leave it verbatim and indicate all the changes you made, like this: "That ... pack of thieves up there [in Washington] ... are [*sic*] in bed with them [the health-care industry]." The more you have to do to make a quotation work, the worse it gets, although it's clearer.

All of these tactics, even verbatim quoting, are a form of fiction. What you publish is not exactly what the person said or how it was said. You have to judge just how fictional you want to be. In hard cases, consult your editor.

You have one other option: Leave the quotation out. Ask yourself, "Will this quotation add to my readers' understanding, or do I just like it? Is it worth all the apparatus I'll need to make it clear?" More often than not, you'll delete both the quotation and the problem.

You can also clarify quotations during interviews. You hear what could make a good quotation, but it's a mess. So you lean forward and say to your subject, "Uhh, excuse me, that's good, but I didn't get it all down. Could you say it again?" And it comes out better the second time. I once asked a source to repeat what she had just said, substituting nouns for the unclear pronouns. It worked.

SOME PEOPLE JUST CAN'T TALK

Writers love quotations because they add human interest and immediacy, but most people don't talk clearly enough to quote.

You use a quotation when it's the best way to explain something or to capture character. But quoting requires a lot of apparatus (attribution, identifying speakers, and context), so you should use it sparingly. Don't quote just to quote. And apply even more rigor to poorly phrased quotations. So first, just leave them out.

Some paraphrases include short bits of quoted material, a "partial" or "fragmentary" quotation. For example, your source says about his mother: "Well, you know, she's sorta with it, stalls, you know, or not, um, in, out of it, um, you know, just occasionally lucid." That mess is not worth its space or confusion, but you like the way it characterizes the speaker's frustration with his mother. So you can drop a partial quotation into a paraphrase, like this: "Jack's mother, 'just occasionally lucid,' seldom finishes her sentences."

Partial quoting taxes your readers' patience. Readers wonder what the rest of the sentence said, what you've left out. And two voices in the same sentence always have the potential to confuse. Fragmentary quotations are so easy they become a habit.

The best solution is to fix the quotation as you hear it and realize it has problems. You respond, "Can you say that again?" or "I don't understand that," and your source will probably say it better. You can also paraphrase on the spot, "What I hear you saying is …." Some writers, not including me, will then write what *the writer* just said and, if the speaker agrees, punctuate it as a quotation. I regard that procedure as making up facts, because it results from conversations like this:

> **WRITER:** Bubba, do you envision using kinesthetic principles to improve your batting average 12 percent in the next fortnight?"
>
> **BUBBA:** Yeah.

If you don't improve the quotation on the spot, you can always call the source later and ask the question again. In my experience, you get a better quotation, and often new information, from follow-up questions.

Sometimes speakers are articulate, but they talk jargon your readers can't understand, like an astronomer describing the precession of the equinoxes. Rather than quote them, ask them to help you with the wording of the explanation. I call this a "negotiated paraphrase." But don't punctuate it as a quotation because it won't be in the subject's language.

SWEARING AND SMUT

The world is full of obscenity and swearing, but humans beings have inherited traditions that mostly suppress them in print, less in visual media. Any swearing, even *heck* or *darn*, will offend somebody, and publications differ in how offensive they choose to appear. Decisions on quoting obscenity and profanity depend on the policies of the publication, usually enforced by editors. If you don't know, ask. *Rolling Stone* and *Taste of Home* publish in different universes.

An arsenal of tactics for dealing with obscenity and profanity exist: deleting it, quoting it verbatim, paraphrasing it, labeling it, writing around it, and coding the offensive words.

Sometimes you just quote it. If you're writing about what someone said, and how it was said is important, your readers will wonder what you're talking about if you don't tell them. When former Vice President Cheney hurled an obscenity in public, the public had a right to know what he said that caused the fuss. Whatever readers imagined was probably worse than the actual quotation.

You can try to hide the offending words by encoding them. A famous blast of expletives erupted at the end of a football game in Tampa between the Jets and the Bucs. Millions of fans heard it all as parabolic microphones broadcast the exchanges on television. Here are some excerpts from a local newspaper trying to capture the action without damaging kiddies or offending old folks:

1. What the Jets said was, "% %&**!!!" or words to that effect.

2. A gutter of four-letter words bubbled from angry New York Jets.

3. "McKay, you're an -------," screamed one New York Jet.

4. "McKay, you're an a--hole," shouted offensive lineman Ted Banker.

5. "F--- you," McKay shot back.

The first two examples leave readers wondering what was yelled. The third one, my favorite, tries to hide the word *asshole* by coding it with dashes. Readers, of course, will feel compelled to decode it, so they have to search their entire obscene vocabulary for a seven-letter noun beginning with a vowel. Numbers four and five don't hide anything; They only create an appearance of propriety.

You may end up emphasizing obscenity by not quoting it and playing with the naughtiness of language, like this: "the-you-know-what hit the fan." Political correctness winks at offensive language when people use such common euphemisms as "the N-word" or "the F-word." The insertion "[Expletive deleted]" calls attention to the fact that the speaker used an obscenity; readers usually assume the worst. Remember the Nixon tapes?

Go back to first principles and ask yourself why you would ever publish obscenity or profanity:

- Readers need to know exactly what was said.
- You want to characterize someone who swears a lot.
- The obscene quotation is necessary to your piece.

In any context, in any publication, obscenity and profanity jump off the page or screen and can distract readers, even very sophisticated or dirty-minded readers. It's important to balance this distraction, this break in the flow of reading, against the specificity of the wording. Every word you write must have meaning and purpose, so you would never use obscenity or profanity gratuitously. You would delete it unless it's germane. If you must use an obscenity or profanity, I believe you should publish it verbatim, full force, again depending on the publication.

Here's a tricky exception. Obscenity and profanity may be part of your voice, and you write for a publication that allows it. In that case, let 'er rip.

ALPHABET SOUP

Our world is full of acronyms, alphabetical abbreviations, such as USA or FBI or CIA. They save space, and are easier to write and read than United States of America or Federal Bureau of Investigation or Culinary Institute of America. They're used all the time, so that means everyone understands them, right? Not necessarily.

Readers appreciate explanation, and they don't resent your explaining things they might know but might not. So you spell out acronyms the first time you use them in a piece, followed by the acronym in parentheses. After that, you simply use the abbreviation: "After graduating, she joined the Transportation Security Administration (TSA). Three years later, she developed innovative pat-down techniques that caused less embarrassment for TSA officers."

Remember that one acronym can stand for a number of things. The acronym RSI, can mean any of the following:

- Repetitive Stress Injury, or Repetitive Strain Injury
- Relative Strength Index
- Research Science Institute
- Restaurant Services, Inc.
- Resource Services, Inc.
- Review of Scientific Instruments

You can't assume that your readers will decode the right one.

Clusters of acronyms, so-called "alphabet soup," can confuse readers:

> ARUFON sent a FOIA request on UFOs to the CIA.

You can't make a rule about how many acronyms one sentence can contain. Like everything in writing, it's a balancing act among common usage, brevity, and clarity. But the greatest of these is clarity.

How do you know if your readers will understand an acronym? Ask three other writers who don't cover the subject what the letters mean. If two of them miss it, spell it out for your readers. If in doubt, spell it out.

WHO SAID THAT?

Your readers judge the validity of information by knowing where you got it.

Books, scholarly articles, and some magazines can tell them in footnotes. Sometimes you inform readers in a box, an editor's note at the end of the article, or a background passage, but mostly you attribute in the text right next to the information. That way, your readers get information and its source together without having to look elsewhere. Here's a simple example:

> "To be absolutely politically correct," Janice snapped, "you'd have to call a man named Norman Goodman, 'Nor-person Good-person.'"

The attribution, "Janice snapped," identifies her as the source, and tells how she said it. Many writing handbooks advise against using any attribution verb except *said*. But I won't give up such a valuable tool for characterization. How speakers say something, not just what they say, tells readers a lot about them.

On the other hand, waxing too poetic or using too many different attribution verbs gets tiresome to read. Avoid attributions that call attention to themselves, such as "she snorted" or "they blithered" or "he pompoted." (I made up that last verb, meaning "to speak pompously.") The greatest exception to this principle comes from Ring Lardner's dialogue of a father and son:

> "Are you lost, Daddy?" I asked tenderly.
> "Shut up," he explained.

Notice the adverb *tenderly* modifying the verb, *i.e.*, telling how the son asked. Some verbs have manner built in, such as *mumbled* or *shouted*. So you wouldn't duplicate the action with an adverb, "shouted loudly."

Where do you put the attribution for a quotation? It depends on what you want to emphasize. Traditionally writers put it at the end: "'I'm sick and tired of being mayor,' said the mayor." But the end of a sentence is its most emphatic point, followed by the beginning. Only rarely would you want to emphasize the attribution.

NEXT MOST EMPHATIC (#2)
not emphatic (no)
MOST EMPHATIC (#1)

Check out these variant positions for attribution:

1. "Free at last! free at last! thank God Almighty, we are free at last!" said Martin Luther King.
2. Martin Luther King said, "Free at last! free at last! thank God Almighty, we are free at last!"
3. "Free at last! free at last!" said Martin Luther King, "thank God Almighty, we are free at last!"

In the third version, attributing in the middle puts the two strong elements in the two emphatic positions and magnifies the repetition.

You also attribute facts to let readers judge them by where they came from. How would you attribute the two sentences quoted above from Ring Lardner? You could say in the text that the quotation came from Ring Lardner's 1920 novel *The Young Immigrunts*. Or you could write a footnote:

> Lardner, Ring W., jr. The young immigrunts. (Indianapolis: Bobbs-Merrill, [circa 1920]). 78.

I found the reference on the Internet at http://www.quotationspage.com/quote/21226.html, like this:

> Quotation #21226 from Rand Lindsly's Quotations:
> Shut up he explained.
> Ring Lardner, The Young Immigrants, 1920
> US author (1885-1933).

Now for an object lesson. If you stop digging when you find an easy Internet source, you might miss things and make mistakes.

ASSUME THAT EVERYTHING ON THE INTERNET IS WRONG UNTIL CHECKED.

Quotation #21226 above has misspelled a word in the title, which is "immigrunts," not "immigrants." The whole book, supposedly written by a four-year-old boy, includes the child's erratic spelling, and so does the title. Pursuing the original source, the book itself, I discovered that I had changed the spelling and punctuation of the exchange. "Picky, picky," you're thinking. "Accurate, accurate," I'm thinking.

You never want readers to wonder where something came from, because a wondering reader is not paying attention. The test is not attributing everything. The test is giving your readers what they need to know about your information. This transparency also enhances your authority.

Finally, attribution thanks the people whose information you borrowed.

BACK IT UP, THEN BACK THAT UP

Every writer I know has lost a document at one time or another. A fuzzy-minded professor friend of mine left the only copy of a book he had just drafted in his briefcase in the back seat of his Volkswagen. He returned from lunch to find it all gone: typescript, briefcase, car. Word processors can always find a way to erase your only copy of something. You should never have a document existing in only one copy.

NOTHING IS SAFE IN ONLY ONE COPY.

My thesis director at UC Berkeley managed to lose three different copies of my dissertation, but luckily, I had taken the precaution of mailing a photocopy of each chapter to my mother in Raleigh. Actually, I was trying to protect myself from earthquakes more than faculty clumsiness. But that incident taught me to keep backup copies, and backups of backups, as the world entered the electronic era.

The simplest form of backing up is hitting the Save key after every paragraph, and every time the phone rings. I also back up in several places on my computer, sometimes onto other computers, and frequently onto removable drives. I stash electronic copies in my wife's office desk drawer, in our Maine summerhouse, and in the archives of the Poynter Institute. But nothing is truly backed up unless it exists somewhere else in hard copy, so I print a paper copy now and then.

Sounds like overkill, doesn't it? But this kind of overkill may save your neck, your sanity, and your career. And I've just hit the Save key, as you should always do at the end of the DRAFT stage. Now on to REVISION.

eight

STAGE FIVE: GETTING IT RIGHT

Now that you've got it down, you can get it right. In the previous stage, DRAFT, you created the framework and a rough version of the words, perhaps with pictures and sound. In the REVISE stage, you will finish the piece. The term *revise* comes from the Latin, meaning "to look back." You look back at what you've already produced, and then look forward to your readers reading it. You figure out what you have to change in the draft by anticipating what your readers will need.

> THINK ABOUT WHAT YOUR READERS NEED ALL THE TIME.

FIX BIG, THEN LITTLE

Most writers revise by crawling through their text word by word and changing anything they don't like. That's a perfectly fine method, but it's slow and only improves the text in spots. Many writers revise heavily and continuously as they draft, and that's why they're so slow, particularly since they keep revising things they've already revised. The longest way to revise is to just keep writing sentences and revising them, and changing anything your revision damages.

What's the fastest way? You draft the entire piece with no revision whatever, and then revise the whole thing once or sometimes twice, if you have more time.

> GET IT DOWN. THEN GET IT RIGHT.

Few writers do it that way because they can't stand to leave anything wrong or misspelled or poorly phrased on the screen. Writing with the screen off helps them see that they can draft without revising, although I don't recommend the blank screen as a normal way of composing. I draft at my top speed (twenty-five words per minute) and then revise separately.

If you revise as a separate step, you're making changes to a complete draft, rather than just part of it. Each sentence gets revised with all the other sentences in mind, which helps unify the piece.

Instead of starting small, at the sentence level, revise the structure of the whole piece first. A lot of phrasing problems vanish when you figure out first what you want to say and how. Rapid drafting creates the structure fast.

How can you sort out something with lots of bits and pieces? This chapter has twelve separate parts, which I wrote as blog posts in the order they occurred to me. To revise them, I wrote down a code for each of the parts on a yellow sticky note. Then I rearranged the stickies until I found an order that made sense. Rearranging was unusual for me; I normally work from a plan and seldom move anything.

Rearrange first for the structure you want, then fix the transitions, and finally the sentences. Otherwise you may have to keep rewriting the transitions as you change the structure. Some people finish the transitions last.

Some writers get a friend (or two or ten) to read their draft and tell them what works and what needs work. Such test readers point out assumptions and holes you can't see. Oddly enough, the less-expert test reader will more likely uncover problems by experiencing them as a reader; experts tend to get picky and focus on detail. I ask my test readers to mark only what they don't understand.

Another tactic involves reading a printed version of your draft aloud, putting a check in the margin beside anything that bothers you, anything you want to change. Then you have a marginal index of everything that needs work.

Finally, you need to stop revising when the piece is finished. At a certain point, further revision makes a piece heavy and less readable. As a writing coach, I find that quick revisers like their pieces better. Fast drafters and revisers worry less, struggle less with their internal critic, and get less tired. They also tend to make deadlines, and get along better with editors.

ALOUD MEANS OUT LOUD

Revision goes faster if you know what you need to revise, and you can find out by reading your draft aloud. Simply print a copy and read it out loud with a pencil in your hand.

By "out loud," I don't mean under your breath. You want your words to leave your mouth and enter your ear, so you can hear them. When you read silently, you bounce along the phrases, not reading the individual words. When you read aloud, you have to pronounce every word. And many problems in clarity and rhythm result from little words colliding with big ones. When words clash in your mouth and ear, you'll feel it.

Make a mark in the margin as you read aloud beside anything that bothers you. Don't stop to fix it; keep reading and marking. Bumps include running out of breath, misspelled words, lapses in grammar and usage, sentences that don't make sense, missing stuff, and rough phrasing. Also put a mark beside things you want to check. When you finish reading, the marks in the margin will show you everything you need to deal with.

Reading aloud also gives you some idea of your readers' experience to come. They don't read aloud, of course, but you're sampling how your own voice will sound in their heads. Tick the margin for anything that doesn't sound like you. Remember that voice is an artifact, created by the devices you use consistently. You'll notice when you don't sound like yourself. This constant tuning makes your writing voice more consistent.

Here's an example. In that last paragraph, I originally typed, "but you're approximating how your own voice will sound in their heads." *Approximating* is a fine word and accurate, but it's a higher level of diction than my blog voice normally uses. I read aloud as I type, so I bumped on that word before I finished the sentence. I tried several rephrasings: "edging up to," "closing in on," "testing," and finally "sampling." I chose *sampling* because of its associations with sound and music. Then I thought of *tasting*, a nice metaphor, but maybe too tricky.

When you've finished reading aloud, you'll know everything that's in the piece, and where it is. Especially with long pieces and books, you can forget that whole sections exist.

Reading aloud will also allow you to experience the readers' pace and expectation of length. You're droning along and find yourself thinking, "Hmmm, this seems long." It feels long to you because it is, and now you know where to shorten it.

REWRITING GOOD SENTENCES

Next I'll revise a sentence in multiple ways to show what effects doing so can achieve. Here's a good test sentence, one of my favorites: "Attribution is the writer's primary device for indicating the validity of information."

I think like that, but I don't have to write that way. Writers phrase their sentences to fit their audiences, what they want to say, and the rest of the piece.

If you read that sentence aloud, it flows, and the meaning is perfectly clear. A fine sentence, if readers know the technical term *attribution*, and if they would know for sure whether *validity* refers to truth or accuracy. This sentence makes several assumptions that would be clear to academics, depending on the context, but maybe not to others.

Now shift the focus from the writer to the reader: "Attribution is the reader's primary device for judging the validity of information." This version features the receiver, but the problems with technical terms persist.

Now try again, defining *attribution* and *validity*: "Knowing where information came from is the readers' primary means for judging if it's true." You can make the sentence more immediate by changing the past-tense verb *came* to the present tense *comes*: "Knowing where information comes from is the readers' primary means for judging if it's true." That last phrase, "if it's true" chooses truth over accuracy, and I could blur the distinction by saying "if it's valid." (As an explainer, I prefer to keep things clear, but sometimes....)

NEXT MOST EMPHATIC (#2)
not emphatic (no)
MOST EMPHATIC (#1)

The word *readers* now sits in the unemphatic middle of the sentence. You can emphasize the readers and attribution by moving them to the beginning and end: "Readers judge the validity of information based on where it comes from."

To get the readers' knowledge into the sentence, try: "Readers judge the validity of information by knowing where it comes from." Less abstract than the phrase "based on."

The sentence is still a little academic and formal, so aim it directly at the reader rather than the writer: "How do you know something is true? First, by asking where it comes from."

All of these sentences are good sentences, and they all say essentially the same thing. But they say it in different ways, with differing effects. Which one would you choose? It depends on what you're trying to say, who your readers are, and how you want them to understand it.

DAUNT TRUSS YORE SPIEL CHUCKER

Spell-checkers do not check spelling. But you should always run your finished piece through the software to catch countless subtle and not-so-subtle mistakes.

Spell-checkers compare the text you select with words in their database. If they find the word, they don't say anything. If they don't find a match, they indicate an error. Spell-checkers tell you they don't recognize a word, not that it's misspelled. Mine says in little type: "Not in dictionary." In the opening sentence of this paragraph, I first typed "test," when I meant "text." No spell-checker will catch that misspelling because both words are in the database.

Here's a test sentence: "Yore to feat shoed tin tows," meaning "Your two feet showed ten toes." (Actually, if you spell that badly, you shouldn't be reading this.) Congratulations, my spell-checker finds no problem. The misspelled words in the test sentence are all homonyms, words that sound alike but are spelled differently.

Spell-checkers perform erratically with names. Mine will endorse "Kennedy," but object to "Kenedy," which happens to be the correct spelling for the town and county of Kenedy in Texas; the John G. and Marie Stella Kenedy Memorial Foundation (also in Texas); and the singer Rachel Kenedy.

The spell-checker will tell you that you've left out the space between two words, unless the resultant letters spell a word, as in "andiron" when you meant "and iron." It won't spot two spaces where you intended one.

Most word processors have another form of spell-checker, usually called something like "AutoCorrect," which works on opposite principles. It searches for misspelled rather than correctly spelled words, and fixes them as you type. It compares what you write with its database of misspellings. For instance, I often type *orginization* when I mean *organization*, and spell *chairman* as *chariman*. (Maybe I'm tired of corporate life.) So I added those two misspellings to AutoCorrect, and it fixes them as I go along.

You can also search for words you commonly misspell, and either fix them or use the "Replace All" function. Many editors search for words they don't want ever to appear, such as "pubic" when they mean "public."

All these errors are hard to spot on a screen, but spell-checkers highlight them for you. You can backstop the software by reading aloud, preferably from a printed version.

"CUT, CUT, CUT, CUT."

The second-hardest part of writing is cutting your own work. (The hardest is organizing, *i.e.*, deciding what to say and how.) It's not like trimming your fingernails; every precious word is more like a finger.

My wife, Joan, and I once helped her university colleagues out of a jam. They'd worked for five hours to cut a key political document in half and managed to remove only ten words. We offered to take a crack at it. I chopped out three whole sections and any sentence likely to cause a fight. Then she revised the transitions. Fifty percent cut, 20 minutes flat. Not a miracle, just technique.

Here's the sequence: cut long, cut short, revise.

First of all, cool off. When you've been slaving over a piece, especially a long piece, you get too close and can't see it. Take a break, eat a gelato, scratch your cat's ears, whatever takes your mind off what you're writing. Then come back fresh and see what works and what needs work.

Strunk and White advise, "Omit needless words," but a lot of the words you need to cut may not seem needless. It's difficult to shorten a piece by focusing on individual words or even sentences. Start with whole sections.

Ask yourself what the piece is about, and then examine each section. Does it contribute to the point of the whole thing? If not, *adios* section. Just cut it; anything you chop survives on your computer's Clipboard. Then read through where it used to be, and you'll probably find you didn't need it.

Repeat this procedure for paragraphs.

Read the whole piece aloud from a printed copy, putting a mark in the margin by anything that's hard to read. Then go back and delete each bit that bumped you. Don't rewrite it; chop it. You probably struggled to write it because it didn't belong.

Cut anything you really love. You're reading along and say to yourself, "What a gorgeous sentence! Damn, I'm good." Cut that part. It's probably self-indulgent, written for yourself and not for your readers. If you can't bear to kill that baby, ask how it helps your readers' understanding. Then cut it.

> *"Read over your compositions, and wherever you meet with a passage which you think is particularly fine, strike it out."*
>
> —SAMUEL JOHNSON.

When you've slashed and burned, you need to restore the flow by writing transitions, making sure all the speakers are actually introduced, and checking that readers have all the information they need. Then you've done it, and (surprise!) it reads better.

But sometimes, you just can't cut your own work. You're exhausted or fed up or too close to it. You need somebody else to help you, either by doing the shortening or by asking you questions about what your readers actually need. Don't let this assistance become a habit; you want to control your own work.

I've just read this section over, and it seems long. If it feels long to me, it'll seem even longer to my readers. So I need to cut it. That second paragraph, with its boastful anecdote about me and my heroic wife saving the day, has to go. Whack!

ENDING JUST ONCE

Your reader will remember best whatever you end with. For maximum power and memorability, you need a single ending. A piece with multiple endings will sound wishy-washy.

I use a technique called "the Hand Test" to discover multiple endings. You scroll to the end of your piece and cover everything but the last sentence with your hand. You read that final sentence aloud and ask yourself, "Does that sound like an ending?" If the answer is "yes," you move your hand up one sentence, read the next-to-last aloud, and ask again, "Does that sound like an ending?" And so on, until the answer is "no."

Try this technique on the following passage, the bottom of a draft piece about premium wines. Use the hand test from the bottom, and count the endings.

> Of course, branded winemakers, premium facilities, and careful care don't assure an exceptional wine any more than an Ivy League education ensures a successful graduate, but it helps. And here it delivers.
>
> The lush, rich, deep flavors of the cabernets carry across the three vineyards. The wines wear the regal California Cult Cab bearing those collectors have become accustomed to. Big wines. Forward and exciting. Like a red velvet curtain pulled back to reveal an exclusive party. They are wines most will enjoy, and those attuned to the category will cherish.
>
> Ultimately, the wines deliver because the team demands the wine meet the dimensions of a dynasty, not the evaluation of economics.

How many endings did you find? I count five, all good ones. See how using all those fine endings erodes the power of each one? The author rewrote it like this:

> The lush, rich, deep flavors of the cabernets carry across the three vineyards. The wines wear the regal California Cult Cab bearing those collectors have become accustomed to, like a red velvet curtain pulled back to reveal an exclusive party. Ultimately, the wines deliver because the team demands the wine meet the dimensions of a dynasty, not the evaluation of economics.

Having discovered your multiple endings, you decide which one leaves the readers with what you want them to remember. Then you recycle the other endings into appropriate places above, or cut them.

READERS REMEMBER BEST WHAT THEY READ LAST.

ABSOLUTELY PERFECT COPY

You don't trust people who make mistakes, especially in public.

Smart writers submit flawless copy because it allows them to maintain some control over their work during the production process. It also builds your reputation with editors likely to give you good assignments or employ you again. In the twentieth century, writers could depend on copy editors, proofreaders, and fact-checkers to back them up, but all three groups either vanished or became so overburdened that much of the safety net has been lost. Some book publishers no longer copyedit manuscripts. Luckily for me, Writer's Digest still does. You may have nobody between you and your readers, as in a blog or a self-published book.

FLAWLESS PROSE CREATES AUTHORITY. ERRORS DIMINISH AUTHORITY.

When readers spot mistakes, such as a misspelled name, they start doubting the information and the author. Writers who take responsibility for their own text publish fewer errors. So how do you achieve perfect copy?

Every word must be spelled right, especially names. Spell-checkers catch mistakes that are hard to see on a screen, such as two words running together without a space between them, but they do only a rough job of catching misspelled words.

Reading aloud makes most spelling errors jump out at you, because you have to read every word. Writers who spell poorly should master a book on spelling, read good fiction, and use devices like word-a-day calendars.

Some software will check grammar and usage, but only in crude ways. I asked my word processor to check this sentence, "Writing are fun." No problem, it said. Again, you can best learn grammar and usage by reading good prose. Studying handbooks, such as Strunk and White's *Elements of Style,* will provide a vocabulary for understanding grammar.

How do you check names? Half the writers who mention me in print spell my last name with an *e*, "F-R-Y-E." They make that error by assuming. You get names right by careful gathering in the first place. You ask everybody you talk with for a business card; then you ask them if everything on the card is correct. You ask people to spell their names, even Karen Clark, who replies, "K-A-R-I-N C-L-A-R-K-E."

In final proofreading, you might check names with a phone directory, or with Google. If you use the same name more than once in the same piece, compare them for consistency. If in doubt, call people or send them an e-mail query. You might feel stupid, but the person will admire your persistence. Finally, if you can, check names in photo captions, maps and diagrams, back-of-the-book lists, and all of the out-of-the-way places.

Numbers are harder to check, but you can mislead readers with just one too many zeros or a misplaced decimal point. Check numbers against the best sources, beyond the places you got them from. Do not trust previously published sources, such as clip files. To check a phone number, call it. Go to URLs to make sure they're right and live.

> ASSUME THAT NUMBERS ARE WRONG UNTIL VERIFIED.

Many publications have stylebooks, sets of rules that mostly have to do with format and usage. Soccer players observe the rules of their game, and you should follow the rules of the writing game. Perfect copy honors stylebook conventions; otherwise copy editors will change your writing to make it do so. If you must violate the stylebook, include a note to editors explaining why.

Fact-checking goes beyond verifying things from your notes. Use directories, Google, and phone calls. When I write about tricky technical material, I often call the source and ask if I got it right. By the way, they usually tell me some new things I didn't know.

The most careful writer I know, Bill Adair, has the most thorough checking system. He prints a copy of his finished piece, and then reads it with a red pen in hand. He asks if each fact is correct and each name is spelled correctly, and marks a check if it is. He'll often check the spelling of names he's written dozens of times, just to be sure. Borderline overkill, but Bill has rarely printed corrections. (By the way, I sent him this paragraph to confirm it. He did. Whew.)

Some meticulous writers read a finished piece backwards, word by word, to check it.

HOW TO STOP YOURSELF

When is a piece finished? Never. One advantage writing has over speech is that you can revise it forever, even after you publish it. The harder question is when to stop revising. When and how do you launch your baby into the world?

You're almost finished when you've run through the techniques I described in the previous section on submitting perfect copy. Use the spelling and grammar and usage checkers (trusting none of them), read aloud, and check names and numbers and facts.

Adair Lara says you're finished "when you catch yourself changing stuff and then putting it back to the way you had it before."[49] I would modify that to say "when you keep changing stuff." You can use the computer's Clipboard to hold alternative versions of short passages, and choose your favorite after reading them aloud.

Two questions can stretch out revision endlessly: "How can I make this perfect?" and "Can I make this better?" No writing is ever perfect, just as no person (especially a writer) is anywhere close to perfect. Striving for absolute perfection leads to slowness at best and never publishing at worst. Maybe even insanity.

Any writing can be made better, but the improvement may not be worth the effort or time. You're more likely to make useful changes in response to questions and suggestions from a helpful editor or friend. But they can't react to what you don't turn in. So hand it over.

One good test has to do with voice. Read the whole piece aloud and mark anything that doesn't sound like you. Change those passages until you hear your own voice flowing.

You can also test your work using the two magic questions: "What works, and what needs work?" The key word is *needs*, and the target is the reader. The deep question is "What do I need to do so my readers will understand this and read it to the end?" After that you might add: "... and make them want to read me a whole lot more?" Watch out. You're about to start thinking about yourself, and your internal critic is about to sneer, "What if this book isn't as successful as the first one?" And your finger will freeze above the Send key.

Sometimes you just surrender it. After twenty-four years, E.V.K. Dobbie finished editing six dense tomes of Anglo-Saxon poetry, saying, "No doubt this volume would be a better book if I had spent a year or two more on it, but as G.P.K. [his collaborator] used to tell me, one must always leave something for the reviewers to say."[50]

BEATING YOUR DEADLINE

The clock is your enemy, but you can turn it into a writing tool.

Except for blogs, publication usually involves people working together in production teams, mostly end to end. Your success as a writer depends on the editors, graphic artists, photographers, copy editors, and others who turn your text into publishable form. You'll get better results by helping your colleagues, by submitting perfect copy on time, and by making deadlines.

Some prima donnas pride themselves on violating deadlines. They fantasize that they're showing their creativity by not playing the game of the management types. They think they're so important that others can wait. They're missing a key factor they would never think of:

> WRITERS WHO TURN WORK IN EARLY, EVEN ON TIME, GET BETTER EDITING, BETTER VISUALS, AND BETTER PLAY.

The secret is not just making the deadline. The secret is turning things in early.

First of all, you need a deadline, and it has to be real and understood. Effective deadlines are exact dates and times. If your editors don't specify a deadline, ask them for one. If they still don't set a deadline, set your own. Writers without deadlines are likely to write long, both in space and time, and to turn in working drafts rather than finished pieces.

Sometimes you can't make your deadline, for perfectly good (but rare) reasons. So you put up a warning flare early, alerting the rest of the production team to adjust their time scheme. Sometimes editors can modify the assignment to preserve the deadline.

Many writers struggle to complete pieces at all, so how do you finish them early? First, you use the methods in this book to tune your writing process. Many of the techniques you've learned in the past actually make you slow, so change them. Your new effective process, with its sequence of techniques, will speed you up once you get used to it. And you keep tuning your process throughout your career to get even faster. The assignments get more complex, the subjects harder, and you get more efficient. Bill Blundell, the fastest writer I ever met, loved gathering information. He told me, "If I write fast, I can report longer."

Here's a magic technique for speeding up long, complicated pieces, which works especially well for books. You divide the project into parts, such as the chapters of a dissertation. Working back from your final deadline, you set individual deadlines for each of those parts. Then you draft as fast as you can toward the first deadline. If you make it earlier than scheduled, you move all the other deadlines that much closer.

For example, you're writing a five-part book, and you schedule five section deadlines plus a final deadline:

Drafts: February 1, April 1, June 1, August 1, October 1. **Final:** December 1.

You write fast, and reach your first-section draft deadline on January 24th, not February 1st. Then you move all your other deadlines one week closer.

Drafts: March 24, May 24, July 24, September 24. **Final:** November 24.

You keep beating deadlines and rescheduling. My doctoral students finished their dissertations in half the time using this technique.

As a writing coach, I can tell you that fast writers have fewer problems than slow ones. And freelancers who beat deadlines get invited again.

DOES IT MAKE SENSE?

Once you've drafted a piece, you can't really see it as your readers will read it. Things in your head interfere. You read one of your sentences, and it makes perfect sense to you, because of information in your head, but not on the screen. Your readers won't have that information to help them unless you type it. So how can you read your finished draft with the innocent eyes of a general reader? You can't. You need a test reader.

Bobbi Alsina was my brilliant program assistant at the Poynter Institute. She read my drafts and simply put a check in the margin beside anything she didn't understand. I didn't want her to edit the piece or even like it. I just wanted her to spot holes and lapses of clarity. She was a perfect test reader because she didn't know the subjects I wrote about.

If a test reader who doesn't know the material can understand your piece, you probably do too, and so will your readers.

Most writers use their editor as their first and only test reader. That's what they're for, to represent the readers' needs. But editors usually don't read drafts, and they know too much. They're not the general reader you're after.

Some test readers do need to know a lot about the subject. If you've written a cookbook, don't invite me as a test reader; I can't cook. You need someone who does cook, who will test the recipes to see if they work. You might need expert test readers in medical or military writing. I recruited two top writing coach friends, Toni Allegra and Roy Clark, to test this book, then farmed it out to ten top writer friends.

Where do you get such test readers? You tap family, friends, clients, sources, agents, and especially other writers. You can take turns helping each other. Smart writers recruit a circle of helpers.

WRITING IS TOO HARD TO DO ALONE.

SENDING NOTES TO INSIDERS

You need ways to send short notes to your editors on the fly. The software at many publications includes a device called the "Notes Mode." This handy feature allows writers to include messages to editors inside the texts. The computer prevents these insertions from printing or appearing on readers' screens. Unfortunately, sometimes the system fails to block them.

The commonest message is "CQ," which means, "I have checked this, and it's correct." Writers use it to mark things like names, phone numbers, and URLs. CQ essentially tells the editors that they don't have to check this item. (Smart editors take that with a grain of salt.) The passage might look like this, depending on the system: "The latest blog post appears at http://donfry.wordpress.com/2009/09/02/never-trust-spell-checkers/ [CQ] and at http://tinyurl.com/ktp8bu [CQ]."

Any violation of the publication's stylebook, profanity or obscenity, or deliberate misspelling should be marked and explained. When copy editors encounter such variants without explanation, they tend to chop them out without checking with the author first.

For example, the "Second Reference Rule," followed by many publications, says that people lose their titles when they appear for a second time in a piece. So "Circuit Judge Henry Smith" on first reference becomes "Smith" on the second. If you violate that rule, you explain it in the notes mode, like this: "[BOTH THE DEFENSE ATTORNEY AND THE JUDGE ARE NAMED 'SMITH,' SO I HAVE USED THEIR TITLES IN LATER REFERENCES.]"

You might indicate deliberate misspellings, as in this sentence from the section above on spell-checkers: "For instance, I often type *orginization* when I mean *organization*, and spell *chairman* as *chariman*." The note might read, "[NOTE TWO WORDS MISSPELLED ON PURPOSE.]" If you followed the misspelled words with "[CQ]," the editors would get confused.

You can indicate potential cuts in the notes mode, a trick I learned from my favorite humor columnist Dave Barry. Knowing that your editors might have to shorten your piece later, you help them by marking passages to cut, including the order of removal. Just before the cuttable bit, you insert "[BEGIN POTENTIAL CUT ONE]." At the end of it, you add "[END POTENTIAL CUT ONE]." Paranoid writers assure me that anything you mark as cuttable will get whacked. My experience is the opposite. Editors don't cut me; they cut people who write long and don't help their colleagues on the desk.

WARNING. The software sometimes fails, particularly when a print piece gets posted online later, so do not include anything in the notes mode that you don't want to appear in public, like this: "[I DON'T HAVE A RESPONSE FROM THE CHEF BECAUSE THAT ASSHOLE WON'T RETURN MY CALLS!]"

As a freelance book reviewer, I don't have a notes mode; so I create my own. I insert messages in brackets and all caps, like this: [[[I CAN'T FIND THE PRICE OF THIS BOOK]]]." I hope my editors will take that out, but just in case, I'm very careful what I put in my jury-rigged notes mode.

DON'T PUT ANYTHING IN THE NOTES MODE YOU DON'T WANT PUBLIC.

DO NOT DEBATE WITH EDITORS

Finally you finish a piece and turn it in, only to have your editor announce that he wants to "talk about it." And you're locked into a debate over how to do this and that. If you consider this conversation a contest, you'll lose, because your editor always outranks you. By the way, if the editor "wins," your relationship suffers.

How do you discuss changes with editors without losing your voice, your mind, or your soul?

(First, a disclaimer. You can't write risky without a good editor to ask you tough questions. I write risky columns without any editors, which scares me to death.)

Some good and useful discussions between writers and editors get down to real issues, but many such exchanges turn into "It doesn't work for me" versus "Well, I like it." The ranking editor wins. Your likes and dislikes and your editor's are both irrelevant. You need another person in this discussion: your reader. All conversations over copy should keep the target reader in mind, and that target reader is never the editor or the writer. So instead of arguing about what you like or dislike, you should talk about what your readers need.

First of all, build a baseline of quality. Ask "What works?" and "What needs work?" That first question usually removes 95 percent of the piece from the discussion, the part that you both agree already works. By asking "What needs work?" you acknowledge that the rest can be repaired. And the full question is "What needs work so readers will understand this?" The magic question is always "What's this about?" That question refocuses both material and thought. If either of you can't answer it, the piece is not organized and not finished. The writer should take it back and rework it.

You should discuss individual passages in terms of the readers' understanding. Does the reader have enough information at this point? This is where the author runs into a problem of humility. The author understands the passage, so what's wrong with the dopey editor that he doesn't get it? The problem is often that the key information is still in the writer's head, but not on the screen. At this point, if I were the editor, I would read the problematic passage aloud, cover it up, and ask the writer, "What did that say?" And the writer says, "so and so," and I uncover the text and ask, "*Where* does it say that?" You can do this alone, playing both roles.

Keep your focus on the text and not on the personality of the two players. If either of you says something like "Well, maybe you just hate description," you're now debating each other's character, not the writing. Focus on the text and the readers.

With ethical questions, you need to ask first, "Do we know enough?" Many ethical dilemmas are solved with one phone call. Then you ask each other, "What's our professional reason for doing this?" The key word here is *professional*. Ethical discussions often stray into emotion, especially fear, away from professional practice.

Questions of wording often turn around preserving voice. If you think a suggested change violates your voice, read the paragraph aloud to the editor to see if it sounds like the surrounding paragraphs.

Now for the real secret of not debating. Debates assume that one side is right and the other is wrong. One side wins; the other side loses. In good decision making, usually the right answer, the useful answer, is a mixture of both sides. Instead of black versus white, the solution may be gray. Or taupe. By talking about what readers need, you can escape your egos and find common ground.

When you resolve the problem, thank each other. You encourage editors to discuss rather than argue by thanking them when conversation reaches a good conclusion.

WRITING SIDE BY SIDE

Our romantic notion pictures writers scribbling alone in an attic, dying young of tuberculosis. But most writers work in teams, with others finishing their writing.

All professional writing outside of blogs needs to be collaborative. Writers may fantasize about serving as their own editor and publisher, thinking they could do whatever they please. Some egotistical columnists demand a no-editing clause in their contracts.

But you can't see your own writing with an objective eye. You won't notice things missing from your text, because they're in your head even if they're not on the screen. You know the recipes in your cookbook work because you wrote them, but you still need somebody else to test them. You need a good editor, particularly if you write risky and complex pieces. You can't serve as your readers' representative; your editor/partner plays that role.

Collaborating with other people can be a dream or a horror depending on how you set it up and go about it. Generally speaking, the secret of collaboration is equality and communication. I know of some joint ventures where one writer outranks the other, but they tend to turn into power struggles and messy misunderstandings.

Alicia Ross and Beverly Mills Gyllenhaal have collaborated for fifteen years on a syndicated column, three cookbooks, and a cooking/lifestyle website. They succeed by "setting aside ego and/or adopting a sort of Wiki mentality," including their own special lingo that ensures coordinated action.

Equality works best if the partners do what they do best. For instance, some collaborations involve a doer and a writer. Typically the doer makes things, and the writer describes what the doer did. Cookbooks by chefs often work this way. Or one partner reminisces, and the writer turns the memories into narrative form. Ghostwriters tend to work the same way, but without credit.

In some cases, one partner thinks, and the other clarifies. Sometimes an ace investigator will team up with an organized writer for difficult projects. A friend of mine writes philosophical novels in French, and his wife turns them into action tales as she translates them into English. I asked her if she could translate a novel I wrote about the Eighth Air Force into a French philosophical novel; she just rolled her eyes.

Roy Clark and I have collaborated for twenty-five years by dividing tasks according to our strengths. Roy's terrific with ideas, and I'm logical. We would eat lunch at Pizza Hut, where Roy would toss off two or three ideas a minute, and I'd write down maybe half of them. Then we'd look at the list and decide what to write about. As the organized member, I would compose the first draft. Roy's funny, and I'm not, so he would lighten up my clear but heavy draft with comic grace. Then we'd trade the text back and forth, revising and revising, until we both liked the way it read. "Pizza Hut" became a verb, as in "Let's pizza-hut this piece on dogs as writing coaches."

Some collaborators divvy up the parts of the project, and revise separately or together. Andrew Schloss and David Joachim wrote their *Science of Good Food* in A-to-Z format. They divided the alphabet evenly until they discovered that food terms clustered in three letters (*C, M,* and *S*), so they redivided the assignments.

And some collaborations aren't so much collaborative as collections of separate works, such as alternating chapters in a book. My son Jason alternates blog posts on the New York Mets with his pal Gregory Prince (http://www.faithandfearinflushing.com/.)

Collaborators should agree ahead of time on credit. Many teams fall apart because of misunderstandings at the end of the process over who gets a byline, in what order, *etc.* Again, equality usually works best. Roy Clark and I use alphabetical credits, perhaps because Roy never caught on that readers remember best what they read last.

And that's the REVISE stage, the end of the WRITING PROCESS. Next I'll talk about VOICE.

nine

CREATING YOUR OWN VOICE

The oldest surviving inscription in Attic Greek, from about 720 B.C.E., circles the shoulder of a small wine pitcher. It says, "Whoso now of all the dancers most playfully sports [wins me]."[51] The little pot is the prize in a dancing contest. It speaks to the contestants through the voice of its inscription. And that's the basic metaphor of all writing: the text speaks to the reader.

Readers experience the illusion of a person speaking to them through the page or from the screen. They assign personality to that illusion, which is called "the *persona*." This *persona* is not the author but an artifact created by the author. You could think of the *persona* or voice as a mask between the author and the reader, similar to the metaphorical masks people use when they talk with other people.

What is voice? Voice is a collection of devices used consistently to create the illusion of a person speaking through the text. Writers create their voices by repeating the same devices over and over, such as sentence complexity and length, level of language, and sophistication of reference. Voice differs from tone, the emotional cast. The same voice can sound elated or sad, even in the same text. Some people equate voice with style, although the latter usually refers to larger issues, such as "epic style."

The following examples will give a sense of the range of voices these devices can create for you. Read each example aloud to hear what I'm describing. Here's the first paragraph of my friend Roy Peter Clark's *Writing Tools*, a terrific book, by the way:

> Americans do not write for many reasons. One big reason is the writer's struggle. Too many writers talk and act as if writing were slow torture, a form of procreation without arousal and romance—all dilation and contraction, grunting and pushing. As New York sports writer Red Smith once observed, "Writing is easy. All you do is sit down at a typewriter and open a vein." The agony in Madison Square Garden.[52]

What devices make this paragraph sound like Roy? He varies his sentence lengths, including some quite long ones ("Too many ... pushing."). He uses everyday language mixed with higher levels of diction ("procreation"), and strong nouns and verbs. He has few adverbs ("once observed"). He uses images of sex ("arousal and romance") and birth ("dilation and contraction") and sports (Red Smith) and New York. Roy simply can't write without coupling procreation and sports. And he puts a religious pun ("agony ... Garden") in the final, emphatic position. Everything Roy writes will sound like that. Roy sounds like Roy, and that's what voice means.

JULIA CHILD

Here's one of America's favorite voices, Julia Child, writing about peeling hard-boiled eggs:

> The perfect hard-boiled egg is one that is perfectly unblemished when peeled; its white is tender, its yolk is nicely centered and just set, and no dark line surrounds it. Excess heat toughens the egg, and excess heat also causes that dark line between yolk and white....
>
> Because of the egg's commercial importance, scientists at the University of Georgia undertook a study involving over 800 of them and concluded that the best way of shrinking the egg body from the shell, to make for easy peeling, was to plunge the just-boiled eggs into iced water for one minute, meanwhile bringing the cooking water back to the boil, then to plunge the eggs into boiling water for ten seconds, and right after that to peel them. The iced water shrinks egg from shell and the subsequent short boil expands shell from egg.
>
> I tried out the Georgia method, found it good, and described it in my monthly column for *McCall's* magazine, thereby receiving even more new suggestions, including one from a testy 74-year-old asking if the U. of Georgia had nothing better to do! They should ask their grandmothers, said she who has been boiling eggs since she was a little girl: she boils them 12 to 15 minutes, plunges them into cold water, and has never had the slightest bit of trouble peeling them.[53]

Sounds like Julia, doesn't it, but why? (Remember that I'm talking about her writing voice, not how she spoke on television.) First, notice the very long but clear sentences, the repetition of key words and phrases, the simple language, the lists of actions in order, and eccentric punctuation. Julia simplifies the science ("that dark line"), cites recent food research, and then invokes the wisdom of grandmothers. This authoritative voice convinces you that you're listening to a real person who's a real expert. She assures you by her confident tone that she knows what she's talking about, and you can do it, too. Just the sort of person you want to eat *Charlotte Malakoff aux Fraises* with. *Bon Appétit.*

THOMAS JEFFERSON

Now study the voice of the most important sentence in American history, the beginning of *The Declaration of Independence* (in Jefferson's original spelling):

> We hold these truths to be self-evident: that all men are created equal; that they are endowed by their creator with certain inalienable rights; that among these are life, liberty, & the pursuit of happiness; that to secure these rights, governments are instituted among men, deriving their just powers from the consent of the governed; that whenever any form of government becomes destructive of these ends, it is the right of the people to alter or abolish it, & to institute new government, laying it's foundation on such principles, & organizing it's powers in such form, as to them shall seem most likely to effect their safety & happiness.[54]

Walter Isaacson describes Thomas Jefferson's prose as "graced with rolling cadences and mellifluous phrases."[55] (*Mellifluous* from Latin *mel* 'honey' + *fluus* 'flowing.') Jefferson writes long, but reads short. He uses long, parallel clauses, with repeated openings ("that...."). His language mixes simple words ("all men are created equal") with elevated diction ("endowed," "inalienable," "instituted"). He lists our rights ("life, liberty, & the pursuit of happiness") and then tells us what we have to do to keep them, moving from abstraction to action. His absolutely assured tone leaves no room for argument ("We hold these truths to be self-evident...."). He doesn't give you time to decide if you want to be part of that initial "We"; he just pulls you along with his driving prose until you reach the end, and you think, "Yes, of course, 'safety & happiness.' Sign me up." You can't write that sentence, nobody else could, but you can sound like it, and that's what voice does.

JANE AUSTEN

Here's another familiar voice offering self-evident truth, Jane Austen:

> It is a truth universally acknowledged, that a single man in possession of a good fortune, must be in want of a wife.

> However little known the feelings or views of such a man may be on his first entering a neighbourhood, this truth is so well fixed in the minds of the surrounding families, that he is considered as the rightful property of some one or other of their daughters.[56]

This voice also depends on long, complex sentences that deliver their key words at the end ("wife," "daughters"). It's aphoristic, wry, and edgy. Austen uses linking verbs ("is") rather than action verbs, giving a conversational feel, and she uses simple language interspersed with abstractions ("truth" twice). And the point of view is always rural, domestic, and female. Like Jefferson's, you can't argue against this voice's assurance.

ERNEST HEMINGWAY

Take a look at one of fiction's most recognizable voices, Ernest Hemingway:

> In the morning it was raining. A fog had come over the mountains from the sea. You could not see the tops of the mountains. The plateau was dull and gloomy, and the shapes of the trees and the houses were changed. I walked out beyond the town to look at the weather. The bad weather was coming over the mountains from the sea.[57]

Every clause has essentially the same rhythm and structure: subject, verb, then more in the right branch. Hemingway keeps showing the reader aspects of the same things from different viewpoints. He uses the simplest language with lots of repeated images and words. Every word counts, and you can't remove even one without causing damage. You might characterize this voice as somewhat flat, restrained, and weary, but absolutely under control.

GAIL COLLINS

Columnist Gail Collins has a witty voice that delivers devastating judgments deftly:

> "Sometimes you misunderestimated me," Bush told the Washington press corps. This is not the first time our president has worried about misunderestimation, so it's fair to regard this not as a slip of the tongue, but as something the president of the United States thinks is a word. The rhetoric is the one part of the administration we're surely going to miss. We are about to enter a world in which our commander in chief speaks in full sentences, and I do not know what we're going to do to divert ourselves on slow days.[58]

Collins has a sharp ear for other people's language, which she treats as a key to their character. She plays with their wording ("misunderestimated") in her own long sentences and simple, everyday language. In a piece about Bush's silly lingo, she elevates president-elect Obama to "commander in chief." Her wit is wry, and a little weary ("divert ourselves"). Her voice speaks in the context of the other voices on the op-ed page, which tend toward high seriousness and abstractions. She sounds like the ordinary person amid the titans. It takes great effort, skill, and attention for Gail Collins to sound effortless and consistently funny.

E.B. WHITE

Every writer should own a copy of Strunk and White's *Elements of Style*. Here is White's voice, describing Strunk's teaching style and its effect.

> "Omit needless words!" cries the author on page 23, and into that imperative Will Strunk really put his heart and soul. In the days when I was sitting in his class, he omitted so many needless words, and omitted them so forcibly and with such eagerness and obvious relish, that he often seemed in the position of having shortchanged himself—a man left with nothing more to say yet with time to fill, a radio prophet who had outdistanced the clock. Will Strunk got out of this predicament by a simple trick: he uttered every sentence three times. When he delivered his oration on brevity to the class, he leaned forward over his desk, grasped his coat lapels in his hands, and, in a husky, conspiratorial voice, said, "Rule Seventeen. Omit needless words! Omit needless words! Omit needless words!"
>
> He was a memorable man, friendly and funny. Under the remembered sting of his kindly lash, I have been trying to omit needless words since 1919, and although there are still many words that cry for omission and the huge task will never be accomplished, it is exciting to me to reread the masterly Strunkian elaboration of this noble theme. It goes: [now quoting Strunk]
>
> *Vigorous writing is concise. A sentence should contain no unnecessary words, a paragraph no unnecessary sentences, for the same reason that a drawing should have no unnecessary lines and a machine no unnecessary parts. This requires not that the writer make all his sentences short, or that he avoid all detail and treat his subjects only in outline, but that every word tell.*[59]

I would describe White's *persona* as bemused, wry and witty, richly observant, playful, and authoritative. White mixes levels of diction (high and medium) and formality, swooping from one to another, clause by clause. He piles phrases and clauses on top of one another, making long sentences that take a while to land, alternating with medium lengths. He repeats key phrases; this passage is about repetition, after all. He exaggerates as he describes actions sharply, uses no contractions, and invents words ("Strunkian"). He makes fun of himself with his mock-serious high tone. His voice resembles Gail Collins, but with more complex and playful sentences.

White ends by quoting a paragraph of Strunk, so go ahead and analyze his voice too, which White calls "Sergeant Strunk snapping orders to his platoon." Strunk's forceful tone drives the reader to his conclusion at the emphatic end of the third sentence, five plain words ("but that every word tell.") He uses simple, everyday, masculine diction, with lots of repetition ("no unnecessary" four times). The middle sentence has four parallel clauses, saying the same thing with different references. You have no doubt what Strunk means, so you just salute.

NATALIE ANGIER

Natalie Angier has an appealing voice that explains the most abstruse concepts of modern science, here the orbits of the inner planets:

> Location is everything, and it was ours during the birth of the solar system that granted us our annum. Earth sails around its orbit of more than half a billion miles at 66,600 miles per hour because of its distance relative to the gravitational master, the sun. Venus, by contrast, is 26 million miles closer to the sun than we are, which means that (a) its orbit is shorter than ours; (b) the comparatively greater gravitational pull of the sun prompts Venus to dash through each lap at a heightened pace (78,400 miles per hour); and (c) a year there lasts only 226 Earth days, another unpleasant thought for book writers with contracts to fulfill. And let's not dwell on that solar toady of a planet named after the Roman god with feathers on his shoes, where a "year" lasts less than three months.[60]

I would describe this *persona* as chatty and witty, wry and learned, sophisticated, conversational and friendly, extremely clear, and therefore authoritative. Now look at the devices that compose that voice.

<[LEFT BRANCH] SUBJECT + VERB [RIGHT BRANCH]>

Her clear explanation flows from long but simple sentences: start with subject and verb, open to the right, put things end to end. The third, long sentence ("Venus… fulfill.") has one main simple clause, which leads to a list consisting of three simple clauses. She uses ordinary language throughout, with only three technical terms: "solar," "gravitational," and "orbit," each appearing twice. She plays with language in the first sentence, using Latin *annum* for "year," but doesn't explain it. In the last sentence, she calls Mercury "a planet named after the Roman god with feathers on his shoes," again with no explanation. Her allusions assume that you share her classical background.

Angier drops comic asides, such as "another unpleasant thought for book writers with contracts to fulfill," implying her literate and professional audience. She mixes active, passive, and linking verbs for conversational feel, with graphic action verbs. She moves readers along rapidly through complex materials by putting witty bits at the ends of paragraphs.

ABRAHAM LINCOLN

Abraham Lincoln had a powerful and distinctive voice, best heard in his Gettysburg Address:

> Four score and seven years ago our fathers brought forth, upon this continent, a new nation, conceived in Liberty, and dedicated to the proposition that all men are created equal.
>
> Now we are engaged in a great civil war, testing whether that nation, or any nation so conceived, and so dedicated, can long endure. We are met here on a great battlefield of that war. We have come to dedicate a portion of it as a final resting place for those who here gave their lives that that nation might live. It is altogether fitting and proper that we should do this.
>
> But in a larger sense we can not dedicate—we can not consecrate—we can not hallow this ground. The brave men, living and dead, who struggled, here, have consecrated it far above our poor power to add or detract. The world will little note, nor long remember, what we say here, but can never forget what they did here.
>
> It is for us, the living, rather to be dedicated here to the unfinished work which they have, thus far, so nobly carried on. It is rather for us to be here dedicated to the great task remaining be-

> fore us—that from these honored dead we take increased devotion to that cause for which they here gave the last full measure of devotion—that we here highly resolve that these dead shall not have died in vain; that this nation shall have a new birth of freedom; and that this government of the people, by the people, for the people, shall not perish from the Earth.[61]

Ten sentences, 272 words of luminous prose. What devices make this voice distinctive?

Lincoln begins with archaic language and phrasing, not "in 1776" or "87 years ago," but "four score and seven years ago." "Brought forth, upon this continent" has the sweep and ring of the King James Bible. He ends his first paragraph by quoting Thomas Jefferson and *The Declaration of Independence*: "all men are created equal," echoed in the closing: "this government of the people, by the people, for the people, shall not perish from the earth."

Lincoln uses simple diction throughout, with some middle level: "conceive," "dedicate" five times, "devotion," "resolve," "perish." He repeats simple words: "here" nine times, "we" ten, "us" four, "nation" five, and "dedicate" five, creating a sense of unity. His powerful verbs picture actions.

Mostly he writes sentences that branch to the right, with a few short insertions, creating a flowing rhythm and great clarity. His sentences turn on parallel phrasing:

> "any nation so conceived, and so dedicated"
>
> "we are engaged.... We are met .... We have come...."
>
> "we can not dedicate—we can not consecrate—we can not hallow this ground."
>
> "It is for us.... It is rather for us...."
>
> "what we say here, ... what they did here."
>
> "government of the people, by the people, for the people."

Most of his sentences are roughly the same length, until he gets to the last one, 84 words long, almost a third of the whole address. The entire speech is heavily punctuated except the last sentence. The shorter sentences build up a rolling rhythm, and that last, long sentence delivers his message in powerful, memorable form.

Lincoln mixes imagery of birth and death with references to land and ground and fields, appropriate for a funeral oration.

Forgetting for a moment what you know about Lincoln, what personality emerges from these devices? I would call it strong and determined, simple and sincere, patriotic, clear, and absolutely compelling. As with Jefferson, readers want to follow anyone who talks and writes like that.

FRANK McCOURT

Now you'll analyze Frank McCourt's voice and see how he creates it. In this typical passage from *Angela's Ashes*, Frank and his brother Malachy take their infant brother Alphie for a stroll in his baby carriage:

> We play games with Alphie and the pram. I stand at the top of Barrack Hill and Malachy is at the bottom. When I give the pram a push down the hill Malachy is supposed to stop it but he's looking at a pal on roller skates and it speeds by him across the street and through the doors of Leniston's pub where men are having a peaceful pint and not expecting a pram with a dirty-faced child saying Goo goo goo goo. The barman shouts this is a disgrace, there must be a law against this class of behavior, babies roaring through the door in bockety prams, he'll call the guards on us, and Alphie waves at him and smiles and he says, all right, all right, the child can have a sweet and a lemonade, the brothers can have lemonade too, that raggedy pair, and God above, 'tis a hard world, the minute you think you're getting ahead a pram comes crashing through the door and you're dishing out sweets and lemonade right and left, the two of ye take that child and go home to yeer mother.[62]

How would you describe the vivid personality speaking here? He's remembering something that happened decades earlier, and impersonating himself then. He comes off as a bemused outlaw, an almost-innocent criminal, knowingly committing a reckless, silly, dangerous, potentially tragic act. He shows no sense of remorse, then or now, and thoroughly enjoys the retelling. He's enthusiastic in the boyish act. Neither child apologizes to the barman, yet McCourt is clearly sympathetic with the bartender's rant. And this speaker has a good ear for common speech. He's a clear storyteller.

What devices produce this personality, this voice?

McCourt sets up the scene and the action with firm geography and expectations about what each character will do, then shoves the pram downhill. The sense of pell-mell action results from a lack of punctuation for the rest of the sentence, and the contrast of chaos and normality. The speeding pram interrupts the men drinking "a peaceful pint," and halts with the baby saying "Goo goo goo goo."

The second half of the paragraph is all one sentence of the barman's reaction, again speeded along with sparse punctuation. His speech alternates direct and indirect quoting without quotation marks. He speaks a little bit of dialect and slang: "bockety," "ye," "yeer." The whole paragraph races along with strong action verbs, lots of repetition, and mostly short, ordinary words. McCourt tells the anecdote entirely in the present tense, giving it immediacy; you, the reader, are right there.

Now go back and read the selection aloud. Don't you agree that this is an attractive voice, a storyteller you want to listen to, even as he tells you the most appalling things?

GARRISON KEILLOR

Here's a familiar voice that most people listen to rather than read. Actually, Garrison Keillor's radio and writing voices are close, because he normally writes for reading aloud. This selection comes from a whimsical survey of six state fairs. He expands the third item in a list of "Ten Chief Joys of the State Fair":

> Of the ten joys, the one that we Midwesterners are loath to cop to is number three, the mingling and jostling, a pleasure that Google and Facebook can't provide. American life tends more and more to put you in front of a computer screen in a cubicle, then into a car and head you toward home in the suburbs, where you drive directly into the garage and step into your kitchen without brushing elbows with anybody. People seem to want this, as opposed to urban tumult and squalor. But we have needs we can't admit, and one is to be in a scrum of thinly clad corpulence milling in brilliant sun in front of the deep-fried-ice-cream stand and feel the brush of wings, hip bumps, hands touching your arm ("Oh, excuse me!"), the heat of humanity with its many smells (citrus deodorant, sweat and musk, bouquet of beer, hair oil, stale cigar, methane), the solid, big-rump bodies of Brueghel peasants all around you like dogs in a pack, and you—yes, elegant you of the refined taste and the commitment to the arts—are one of these dogs. All your life you dreamed of attaining swanhood or equinity, but your fellow dogs know better. They sniff you and turn away, satisfied.[63]

How would you characterize the *persona* speaking here? (Forget that you've heard and seen him; just consider his prose.) You would probably judge it as wry and comic, ironic, edgy, hip, suburban, comfortable and uncomfortable, and vigorous, as well as homely and sophisticated at the same time. A voice filled with contradictions.

What devices create this familiar voice? First, you notice the long, sprawling sentences. Despite their length, they're clear because Keillor gives you the subject and verb early, and keeps expanding to the right. His parenthetical insertions fall at places that don't impede the flow. These sentences would be even easier to follow on radio, with his voice punctuating, although he wrote this piece for *National Geographic*. The effect is a rich, compelling, clear explainer.

Most people think of state fairs as rural, but the worldview here is suburban, with the sensibility between the farm and city. The first-person plural pronoun "We," beginning with "We midwesterners," actually refers to all Americans.

Keillor propels the reader with strong verbs and rolling sentences. He uses mostly simple words, mixed with more sophisticated vocabulary: "tumult and squalor," "scrum," "corpulence," "bouquet of beer," "commitment." He even makes up words: "swanhood" and "equinity."

He tosses off a reference from the fine arts ("solid, big-rump bodies of Brueghel peasants") without explicating it. He presents all the imagery of the state fair without explanation; he assumes you know what he's talking about, and probably have experienced it. Even if you haven't, he puts you there.

Garrison Keillor, this very American voice says, is our representative, our point of view, immersed in a situation that characterizes us.

BARACK OBAMA

Now analyze candidate Barack Obama's voice in his 2008 victory speech after winning the Iowa caucuses. It begins like this:

> Thank you, Iowa.
>
> You know, they said this day would never come.
>
> They said our sights were set too high. They said this country was too divided, too disillusioned to ever come together around a common purpose.
>
> But on this January night, at this defining moment in history, you have done what the cynics said we couldn't do.
>
> You have done what the state of New Hampshire can do in five days. You have done what America can do in this new year, 2008.
>
> In lines that stretched around schools and churches, in small towns and in big cities, you came together as Democrats, Republicans and independents, to stand up and say that we are one nation. We are one people. And our time for change has come.

> You said the time has come to move beyond the bitterness and pettiness and anger that's consumed Washington.
>
> To end the political strategy that's been all about division, and instead make it about addition. To build a coalition for change that stretches through red states and blue states.
>
> Because that's how we'll win in November, and that's how we'll finally meet the challenges that we face as a nation.[64]

Obama starts conversationally, "You know…," and keeps his language simple and direct. His driving rhythm results mostly from repetition of short phrases:

> "They said.... They said.... what the cynics said....You said...."
> "too divided, too disillusioned...."
> "said we couldn't do.... You have done.... You have done...."
> "...can do in five days.... can do in this new year, 2008."
> "to move beyond the bitterness.... To end the political strategy.... To build a coalition...."

He revs up some sentences with opening phrases that delay the subject:

> "But on this January night, at this defining moment in history...."
>
> "In lines that stretched around schools and churches, in small towns and in big cities...."

The whole passage turns on imagery of time and space, from lines stretching to the whole nation. He uses contrasting pronouns: "they" versus "you" and "we." His tone is absolutely assured, without qualifiers.

Most of his sentences are either long or medium length, except for two: "We are one people. And our time for change has come." And those two sentences, emphatic by their short punchiness, are the heart of his message in this speech. Barack Obama sounds like Lincoln and Martin Luther King Jr.

DAVID BROOKS

David Brooks has a firm voice, as in this excerpt from his book, *The Social Animal*:

> If the conscious mind is like a general atop a platform, who sees the world from a distance and analyzes things linearly and linguistically, the unconscious mind is like a million little scouts. The scouts careen across the landscape, sending back a constant flow of signals and generating instant responses. They maintain

> no distance from the environment around them, but are immersed in it. They scurry about, interpenetrating other minds, landscapes, and ideas.
>
> These scouts coat things with emotional significance. They come across an old friend and send back a surge of affection. They descend into a dark cave and send back a surge of fear. Contact with a beautiful landscape produces a feeling of sublime elevation. Contact with a brilliant insight produces delight, while contact with unfairness produces righteous anger. Each perception has its own flavor, texture, and force, and reactions loop around the mind in a stream of sensations, impulses, judgments, and desires.
>
> These signals don't control our lives, but they shape our interpretation of the world and they guide us, like a spiritual GPS, as we chart our courses. If the general thinks in data and speaks in prose, the scouts crystallize with emotion, and their work is best expressed in stories, poetry, music, image, prayer, and myth.[65]

How would we characterize Brooks's *persona*? It's authoritative and strong, learned but unpretentious, moral, and a bit skeptical at the human condition.

What devices create this personality? The passage is stunningly clear, which creates the sense of powerful authority. This guy knows what he's talking about. He takes his time to explain things, rather than jamming heavy concepts into dense, academic prose.

The language is mostly simple, with a mixture of slightly technical words: "linearly," "linguistically," "perception," "interpenetrating," *etc.*, all used in ways that make their meaning clear without explication, setting what sounds like common sense into a philosophical frame, lightly worn.

His sentences are long and straightforward, with a clear subject and verb, nothing inserted between them. He rarely uses contractions, and repeats "we" and "our" and "us" to personalize his applications.

Brooks unifies his argument by repetition. He chains ideas together by repeating and varying a word in one clause in the next:

> "<u>If the conscious mind is like a</u> general atop a platform, who sees the world from a distance and analyzes things linearly and linguistically, <u>the unconscious mind is like a</u> ...."

He begins related clauses with the same structure:

> "The scouts careen...."
> "These scouts coat...."
> "...the scouts crystallize...."

Brooks always injects a wistful note. He has high hopes for the human race, but is skeptical about whether we actually direct our own lives. The clarity of this voice creates authority and power and understanding.

JOAN DIDION

Joan Didion has an influential voice, as in this selection from "Goodbye to All That":

> I am not sure that it is possible for anyone brought up in the East to appreciate entirely what New York, the idea of New York, means to those of us who came out of the West and the South. To an Eastern child, particularly a child who has always had an uncle on Wall Street and who has spent several hundred Saturdays first at F.A.O. Schwarz and being fitted for shoes at Best's and then waiting under the Biltmore clock and dancing to Lester Lanin, New York is just a city, albeit the city, a plausible place for people to live. But to those of us who came from places where no one had heard of Lester Lanin and Grand Central Station was a Saturday radio program, where Wall Street and Fifth Avenue and Madison Avenue were not places at all but abstractions ("Money," and "High Fashion," and "The Hucksters"), New York was no mere city. It was instead an infinitely romantic notion, the mysterious nexus of all love and money and power, the shining and perishable dream itself. To think of "living" there was to reduce the miraculous to the mundane; one does not "live" at Xanadu.[66]

I would characterize the *persona* speaking here as sophisticated, world weary, sardonic and edgy, intense, knowing, and sad. What devices create this voice?

Her sentences are long and complex, even the short ones. She creates rolling rhythms, mostly with simple words and lengthy clauses, with lots of things inserted into them. She does not use contractions, which lifts the formality slightly. She repeats parallel phrases. Some of her sentences have extended, introductory, dependent clauses. She builds toward powerful images at the ends of sentences: "the shining and perishable dream itself," "one does not 'live' at Xanadu." She uses specific lists of stores and places to build up a sense of plenitude pointing toward abstractions. Readers have a sense that she's thinking in front of them, in her back-and-forth clauses and phrases, all tightly controlled by precise sentences.

WILLIAM FAULKNER

William Faulkner was famous for long, complex sentences, some over a page long. You can't imitate his voice without parody, but you can analyze it for devices. This passage begins his 1950 Nobel Prize acceptance speech:

> I feel that this award was not made to me as a man, but to my work—a life's work in the agony and sweat of the human spirit, not for glory and least of all for profit, but to create out of the materials of the human spirit something which did not exist before. So this award is only mine in trust. It will not be difficult to find a dedication for the money part of it commensurate with the purpose and significance of its origin. But I would like to do the same with the acclaim too, by using this moment as a pinnacle from which I might be listened to by the young men and women already dedicated to the same anguish and travail, among whom is already that one who will some day stand here where I am standing.[67]

Forget what you know about how Faulkner looked (tiny, elegant) and spoke (deeply Southern), as you ask what kind of personality speaks from this paragraph. I would call it tricky and witty, alternately simple and complex, idealistic, humble and aloof, and deeply authoritative. What devices create this *persona*?

First, he uses no qualifiers, but speaks with the absolute assurance of a person who knows who he is and what he is talking about, not that hard to do if you've just won the Nobel Prize. His sentences are either long and simple, or short and simple. The flanking sentences ("I feel...." and "But I would like...."), each fifty-six words long, open to the right after the subject and verb, and put new things end to end, not inside something else. He uses fairly simple diction, with only a few longer words: "commensurate," "significance," "pinnacle." He includes slang, "the money part," and some archaic terms: "anguish," "travail," "agony," "acclaim." He mixes ordinary imagery, such as "sweat," with abstractions: "human spirit" and "glory." And he repeats words and phrases and images.

Finally, he's very down to earth about how to win the Nobel Prize: It takes work and suffering and determination. As he achieved this honor, all his novels were out of print.

CREATING ANOTHER VOICE, MY THIRD

I keep reinventing myself. My voice is the illusion that my text speaks, and my readers assign it a personality. So when I become a new person, I need a new *persona*, a new voice. My three voices so far are professor, writing teacher, and blogger.

My first *persona* had an academic voice, suitable for a brand-new assistant professor of English, a former navy lieutenant, who signed himself "Donald K. Fry." I wanted to write with striking power and clarity, so I turned Strunk and White's *Elements of Style* into a voice. I used all their devices of clarity, and avoided anything that sounded conversational, such as the verb "to be." My academic colleagues criticized that first voice as too clear. One sniped, "You don't sound like a professor; people can understand you."

I created a friendlier, less academic voice in 1984, when I changed professions to teaching journalism and renamed myself "Don Fry." I still valued clarity and power, but I also wanted to engage my audiences, to impel them to act on what I wrote about. This new voice kept the formality of Strunk and White, but admitted some conversational devices, such as an occasional "to be" and contractions. I used the second person singular *you* to draw readers into action. My second voice worked. One editor observed, "You could cut yourself on Don Fry's prose." I think that was a compliment.

You're reading my third voice now, drafted by a character named "donfry," who writes a blog. I realized that my first voice sounded like a book because I thought of myself as a book writer. My second voice sounded like someone standing up because that's what I did; I stood up and talked AT people. My third voice speaks in our brave new world of electronic exchanges, where readers and writers keep switching roles, talking WITH each other, not AT each other. In my earlier voices, I might have called it "multidirectional." Now I call it fun.

What makes this new, third voice sound the way it does? It still uses all the devices of clarity and power, as well as chatty contractions and sprinkles of the verb "to be." Strunk commanded, "Omit needless words," but now I leave some in. I ended that last sentence with a preposition, perfectly good grammar but informal. I'm also writing about myself, which I rarely did before. As I wrote this chapter, I realized that this third voice allows me to escape my later teachers, Strunk and White, especially "Sergeant Strunk."

I find myself analyzing the prose of respondents to my new style. Whoa, that sentence is in my second voice, not my third. I'll try it again: "I'm watching how friends talk back to my blog." Better.

Most of my writer friends seem to have blogging down pat, writing like bar talk. I'm still experimenting with this new voice and virtual self in front of you, in this book.

CREATING YOUR OWN VOICE

And now I'll show you how to create and re-create your own new voice, as I continue to create mine. There are three ways to build a voice of your own: just let it happen, imitate other writers, and design it from devices.

Most writers create a voice unconsciously. You just write over a period of years, paying no attention to the kind of thinking about *persona* and devices discussed above. Eventually you get a sense of what sounds right to you, how to sound like yourself. You may unconsciously modify that evolved voice by adopting new techniques you learn and like.

This passive method works by default, and it has two drawbacks. Such writers lack the vocabulary and awareness of devices that allows them to discuss their voice with others. They can't describe their voice technically, and find it hard to change. It's difficult to think about something if you don't have the vocabulary for it. Perhaps they object to an editor changing their voice in a piece but aren't equipped to say, "I never begin sentences with dependent clauses." They end up saying, "It doesn't sound right to me." Neither the editor nor the writer knows why. By the end of this section, you'll know why.

Second, you can create your voice by imitation. My son, Jason, started writing seriously at the age of eleven in 1980, the year we bought our first computer, an IBM PC Model 1. With no help from me, he set out to develop his own voice by imitating writers he admired, one per year. The first year, unfortunately for his parents, he imitated the Conan the Barbarian series, all preposterous weapons and overblown language and busty women warriors. But the next year, he took on Arthur C. Clarke. His parodies did sound like the authors he modeled himself on. Later, he settled into his own voice as a columnist and blogger.

So how do you imitate a voice? You choose a writer you want to sound like and read a lot of that person's work, especially on subjects close to what you're likely to write about. It helps to read it aloud. Then you try to imitate that writer's style. Actually, it works better if you parody it, overdo it rather than hit it exactly. Then you keep experimenting until you achieve the voice you want.

Voice is all about sound, and you can use a recorder to test your imitations. Write a piece, and read it into a machine. Then listen to it, paying attention to what sounds the way you want, and what does not, the familiar formula: What works, and what needs work? And then experiment some more. It takes a while.

One drawback: You need a good ear to imitate another writer. You might want to tune your ear by writing fictional dialogue first.

Finally, you can design your own voice from scratch as a collection of devices used consistently, which is the point of this chapter. I've shown you above examples of voices analyzed for personality, *persona*, and devices. Now I'll discuss those devices individually in terms of the effects they create.

Remember that no device creates voice by itself, and all devices interact within a context. For example, the level of diction is relative to the language normally expected in the publication or subject. Think about two magazines: *Foreign Affairs* versus *Seventeen*. All effects lie along a spectrum, from absent to overdone.

DEVICES THAT CREATE VOICE

LEVEL OF DICTION

Readers perceive first the level of language in a piece: high, medium, or low. Medium would be the normal wording used in everyday speech by educated people, *i.e.*, conversational but moderately correct. You're reading medium-level diction now. You can change the level for different effects:

> **MIDDLE:** You're reading medium-level diction now.
> **LOW:** This's the way folks talk.
> **HIGH:** Readers would experience the diction embodying this document as appropriate to the discourse community of educated, middle-class speech. (Okay, that's a parody.)

This first impression, largely based on diction level, helps readers estimate if they'll understand the piece. If the diction is wrong for the context, readers will grow suspicious of the voice. It "violates decorum." High diction in a low context sounds pompous, and low diction in a high setting sounds cute and condescending.

Breadth of vocabulary also registers here. Most people use the same thousand or so words in their daily speech, and recognize a few thousand more. Using words beyond that range will make the voice seem elevated, sophisticated, and even stuffy. Using "street language" would imply youth, hipness, and lack of seriousness.

Readers don't say to themselves, "Oh, I see this is written in medium-level diction, which fits my education, so I'll understand this." Most of these reader perceptions are unconscious.

UNUSUAL LANGUAGE: SLANG, DIALECT, ARCHAIC

SLANG makes prose sound conversational, and lots of hip slang makes it sound young. Slang can shade over into jargon, as any adult can tell you after listening to teenagers discussing the gadgets under their thumbs. Extreme use of professional slang and jargon creates distance between the *persona* and readers. Your doctor says, "You've got a bump on your leg," or "You have an induration on your lower extremity."

DIALECT always creates such a gap, since it is perceived (unfairly) as a mark of someone who does not or cannot speak Standard English. Even a charming dialect, such as an Irish brogue, may elicit snobbery. If you must use dialect, use very little, except for comic purposes. Remember the McCourt passage above had only three words of dialect in it.

ARCHAIC language has the same effect as a wide and unusual vocabulary, and can lapse into quaintness. Even used in quotations, it makes the voice sound older and odder. Think about words like "wraith," "vainglory," and "happenstance." Take a look at any page in Tolkien's *Lord of the Rings* trilogy.

FORMALITY OF GRAMMAR AND USAGE

Readers don't have to know much, if anything, about grammar or usage to notice formality. Distinctions such as *that* versus *which* or *who* versus *whom* raise the level of formality. Stricter, more formal grammar and usage create a sense of distance and sophistication, which can be welcoming or forbidding, depending on context. You would use *disinterested* formally in *Harper's* and informally (or not at all) in *Parade Magazine.* If you write formally and then use a colloquial verb like *ain't* for effect, it leaps off the screen or page.

PUNCTUATION

Skilled punctuation makes sentences easy to read, and lack of punctuation makes your readers struggle. Easy sentences create authority and trust, and a sense of friendliness. Hard sentences can give a sense of sophistication, unless they become impenetrable. Hard sentences increase distance between *persona* and reader, except in academic writing, where such sentences imply deep thought.

SENTENCE CLARITY

I've discussed sentence clarity at length above, noting that it mostly flows from simplicity: short or no left branch, subject and verb together, open to the right, and nothing inserted inside anything else.

Readers don't share that template, but they experience the simplicity or complexity of sentences. Simple sentences seem conversational. Oddly enough, even long simple sentences can sound like conversation. Complex sentences, regardless of length, prove daunting. They create distance, and suggest learning and sophistication. In extreme form, we associate complex sentences with intelligence. It takes more brainpower to write simply. An editor once advised me, "Easy reading takes hard editing." Nathaniel Hawthorne said, "Easy reading is damn hard writing."

SENTENCE LENGTH AND VARIED LENGTH

Readers can see sentence length. A lot of long sentences make the page gray. Big gray pages make most readers want to read something else.

Long sentences make the voice seem tedious, no matter what the complexity. A mixture of sentence lengths creates variety of sound and experience, and moves readers along. A series of sentences about the same length sounds monotonous. But even a negative quality like monotony can be part of voice; remember Hemingway.

DEPENDENT CLAUSES AT THE BEGINNING OF SENTENCES

Such clauses delay the subject and dim the clarity of the sentence. Longer and more complex ones delay it even longer, causing frustration for readers. Lowered clarity lowers authority. I avoid beginning sentences with dependent clauses, not only because I'm a clarity freak, but also because it's part of my voice. Some of these devices help create a *persona* by *not* doing something, such as avoiding contractions.

INSERTIONS

Insertions put one unit (such as this parenthetical aside) inside another unit. They give a sense of a person thinking, unless there are so many that they become confusing, in which case, they make the voice seem wishy-washy. It's a balancing act, like everything else in writing. Insertions, especially those between subject and verb, the two anchors of the sentence, sometimes with insertions inside other insertions, and even going on for half a page, drive readers crazy the way this sentence just drove you crazy. See?

REPETITION: WORDS, PHRASES, IMAGERY

Repetition creates meaning by tying things together. Used clumsily, it links things you didn't intend, and becomes confusing and tedious. The French novelist Stendhal avoided repeating the same word on a page, depriving himself of a powerful device.

Repeating key words and phrases makes them prominent in the readers' memories, unless you repeat them too much, in which case readers notice the repetitions, and they make the voice boring. Repetition puts things in parallel, and invites readers to compare them without saying so.

Repeating meaningful images can spark readers' memory in new contexts. Frank McCourt is the master of this technique, constantly reminding readers of his miserable childhood, Ireland's tragic history, his clotty eyes.

PARALLEL STRUCTURES

Parallels are repetition in form. A series of clauses or sentences with the same shape creates a compelling rhythm, a sense of unity, and authority, unless overdone. Remember Martin Luther King Jr.'s "I have a dream" speech, and especially Winston Churchill's great rallying speech of 4 June 1940:

> We shall go on to the end, we shall fight in France,
> we shall fight on the seas and oceans,
> we shall fight with growing confidence and growing strength in the air,
> we shall defend our Island, whatever the cost may be,
> we shall fight on the beaches,
> we shall fight on the landing grounds,
> we shall fight in the fields and in the streets,
> we shall fight in the hills;
> we shall never surrender.[68]

Variation increases the power of parallels, as you can see in the slight changes in form after each "we shall. . . ." Parallels have the same compelling quality as chant.

ACTIVE, PASSIVE, AND LINKING VERBS

Active verbs create a sense of power, mostly by being graphic and specific. Passive verbs dilute the voice, and linking verbs ("to be") weaken it. On the other hand, informal American speech uses lots of linking verbs. Using them in prose creates a conversational sound. The active voice used exclusively will sound powerful but formal.

CONTRACTIONS

Contractions combine two words: *isn't* instead of *is not*. They make prose sound conversational, and the more contractions, the more it sounds like speech, unless the readers notice them. A total avoidance of contractions raises the level of formality.

ECONOMY OF WORDING

Again I bring up Strunk's Rule Seventeen: "Omit needless words." Wordy sentences sound more conversational because everyday speech isn't tight or edited. But if you trim sentences skillfully, they flow better, becoming conversational and friendly. On the other hand, extremely tight sentences come off as formal, distancing, and even huffy, like this: "Omit needless words."

I once ended a blog post inviting readers to comment: "Done any experiments with creating a voice?" The following examples add and subtract words to show different effects:

> Have you done any experiments with creating a voice?
> What's been your experience trying to create a voice?
> Have you tried experiments with your voice?
> Ever experiment with voice?

I wouldn't call any of those words "needless," although I could (and would) cut some of them in all three of my voices. I might leave some of them alone if I were trying to sound chummy.

RHYTHM AND FLOW

Rhythms can range from jerky to, as we said of Jefferson, *mellifluous*, which means 'honeyed and flowing.' I'm talking about the sense of movement, how the sounds lead from one to another. Jerky rhythms make the voice seem disorganized, jittery, slightly out of control, even angry. Rolling rhythms create order and unity. Easy flow sounds poetic.

ABSTRACT AND SPECIFIC

Abstractions make the voice seem elevated, sophisticated, and learned. If you use too great a density of abstractions, the prose becomes remote and tedious. Specific words and images create authority by drawing readers in close. Readers experience an illusion of "being there," and a sense of the *persona* as someone who knows things in detail. For greatest power and authority, use a few abstractions to frame a lot of specifics.

PERSON AND TENSE

Journalists avoid the first-person singular *I* because they think it makes them sound un-objective. Overused, *I* sounds egotistical; lightly used, confessional and personal. The first-person plural *we* sounds inclusive; I use *we* a lot in this book to link you with me in the fraternity of writers. The second-person *you*, singular and plural, addresses readers directly (as I just did), and engages them, unless you use it too often or in a commanding way. Third-person is the norm of prose, with a slight distancing effect.

Most writing involves the past tense, again a comfortable norm. Shifting into the present tense creates a sense of immediacy and presence, but staying in the present becomes mannered and tiresome. Writing in the future tense is difficult to sustain, but can be powerful, as in the Churchill masterpiece above: "We shall never surrender."

CONFIDENCE AND ASSURANCE

Speaking of Churchill, a confident tone creates authority because the speaker is sure of what she's saying and also speaks with clarity. Have you ever noticed how scientists seldom sound confident? They're trying to sound scientific, and they put a lot of qualifiers in their sentences. They keep saying they're not sure, concepts are theoretical, the evidence is not totally solid, there might be infinite alternative universes instead of just seventeen, *etc.* Natalie Angier explains, "By accepting that they can never *know* the truth but can only approximate it, scientists end up edging ever closer to the truth."[69] But that hedging makes them sound uncertain. You can adjust assurance by the number of qualifiers you include, especially early in a piece. Here's a wishy-washy example:

> The Prostate-Specific Antigen test, the subject of increasing controversy, measures, with varying degrees of accuracy, the level of PSA in male blood samples as an indicator, subject to interpretation and laboratory error, of the likelihood of prostate cancer, although infection can warp the results.

SOPHISTICATION OF REFERENCE AND EXPLANATION

References to works outside the text create a sense of breadth and depth. A *persona* explaining the reference will come off as helpful, unless the explanation seems condescending. Nineteenth-century British authors often began explanations with "As every schoolboy knows,…." Unexplained references imply sophistication and either learning or hipness, depending on the context.

Natalie Angier says, "Obviously my sense of scale has been out of whack and off the map, a puerile version of Saul Steinberg's often imitated Manhattanite's view of the world."[70] She alludes to the iconic magazine cover that hangs as a poster in millions of rooms. Angier assumes you know it, although she hasn't described or explained it. Density of references and their explanation or lack of one can create a relationship with your readers. You can share what you both know, you can bring in new information, or you can puzzle them with things they've never heard of.

AREAS OF REFERENCE

The references you choose help characterize your *persona*. My friend Bill Blundell only used masculine references; he once said to me, "I went to Houston, and talked to the guy in charge there, and she told me. . . ." I apologize that we're now in the realm of stereotypes, but stereotypes shared with readers help create voice. Lots of sports or military references imply maleness, while domestic imagery suggests the female. And so on.

NAME DROPPING

Personal names form a large part of reference and can create the illusion that the *persona* actually mixes with the people mentioned. Lots of current names suggest a *persona* who's an insider, and the familiarity of the reference can increase it. Machiavelli would put on his best clothes to read in his study, "and in this graver dress . . . enter the antique courts of the ancients and am welcomed by them."[71] He pictured himself hobnobbing with Cicero and Virgil. My son Jason drops names of singing groups I don't get, and I weave in medieval names he doesn't recognize. Even how you frame names has an effect: "First Lady Michelle Obama" versus "Michelle."

ECHOES, ESPECIALLY STANDARD WORKS

Many authors consciously or unconsciously imitate the rhythms, language, and imagery of recognizable texts, especially Shakespeare and the Bible. Melville often sounds like the King James version. (In view of our discussion above of references, notice that I did not spell out Herman Melville or the King James version of what.) Such echoes give depth and a sense of sophistication.

IMAGERY

Imagery functions somewhat like references. Certain images and groupings of images become a signature in voice. Roy Clark falls into image clusters of sex and religion and sports, and I tend toward military and aviation metaphors.

WIT AND HUMOR

Humor is funny, while wit is amusing. Humor (or the lack of it) helps establish voice. The sophistication of the humor determines its effect, whether it elevates or deflates prose. Warning: Don't make humor part of your voice unless you're a funny person. I'm not.

POINT OF VIEW

Point of view is the spot from which the *persona* views the world, mostly determined by references and names. Columnist George Will always speaks from the inside, Woody Allen from the outside. Point of view can also seem spatial. Some voices see everything from high altitude, others up close. Again it's the abstract versus specific. At a larger level, voices can have a worldview, essentially a stance toward nature and the human race. The higher the worldview, the more remote the voice.

ZEST

Some voices show enthusiasm for their subject, and for life in general, and some show the opposite. Cleveland Amory, despite being nutso about cats, was grumpy about almost everything else. Zest engages the reader and suggests youth.

Well, those are some of the devices that, in combinations, create voice.

LET'S CREATE A VOICE

First, you describe the personality you want, and then you select the devices to create that *persona*. Your goal for this exercise is to create a breezy travel writer for *Southern Highways*. This *persona* should be clear, conversational but a little formal, witty and irreverent, and should speak to readers as an equal. The devices you need to use include clear, simple sentences of varied length; light explanation and clear references; slightly loose grammar with medium-level diction, slang, and contractions; occasional second-person address; a sprinkle of wry phrasing; and lots of punctuation. Here's a first try:

> The University of Virginia is restoring a national treasure, the Lawn, a World Heritage site, the Rotunda and ten faculty mansions, called "Pavilions." Any American child would recognize Jefferson's signature style: always red brick with white columns and trim. But recent archaeological research suggests that the columns of Pavilion X should be left tan, the natural color of their stucco, and the woodwork repainted the original taupe. I'd sooner colorize the Parthenon.

Not bad, but diction and reference have to come down a little. The sentences sound more like writing than conversation. Here's my second try:

> The University of Virginia in Charlottesville might mess up a national treasure, "The Lawn." It's a World Heritage site, the famous Rotunda and ten "pavilions," or houses where professors live. You'd recognize Jefferson's style: white columns and trim, with red brick. But researchers studying Pavilion Ten's colors say the columns were originally tan, and the trim was painted taupe. Who could envision that?

Close, but stiff. I'll lighten up the sentences a little more:

> The University of Virginia's messing with a national treasure, "The Lawn." As a school kid, you probably visited the famous Rotunda with its ten "pavilions," or professors' houses. Everybody knows Thomas Jefferson's look: red brick walls with white columns and trim. But now, it turns out that Pavilion Ten had *tan* columns, and the wood was painted *taupe*. Taupe?

And there's your breezy but clear travel-writer voice. I could play with it some more, record it and listen to the results, and keep experimenting until I got it just right.

And that's how voice works. Now you can create your own.

ten

WHAT'S NEXT FOR YOU?

What will you do with what you've learned in this book? Well, you can just keep writing the way you always have. That's fine if you're satisfied with your writing. You now have the tools to understand your writing process and some sense of how your voice works, even if you have no plans to change either.

But I've never met any writers satisfied with their writing. Writers aren't the sort of people who are satisfied with things, especially themselves.

Or you could use this book for what it is, a catalog of techniques for writing, and devices for creating voice. You can try out some of the techniques and add them to your writing process to see if they work for you. Remember that you can only use methods you're equipped for. I envy my pal Roy Clark's fast typing, but I can't do it.

Or you can use the categories and techniques in this book to analyze your writing process and your voice, and make changes that suit you and serve you. How would you do that?

First, you would study your whole writing process, from the beginning of IDEA to the end of REVISE. You would examine every technique, habit, and trick you use, everything you do, in order, and ask about every bit: What works, and what needs work?

What do we mean by, "What works?" Techniques work for you when they make you fast and confident and accurate and powerful and persuasive. Techniques work for you when they magnify your strengths and avoid your weaknesses. Techniques work for you when they function together to streamline your writing process. Techniques work for you if they seem natural.

What do we mean by, "What needs work?" The question implies that anything can be fixed by effort, which isn't quite true. But anything can be *improved* by effort and attention and knowledge and experiment. You can compensate for what you can't change. I'll never type 140 words per minute, but I can use my deep memory, fast drafting without revision, and setting my own deadlines to make myself fast.

Techniques need work when they make you slow, hurt your confidence or accuracy, or weaken your prose. Techniques need work when your writing does not get you what you want, *i.e.*, when it's not persuasive. Techniques need work when they succeed for other people but not for you; for example, plungers who use planner methods tend to stumble, and vice versa. Techniques need work when they don't function together and when they don't mesh with your production teams. Techniques need work when they don't match the requirements of your time scheme. Techniques don't work when they make writing seem tiresome.

So first you figure out what works and what needs work. Then you ask what techniques would strengthen those that already work.

> THE SECRET OF WRITING BETTER: STRENGTHENING THE THINGS YOU DO WELL.

You ask yourself what techniques and combinations of techniques would improve the things that need work. And then you experiment. It helps to get help. Have someone you trust march you through your writing process, asking the key questions and accepting no easy answers. Keep experimenting until you create your own writing process and your own voice.

STARTING OFF FOR BEGINNERS

I aimed this book at writers who want to write better, not at beginners. If you're just starting as a writer and managed to read this whole volume, you may be wondering what to do now. You may not have your own writing process to experiment with and make it work your way. You may not have your own voice. You may feel intimidated by these pages and pages of techniques. So I've designed a simple writing process to help you get started. You can try it for a while and then modify it to make it your own.

IDEA

Focus an idea with these questions: What's this likely to be about? Who might read it? What do they know already? What are the major issues? Do some gathering before you pitch the idea to another person.

GATHER

List things you have to find out and what sources might provide them, then pursue the easiest first. Halfway through, inventory what you've got. Ask "What's this about?" and answer it in writing. Stop when you think you have the information you need.

ORGANIZE

Ask three questions: What's this about? What are the parts of this piece? How long does this need to be? Tell smart people what you intend to write, and pay attention to what they don't understand.

DRAFT

Put your butt in your chair and your fingers on the keys. Draft the piece quickly with as little revision as possible. Type the part you know best first. Don't think about yourself.

REVISE

Read your draft aloud from a printed copy and put marks in the margin beside anything that needs changing. Revise the draft, moving from large units down to words.

Keep writing until you get the hang of it, then read this book again. Good luck.

eleven

WRITING ABOUT YOURSELF: MEMOIRS

We live in an era of personal sharing and confession. No wonder memoir is one of our favorite genres. Writing your memoirs has many benefits:

- Leaving a record of you or your family
- Celebrating family, friends, and yourself
- Learning things about your family
- Making sense of your life
- Justifying what you did
- Taking revenge on your enemies

First, ask why you're writing about yourself. That will determine the size, genre, and structure of the piece. For example, a family history will probably be chronological and will include a lot of less interesting details (just to keep a record of them), as well as mention everybody. But a memoir of your career as the world's authority on river silt will mostly center on deltas and harbors; your family may take up one sentence, and a collaborator half the book.

Here's an example from my life:

> My parents were house-sitting for us one summer, and my mother asked me to teach her how to use a word processor to write her memoirs. I set her up with our IBM-PC and XyWrite, and we left for Greece. When we returned a month later, she'd typed one sentence: "I have lived an interesting life, and I think other people would like to read about it."
>
> I asked if I could read the rest, and she replied, "No, that's what I wanted to say."

I've reduced this month-long incident to a mere anecdote, but I could make it part of a book-length memoir of my ditzy mother, or a key moment in my life growing up in a house where everyone could read, but only I did.

You can organize autobiographical materials in many ways. Usually you focus on people, such as yourself, your families, your teachers, your friends and enemies, celebrities you knew, *etc.* My wife, Joan, would feature her cats, from the fifty she grew up with, to the three nut balls we live with now. Some memoirs narrow to a time and a place, such as Marlena De Blasi's *A Thousand Days in Tuscany* and *A Thousand Days in Venice.*

Autobiographies are usually organized into periods in the subject's life, positions or jobs held, key events, and that kind of thing. The series becomes the spine along which all the details hang, with various high points. And here's a trick: Develop those high points in depth and demote the low points in between, keeping them short. As Elmore Leonard said, "I leave out the parts readers skip."[72]

You can build a narrative toward a conclusion, such as the events leading up to your decision to become a Buddhist monk, followed by the events that then led to your becoming a vegan chef in Montana. Or you can follow several converging narrative lines, such as the series of betrayals that brought you and your future spouse to meet at a party that neither of you wanted to attend.

Where do memoirs go wrong? Go to your local bookstore and sample the memoir section. Half the books consist of whining, whining, followed by whining. How the unfairness of life kept me from winning the Nobel Prize. How I should have played more catch with my father, but he failed me by dying young. How my bitch sister kept my parents from loving me. It's all right to write such a memoir to get it out of your system, just don't inflict it on the world by publishing it. Write a version that other people might enjoy and learn something from.

Autobiography means "self+life+write," but too much self gets tedious. Decide that some of the other people in your life are just as interesting as you are. (Actually, they are. Interview them to find out how.) Then select your characters ruthlessly, leaving out peripheral players unless you need them to explain things. Develop the main characters so readers can see them, hear them, smell them, and understand them as people.

Earlier in the book, I talked about "showing and telling." Keep in mind that memoirs tend to fail from too much telling and little showing. Treat your memoir as a novel based on true things. Which it is, by the way. All memory is a form of fiction. The human brain reconstructs the past from recalled bits and pieces, and we update the past to fit the present without realizing it. You can't write autobiography without making part of it up.

Finally, your internal critic will expand into a group shouting at you as you write about family and friends. You'll start thinking about how Uncle Horace will react if you mention his frog fetish, and you'll tone it down or leave it out. Don't. Write your memoirs full blast, and make decisions later about what to leave in. With luck, maybe Horace will croak before you finish.

twelve

SELECTED LIST OF TECHNIQUES DISCUSSED

IDEA STAGE

- View the world as stories, and tell them.
- Enlarge the context of ideas in a wider perspective or a longer time scheme. Narrow the context by finding people who exemplify large things.
- Ask experts to explain how ordinary things work.
- Find the people who operate things in your community.
- Explore your own emotional reactions for ideas.
- Think about objects to find the past continuing to influence the present.
- Randomize your experiences and points of view.
- Store ideas randomly.
- Take alternate routes to your normal destinations.
- Strike up conversations with people you don't know.
- Lower your standards for what you look at and listen to.
- Eavesdrop to find out what people are doing and thinking.
- Role-play the lives of people with viewpoints different from yours.
- Extend your personal life outside your writer friends and economic group.
- Find ways to experience safely things that frighten you.
- Move around at any event to get as many points of view as possible.
- Ask for business cards, correct them, and keep them in random order.
- Place yourself where other writers aren't.
- If everybody's looking in the same direction, turn 180 degrees.
- Ask sources to recommend other sources and ideas.
- Map out complex issues visually.

- Do some gathering before you pitch ideas to editors.
- Tailor pitches to editors' tastes and quirks.
- Suggest visuals as part of a pitch.
- Pitch hard pieces with a short memo followed by a chat.
- If the pitch fails, write the piece anyway.
- Do dumb assignments as fast as possible to get them out of the way.
- Talk to real people to make dumb ideas come alive.
- Brainstorm an idea to include what the piece might be about, its scale, and the deadline.
- Never surprise an editor.
- Never end a briefing unless you know what you're expected to do.
- Freelancers should ask for a memo spelling out what's expected.
- Know what you're talking about when you pitch an idea.

GATHER STAGE

- Write a plan to focus your gathering of information.
- Plan what you're after on the way to the scene, and plan what you intend to write on the way back.
- Use pathfinders early to lay out the issues and suggest sources.
- Turn sources into pathfinders and vice versa.
- Brainstorm with librarians, photographers, and graphic artists.
- Schedule easier interviews earlier to prepare for harder ones.
- Interview subjects in spaces that are meaningful to them.
- Look for clues to your subject in the waiting room before an interview.
- Start interviews slow and easy to create trust.
- Nod your head and say "uh-huh" to keep subjects talking.
- Ask hard questions in single, simple, and neutral form. Then shut up.
- Interrupt a rambling subject by leaning in and saying, "Hey, that's fascinating."
- Take good notes and listen well for effective follow-up questions.
- Ask interview subjects if you can call back later to check things.
- At the end of an interview, ask, "Anything else you'd like to talk about?"
- Annotate notes while you're still at the interview site.
- Think of yourself as a writer privileged to gather information.
- Effective interview questions are open-ended, active, neutral, simple, and short.
- Ask "dumb" questions to produce answers nobody else thought of.

- Control the pace of interviews by asking subjects to speak slower.
- Improve a quotation by asking the subject to repeat an answer.
- If you use a recorder, note the counter numbers of things you think you'll want to use.
- Record for a Q&A, for historical subjects, and for languages you're not fluent in.
- Develop your own system for annotating notes so you can find things.
- Don't think about yourself or your next question while subjects are talking.
- Use eye contact to keep subjects engaged, and let them see you taking notes.
- Turn "off the record" into "not for attribution" inside the interview.
- Get off-the-record stuff back on the record at the end of an interview.
- Get a business card from everyone you talk with; ask if everything's correct.
- On-site, pick up anything with a picture, diagram, or list on it.
- Write a continuous narrative as an event happens; edit it later.
- Develop your own test to know when you've gathered enough.

ORGANIZE STAGE

- Planners decide what they want to say and then write it; plungers type to find out what they want to say.
- Planners should debrief their plan with someone before they type.
- Plungers should debrief the parts they envision before they type.
- Plungers should type, cut, rearrange, and revise, in that order.
- Use the Stack of Blocks form for maximum understanding.
- Avoid the Inverted Pyramid form, because readers can't understand it.
- Use the Champagne Glass form when telling the tale twice to help readers understand it.
- Start a piece in the middle of the action, and end soon.
- Place "gold coins" just before readers think about stopping reading.
- Organize material into sections of related subject matter in logical order.
- Jot down important things and rearrange them into sections.
- Select characters that help readers understand without lots of apparatus.
- Organize a piece along a "spine," or theme, running all the way through.
- Arrange photos, titles, captions, and text in that order to lead readers into the piece with accurate expectations.
- Treat photographers as equals in a team.
- Always suggest titles, subheads, and captions to editors.
- Move secondary information into boxes to keep the main text simple.

- Slow down in an emergency and plan on the fly.
- In a crisis, turn the screen off and type the whole thing as fast as possible.
- To discover what you think, type without thinking.
- Organize with a series of questions, answer them, then turn the questions into statements.
- Imagine target readers as you decide what to tell them.

DRAFT STAGE

- Draft without revising for maximum speed, and then revise once.
- Write the text in any order, not just beginning to end.
- Don't repair imperfect things on the screen until you revise.
- Begin typing whatever gets you started fastest: the easiest part, or the hardest, or what you know best.
- Type a quick draft, study it for holes, and gather more to fill those gaps.
- Write an online brief first for simultaneous print and online publication.
- Write beginnings that tell readers what the piece is about and why they should read it.
- Establish authority by writing clear and simple beginnings in a confident tone.
- Write the beginning last after you type the main text.
- Use a question as the basis for a draft beginning; revise it later into a statement.
- Anecdotal beginnings work best if the first sentence or the title tells what the piece is about.
- Use nut graphs to tell readers what the piece is about, to relay a key piece of information, or to suggest why readers should read it..
- Tell readers what they need to know before they realize they need it.
- Draft by speaking sentences to the screen, then typing them if they say what you want.
- Draft in your head and dictate to the screen from memory.
- Type with the screen off to learn that you can draft without revising.
- Leave blanks in the text to fill in later.
- Calculate length by how much explanation readers need.
- Write short by leaving things out.
- Write short by starting with your point, describing actions, and limiting quotations.
- Provide background in bits, not in sections.

- Avoid inserted transitions in short writing.
- Achieve brevity by selection, not compression.
- Stop in the middle of a sentence when you're interrupted.
- Hit the Save key whenever your phone rings.
- Pull readers across boundaries with "gold coins" and cliff hangers.
- Use an ending to cement main points in the readers' memory.
- Take breaks to cool off and avoid fatigue.
- Create a quiet zone where you can think and type.
- Cut anything you love that has nothing to do with what your piece is about.
- Avoid writer's block by never thinking of yourself while touching keys.
- If stuck in writer's block, review something your wrote superbly, then say, "I did it then, and I can do it now."
- When stuck, ask: "What am I trying to say here?"
- If you're momentarily stuck, back up one step in your writing process.
- Create a little saying to distract yourself from thinking about failure.
- Shut up your internal critic during drafting, and train him to say useful things during revision.
- Select characters ruthlessly, and introduce them separately.
- Spell names right by multiple checking.
- Assume that clip files, previous publications, and the Internet have errors.
- Use spell-checkers, but always follow up with proofreading.
- Use telling to frame showing.
- Look for telling details, get them in your notes, and select them rigorously.
- Handle emotional materials with extra restraint.
- Write clear sentences by starting with the subject, putting the verb next, continuing to the right, and never inserting anything inside anything else.
- Write clear sentences by picturing actions.
- Use punctuation to show readers the parts of a sentence.
- Avoid the dash.
- Use lists to put lots of information in small space, and use bullets to open lists up.
- Alliterate words to tie them together and create meaning.
- Put things you want to emphasize in emphatic positions.
- Use abstractions to frame specifics, emphasizing the latter.
- Use visible transitions so readers can see the boundaries and structures.
- Place forward-looking subheads to introduce sections.
- Choose active versus passive voice depending on emphasis.

- Writing edgy requires a good editor to keep you from overdoing it.
- Clean up quotations so they make sense to readers.
- Quote inarticulate people with partial quotations and paraphrases.
- If you can write it better than your source said it, you probably should.
- Coding obscenities does not hide them from readers.
- Follow your publication's policy on obscenity. If you don't know it, ask.
- Spell out acronyms if readers might not recognize them.
- Attribute facts so readers can judge their validity.

REVISE STAGE

- Draft without revising for maximum speed, then revise once.
- Revise the structure first, then transitions, and finally the sentences.
- Read a printed version of your draft aloud, marking things you want to revise.
- Revise good sentences to make them easier to read and understand.
- Use spell-checker software, but follow up with proofreading.
- To shorten a piece, cut sections, paragraphs, sentences, and words in that order.
- Cut anything you really love and see if the piece reads better.
- Use the hand test to detect and revise multiple endings.
- Submit perfect copy so editors will trust you and change it less.
- Check all numbers, URLs, addresses, and names.
- Stop revising when the piece is good enough to hand over to production staff.
- Ask "What works, and what needs work?" When the answer to the latter is "Nothing," stop.
- Turn pieces in early to get better editing.
- Set your own deadlines and keep moving them closer.
- Recruit test readers who will tell you what they don't understand.
- Send messages to editors in the Notes mode.
- Avoid debates with editors by asking, "What do readers need here?"
- Collaborate with other writers by agreeing on division of duties and credit.

VOICE

- Develop your own voice by deciding what personality you want readers to experience, then experiment to find devices that create that persona.

APPENDIX:

TURNING MY BLOG INTO THIS BOOK

My son, Jason, came up with the idea to write this book as a blog. Prior to this, I had not considered myself the type who would inflict my daily rambling thoughts on the world. Then he showed me his two blogs, "Reinventing the Newsroom" and "Faith and Fear in Flushing," the latter about the New York Mets, not toilets. I was impressed by the communities he created online, thousands of readers who wrote comments on what he published. I was writing a book on techniques, and he showed me a way to collect other people's techniques.

So I began the blog with my first post, on "That versus Which," the flattest, dullest piece of writing in my entire life. I had no idea how to blog. But I did get responses, some objecting and some suggesting things. I quickly realized that my two previous voices wouldn't do; I had to create a new, bloggy voice.

Blogging turned out to be fun, much to my surprise. I'm a planner who writes plans and follows them rigidly, but this blog had no plan. I just wrote whatever interested me day by day. Usually something sparked my attention, and I wrote about it. Friends and colleagues suggested issues that interested and troubled them. Eventually I made up a list of topics for the blog and book to cover, but I wrote them in no order, just what hit me.

Turning 145 blog posts into a book required addition and subtraction. I began with a two-column list: what I had already written against what the book needed. Then I filled in the holes. Every post had to be freestanding; I couldn't assume the reader knew what I'd written before. For the book version, I had to cut out repeated definitions and context. But readers may not read this book from cover to cover, so I had to put some of it back in.

I was creating my third voice, *i.e.*, my blog voice, while I blogged over the course of a year. The voice keeps evolving, and because of this fact, I had to revise the whole book to arrive at one consistent sound.

This book isn't the end of this project. I intend to keep writing my blog as topics occur to me, and I'll incorporate them into later editions. And now I need your help. First, I want to know what works and what needs work about this book. I particularly want to know if the methods for improving your writing process and creating a voice actually work for you. Second, I want to hear about writing techniques that you use that didn't make it into the blog. Thanks in advance for any help you can give me.

HELPFUL WORKS

The Associated Press Stylebook 2009. 43rd ed. (New York: Basic Books, 2009).

Barr, Chris. *The Yahoo Style Guide: The Ultimate Sourcebook for Writing, Editing, and Creating Content for the Digital World*. (New York: St. Martin's Griffin, 2010).

Best Newspaper Writing. (St. Petersburg: Poynter Institute, annual).

Biagi, Shirley. *Interviews That Work, A Practical Guide for Journalists*. (Belmont: Wadsworth, 1986).

Blundell, William. *The Art and Craft of Feature Writing: Based on The Wall Street Journal Guide*. (New York: New American Library, 1988).

Brande, Dorothea. *Becoming a Writer*. (New York: Harcourt, 1934; repr. New York: Houghton-Mifflin, 1981).

Carey, John. *Eyewitness to History*. (Cambridge: Harvard University Press, 1987).

Clark, Roy Peter. *Free to Write, A Journalist Teaches Young Writers*. (Portsmouth: Heinemann, 1987).

--. *The Glamour of Grammar*. (New York: Little, Brown, 2010).

--. *Help! For Writers*. (New York: Little, Brown, 2011).

--. *Writing Tools. 50 Essential Strategies for Every Writer*. (New York: Little, Brown, 2006).

Clark, Roy Peter, and Don Fry. *Coaching Writers*. 2nd ed. (New York: Bedford/St. Martin's, 2003).

Elbow, Peter. *Writing with Power, Techniques for Mastering the Writing Process*. (New York: Oxford University Press, 1981).

Franklin, Jon. *Writing for Story*. (New York: Athenaeum, 1986).

Hart, Jack. *A Writer's Coach: The Complete Guide to Writing Strategies That Work.* (New York: Anchor Books, 2006).

Jefferson, Thomas. *Writings.* Merrill D. Peterson, ed. Library of America. (New York: Literary Classics of the United States, 1984).

Kerrane, Kevin, and Ben Yagoda. *The Art of Fact.* (New York: Scribner, 1997).

Kramer, Mark, and Wendy Call. *Telling True Stories: A Nonfiction Writers' Guide from the Nieman Foundation at Harvard University.* (New York: Plume, 2007).

Lara, Adair. *Naked, Drunk, and Writing.* (San Francisco: Scottwall, 2009). Rev. ed. (Berkeley: Ten Speed Press, 2010).

Murray, Donald. *The Essential Don Murray: Lessons from America's Greatest Writing Teacher.* Thomas Newkirk and Lisa C. Miller, eds. (Portsmouth: Heinemann, 2009).

Pullum, Geoffrey K. "50 Years of Stupid Grammar Advice." *The Chronicle Review* 55.32 (April 17, 2009). B15; http://chronicle.com/article/50-Years-of-Stupid-Grammar/25497.

Scholes, Robert; Robert Kellogg; and James Phelan. *The Nature of Narrative.* Rev. ed. (New York: Oxford University Press, 2006).

Strunk, William, and E. B. White, *The Elements of Style.* (New York: Macmillan, 1959).

Ways with Words. A Research Report of the Literacy Committee. (American Society of Newspaper Editors. 1993).

Welty, Eudora. *One Writer's Beginnings.* (Cambridge: Harvard University Press, 1984).

Zinsser, William. *On Writing Well, 30th Anniversary Edition: The Classic Guide to Writing Nonfiction.* (New York: Harper and Row, 2006).

--, "How to Write a Memoir. Be yourself, speak freely, and think small." *American Scholar* (2006); http://www.theamericanscholar.org/how-to-write-a-memoir/.

SOME MODELS FOR WRITERS:

Joan Didion, especially *The White Album.* (New York: Pocket Books, 1979).

Tracy Kidder, especially *The Soul of a New Machine.* (New York: Avon, 1981).

John McPhee, especially *Coming into the Country*. (New York: Farrar, Straus, and Giroux, 1977).

George Orwell, *The Orwell Reader, Fiction, Essays, and Reportage*. (New York: Harcourt Brace Jovanovich, 1956), especially "Politics and the English Language" and "Why I Write."

William Shakespeare, anything he wrote.

PUBLICATIONS AND SITES KNOWN FOR GOOD WRITING:

The Atlantic Monthly

The Ecocomist

Harper's

The New York Times

The New Yorker

Slate

The Washington Post

SOURCES

1. Joan Didion. *The White Album.* (New York: Simon and Schuster, 1979). 127.
2. *The New York Times Magazine* (12-13-2009). 32.
3. Hank Stuever. *Off Ramp.* (New York: Holt, 2004). xv.
4. John Donne. "The Ecstasy," 7-8. Arthur Quiller-Couch, ed. *The Oxford Book of English Verse 1250-1900.* (Oxford: Clarendon Press, 1922). 228.
5. Jack Heeger. "What wine goes with Snickers?" *Napa Valley Register* (10-26-2006). B1.
6. *Ways with Words. A Research Report of the Literacy Committee.* (American Society of Newspaper Editors, 1993).
7. Christina K. Cosdon. "Firefighters rescue manatee from crab trap rope," *St. Petersburg Times* (9-25-1987). 4. Copyright 1987, Times Publishing Company. Used with permission.
8. John Noble Wilford, "Earliest Days; Takeoff! How the Wright Brothers Did What No One Else Could," *The New York Times* (12-9-03). E1.
9. Tr. Robert Fagles. (New York: Penguin, 1997). *Odyssey* I.1-12, p. 77.
10. Robbie Brown and Carl Hulse. "Heckler's District Mostly Supports the Outburst." *The New York Times* (9-11-2009). A15.
11. Adam Nicolson. *Seize the Fire. Heroism, Duty, and the Battle of Trafalgar.* (New York: Harper Collins, 2005). 4.
12. Lynn H. Nicholas. *The Rape of Europa.* (New York: Knopf, 1994). 54.
13. Peter Rinearson. "Making it fly: A special report on the conception, design, manufacture, marketing and delivery of a new jetliner—the Boeing 757." (Seattle: Seattle Times, 1984); http://seattletimes.nwsource.com/news/

business/757/part03/. Copyright 1983, Seattle Times Company. Used with permission.

14. *The Daily Progress* (11-2-2009); http://www2.dailyprogress.com/cdp/business/local/article/cbj_women_have_unique_financial_needs/48362/.

15. media.komonews.com/images/090518_ducks_banker.jpg.

16. *The New York Times* (12-1-2009). A14. Photo by Dario Lopez Mills, Associated Press.

17. Adair Lara. *Naked, Drunk, and Writing.* (San Francisco: Scottwall, 2009). 49.

18. Larry Gelbart, quoted on "CBS Sunday Morning" (12-27-2009).

19. Michael Ruhlman, at Symposium for Professional Food Writers, The Greenbrier, May 2009.

20. *The Daily Progress* (8-27-2009); http://www2.dailyprogress.com/cdp/news/local/article/aggressive_fox_bites_2_people_steals_sweater/44546/.

21. Alessandro Treves, "Coding and representation: Time, space, history and beyond." In Henry L. Roediger, Yadin Dudai, and Susan M. Fitzpatrick, eds. *Science of Memory: Concepts.* (New York: Oxford University Press, 2007). 58.

22. Quoted by Eli Saslow. *The Washington Post* (12-18-2008). A01.

23. John Gardner. *The Secret Generations.* (New York: Putnam, 1985). 19.

24. David Finkel, "Their House: It Was Spectacular, But It Is No More," *St. Petersburg Times.* (8-30-1989). 1A. Copyright 1989, Times Publishing Company. Used with permission.

25. V. S. Naipaul. *The Enigma of Arrival.* (New York: Knopf, 1987). 142.

26. William L. Hamilton, "At Home With: Andrew Solomon; Showing The Demons The Door." *The New York Times* (5-17-2001). F1.

27. Matt Bai, "The Brain Mistrust," *The New York Times Magazine* (2-21-2010). 13-14.

28. Brian McKenzie. "Study of commas a splicing headache," *The Daily Progress* (6-1-2009); http://www2.dailyprogress.com/cdp/news/opinion/columnists_bryan_mckenzie/article/study_of_commas_a_splicing_headache/40881/.

29. *The Associated Press Stylebook 2009 (Associated Press Stylebook and Briefing on Media Law).* 43rd ed. (New York: Basic Books, 2009). 42.

30. Edwin T. Layton, *"And I Was There." Pearl Harbor and Midway– Breaking the Secrets.* (New York: Morrow, 1985). 449.

31. Frank McCourt. *'Tis. A Memoir.* (New York: Scribner, 1999). 42.

32. Patricia McLaughlin. "Merit badges are eternally fashionable." *St. Petersburg Times* (3-13-1989). 1D. Copyright 1989, Times Publishing Company. Used with permission.

33. Robin Mather Jenkins, "Cutting through the fat, protein and carbs," *Chicago Tribune* (3-2-2005). 7.1l.

34. Malcolm Gladwell. *Blink.* Expanded ed. (New York: Back Bay, 2007). 182.

35. Jennifer Steinhauer. "Despite Ray Bradbury's Efforts, a California Library Closes." *The New York Times* (12-6-2009). A28.

36. Annie Proulx. *The Shipping News.* (New York: Scribner's, 1993). 60-61.

37. Nicolson, 209.

38. Lisa Jardine. *On a Grander Scale: The Outstanding Life of Sir Christopher Wren.* (New York: Harper Collins, 2002). 295.

39. Natalie Angier. "Fungi, From Killer to Dinner Companion." *The New York Times* (5-26-2009). D1.

40. Media General News Service. "Search continues for missing professor." *The Daily Progress* (2-17-2010). A2.

41. William Safire. "Straw-Man Issue." *The New York Times Magazine* (6-7-2009); http://query.nytimes.com/gst/fullpage.html?res=9A06E3DA153AF934A35755C0A96F9C8B63.

42. V. A. Kolve. *Telling Images. Chaucer and the Imagery of Narrative. II.* (Stanford: Stanford University Press, 2009). 226-228.

43. Ginia Bellafante, "Map Quest." *The New York Times* (6-19-2009); http://www.nytimes.com/2009/06/21/books/review/Bellafante-t.html.

44. S. I. Hayakawa. *Language in Thought and Action.* 5th ed. (San Diego: Harcourt Brace Jovanovich, 1990).

45. Mark Danner. "If Everyone Knew, Who's to Blame?" *The Washington Post* (4-26-2009). B5.

46. David Brooks. "Vanity Fare." *Food & Wine* (4-2001). 54, 56.

47. *The New York Times* (12-16-2007). WK10.

48. Jonathan Swift "A Modest Proposal." (Dublin: Harding, 1729).

49. Lara, Adair. *Naked, Drunk, and Writing.* Revised edition. (Berkeley: Ten Speed Press, 2010). 126.

50. E. V. K. Dobbie, ed. *Beowulf and Judith.* (New York: Columbia University Press, 1953). vi.

51. Kevin Robb. *Literacy and Paideia in Ancient Greece.* (Oxford: Oxford University Press, 1994). 24. Dipylon Oinochoe, National Museum, Athens.

52. Roy Peter Clark. *Writing Tools: 50 Essential Strategies for Every Writer.* (New York: Little, Brown, 2006). 3.

53. "HB Eggs. An unusual and successful way to boil and peel them." *Julia Child, Julia Child & Company.* (New York: Knopf, 1978). 34-35.

54. Merrill D. Peterson, ed. *Thomas Jefferson Writings.* Library of America. (New York: Literary Classics of the United States, 1984). 19.

55. Walter Isaacson. *Benjamin Franklin An American Life.* (New York: Simon & Schuster, 2003). 311.

56. *Pride and Prejudice* (1813). R. W. Chapman, ed. *The Novels of Jane Austen.* (Oxford: Oxford University Press, 1932). 2, 3.

57. *The Sun Also Rises* (1926), ch. 16. Charles Poore, ed. *The Hemingway Reader.* (New York: Scribner's, 1953). 224.

58. "He's Leaving, Really." *The New York Times* (1-15-2009). A27.

59. *The Elements of Style.* 3rd ed. (New York: Macmillan, 1979). xii-xlv.

60. Natalie Angier. *The Canon.* (Boston and New York: Houghton Mifflin, 2008). 73.

61. http://avalon.law.yale.edu/19th_century/gettyb.asp.

62. Frank McCourt. *Angela's Ashes.* (New York: Simon & Schuster, 1999). 249-250.

63. "Top Ten State Fair Joys." *National Geographic* (7-2009). 64-81; http://ngm.nationalgeographic.com/2009/07/state-fairs/keillor-text. Copyright 2009, Garrison Keillor, National Geographic Society. Used with permission.

64. http://www.nytimes.com/2008/01/03/us/politics/03obama-transcript.html.

65. David Brooks: *The Social Animal: the Hidden Sources of Love, Character, and Achievement.* (New York: Random House, 2011). xi-xii.

66. http://www.mtholyoke.edu/~zkurmus/html/didion.html.

67. http://nobelprize.org/nobel_prizes/literature/laureates/1949/faulkner-speech.html.

68. http://www.presentationmagazine.com/winston_churchill_speech_fight_them_on_beaches.htm.

69. Angier, *Canon*, 38.

70. Angier, *Canon*, 72.

71. "Letter to Francesco Vettori," *The Literary Works of Machiavelli*, trans. J.R. Hale. (Oxford: Oxford UP, 1961). 139D.

72. *Elmore Leonard's 10 Rules of Writing* (New York: Morrow, 2007).

ACKNOWLEDGMENTS

The certainties in the publishing world change almost daily, which makes it difficult to publish a book on writing. Most agents and publishers don't want to deal with you. But Liv Blumer did listen and agreed to represent me, and she persuaded Writer's Digest to publish this book.

She pushed me mercilessly to rewrite it four times for general professional writers. And she taught me how to think commercially in the language of publishers. Thanks to Liv and her husband Bill.

I wanted smart editing and aggressive promotion, and Writer's Digest responded, always saying the right things and meaning it. My editor Scott Francis and copy editor Kim Catanzarite preserved my new bloggy voice, while making insightful suggestions.

A number of friends read the book and responded promptly and positively: Jacqui Banaszynski, R. Thomas Berner, Bill Blundell, Jack Hart, Kevin Kerrane, Diane Morgan, Ben Narasin, Sherry Ricchiardi, Kim Severson, and Carl Stepp.

Two of my oldest pals, Toni Allegra and Roy Peter Clark, provided constant encouragement and wise advice. Other friends made suggestions and supplied information: Bill Adair, Jane Bonacci, Jon Bowen, Meg Klosko, Marie Kolchak, Suzanne Palmer, Ashley Parada, David Shedden, Ricky Young, and especially Bill LeBlond and Adair Lara.

Finally, I could have dedicated any of my earlier books to my wife Joan, but this one, my *magnum opus*, is the first one worthy of her.

INDEX

D